"Charles D. Hayes has written an auth̶o̶.̶.̶.̶.̶.̶.̶.̶.̶.̶ book on policing in America. I highly recommend it to anyone looking for a clear, well written, definitive analysis of why this critical institution continues to struggle for credibility and public confidence. His prescriptions are imaginative yet practical and down to earth, reflecting both his considerable research and his time on the streets as a big-city cop. Paraphrasing quoted material from the book, 'Get ready to remember what you are about to read.'"

—NORM STAMPER, Seattle Chief of Police (Ret.), author of
Breaking Rank and *To Protect and Serve*

"While we think of ourselves as rational agents with free will, our behavior is shaped by implicit, subterranean forces that we cannot imagine or control. Hugely important are the implicit biases we carry, determining who counts as an Us or a Them, and few such biases are as consequential as those carried by police officers. In *Blue Bias*, Charles Hayes' goal as an ex-cop is to teach the science underlying implicit bias, and how it impacts the extraordinary capacity for police to help or harm society's vulnerable. He succeeds admirably at this, with clear, insightful, scientifically accurate and often elegant writing. Unexpectedly, the book also is emotionally powerful—one can practically hear this septuagenarian trying to impart wisdom to the young, flawed police officer he once was, half a century ago. This is an important book."

—ROBERT M. SAPOLSKY, author of *Behave* and *Why Zebras Don't Get Ulcers*

"Entrusted to make life-or-death decisions in a split second, peace officers must understand how the brain's rapid threat response system operates. In *Blue Bias*, Charles Hayes assembles the latest research from brain science and psychology to help protect lives—those of police officers and the public citizens they serve and protect."

—R. DOUGLAS FIELDS, PHD, author of
Why We Snap: Understanding the Rage Circuit in Your Brain

"An eye-opening glimpse into what (good) police work entails; a basically reassuring message to all of us who depend on the men and women in blue to live safe lives."

—MIHALY CSIKSZENTMIHALYI, author of *Flow* and *The Evolving Self*

"The author has done a stand-up job from his police experience years ago to being committed to continuous learning throughout his life. While I stayed in policing, Charles left after a number of years. What is most interesting to me is that while we are similar in age, we both came to the same kinds of conclusions about the nature and work of policing a free society. If somehow, I could distill his findings and serve it to every police recruit in America, we would find and field the kind of police we deserve. Policing a democracy is a most difficult task and demands those with high emotional intelligence serve our towns, cities and counties. What Hayes writes here contributes highly to the most lofty (and necessary) goal of American policing."

—DAVID COUPER, Madison Chief of Police (Ret.), author of
Arrested Development and *Telling It Like It Is*

"Charles D. Hayes continues to demonstrate his extraordinary versatility as a visionary thinker and integrative writer in this brilliantly conceived and ingeniously conceptualized—and uncannily timely—book about the systemic shortcomings of existing police training, practice, and management that can foster the conditions for bias. Weaving together theory and research from a diversity of disciplines, Hayes constructs a new and invaluable model for understanding and combating the forces, including the biochemical and psycho-physiological ones, which can compromise the moral character, integrity, philosophical sophistication, and civic responsibility that should form the cornerstone of police consciousness and law enforcement practice. While *Blue Bias* offers a ground-breaking and revolutionary formula for curtailing bias, prejudice, excessive force, and so forth within the arena of law enforcement, it also shows how society generally can elevate and re-moralize itself in order to enhance the quality of human relations and encourage mutual understanding and respect, while reversing the breakdowns of basic humanity that are emanating in all spheres from the growing pathologies of modern culture. Essential reading."

—JOHN F. SCHUMAKER, author of *Wings of Illusion* and *The Age of Insanity*

BLUE BIAS

An Ex-Cop Turned Philosopher Examines
the Learning and Resolve Necessary to
End Hidden Prejudice in Policing

BY CHARLES D. HAYES

AUTODIDACTIC PRESS

WASILLA, ALASKA

Autodidactic Press
P. O. Box 872749
Wasilla, AK 99687
www.autodidactic.com

ISBN 978-1-7330386-0-7 (softcover)
ISBN 978-1-7330386-1-4 (eBook)
LCCN: 2019919546

Printed in USA

10 9 8 7 6 5 4 3 2 1

First Edition

Book design: Shannon Bodie, BookWiseDesign.com
Source image: Shutterstock

Publisher's Cataloging-In-Publication Data
(Prepared by The Donohue Group, Inc.)

Names: Hayes, Charles D. (Charles Douglas), author.
Title: Blue bias : an ex-cop turned philosopher examines the learning
   and resolve necessary to end hidden prejudice in policing /
   Charles D. Hayes.
Description: First edition. | Wasilla, AK : Autodidactic Press, [2020] |
   Includes bibliographical references and index.
Identifiers: ISBN 9781733038607 (softcover) | ISBN 9781733038614
   (ebook)
Subjects: LCSH: Police--Psychology. | Peace officers--Psychology. |
   Discrimination in criminal justice administration--Psycho-
   logical aspects. | Psychophysiology. | Racial profiling in law
   enforcement--Psychological aspects. | Prejudices--Psychological
   aspects.
Classification: LCC HV7936.P75 H39 2020 (print) | LCC HV7936.P75
   (ebook) | DDC 363.2019--dc23

To the Memory of LuAnne Dowling

CONTENTS

INTRODUCTION

How many unarmed citizens must die because the glint of a cellphone is assumed to be a gun or because a movement to pull up one's pants is mistaken for reaching for a weapon? How many police officers must die in the line of duty because they are taken by surprise and fail to perceive a mortal threat?

The purpose of this book is to help address such questions—and to inform and inspire anyone who hopes to become a peace officer or who is able to improve public safety for peace officers and the public. I have also sought to make it accessible to anyone seeking to understand the role of law enforcement in today's multicultural society. After all, criminal justice is everyone's business. (Note, by the way, that I use the terms *police officer* and *peace officer* interchangeably simply for aesthetic reasons, as there are many types of jobs in law enforcement: Sheriffs, deputies, marshals, troopers and more. But for the most part, all are peace officers in that preserving the peace is their most pressing objective.)

Although there is no shortage of educated opinions about how to address the problems described above, too many overlook the importance of increasing our knowledge of human behavior and

1

biological responses. By the time you finish this book, you will better understand why this has been a critical oversight as well as what needs to be done about it to make life safer for the public and for peace officers. And if those of you who are new officers heed its lessons, you will have a more fulfilling, healthier, and longer career in law enforcement than I did—with an opportunity to both fulfill your oath and change your communities for the better—and in doing so, to personally feel the benefit of the "flow state" that comes with impassioned lifelong learning.[1] Finally, in the best-case scenario, your experiences, ideas and studies may lead you to help contribute further solutions.

Policing has changed significantly during the past half century, especially in technological capabilities; recruits spend weeks to months longer in academies, as well as more time after graduation under the supervision of a training officer. But what hasn't changed is the existential nature of the relationship between the police and the public, which is continually shaped by daily interactions as well as sensational media examples that raise fundamental questions about the competence and integrity of law enforcement in America. Helping to address this problem while supporting the police and the public is the purpose of *Blue Bias*.

In the 1960s, I was a police officer in Dallas, Texas, having joined the force when I was 23.[2] I had grown up in Oklahoma and Texas during the 1940s and '50s as part of a racist family, in a racist community, in a racist state, and in a racist region of the country. But at the time, I had no idea that I was just as racist as my surroundings; in fact, I was convinced I was socially objective, open-minded, and not in the least bit prejudiced.

It so happens that, around the same time I was growing up, one of the preeminent social psychologists of the twentieth century, Gordon Allport, was studying prejudice. In 1954, he published *The*

Nature of Prejudice, a classic which provides the following definition: "Prejudice is a pattern of hostility in interpersonal relations which is directed against an entire group, or against its members; it fulfills a specific irrational function for its bearer."[3]

The passion with which people promote and defend their prejudices can indeed reach irrational heights. In my part of the country, for example, people used the N-word openly without worrying about anyone taking exception, because protesting would have incurred a public wrath that makes the current notion of political correctness as a form of censorship seem naïve. In those days, no one speculated about the existence of implicit (or hidden) bias that might be formed by unconscious assumptions, because explicit bias—in the form of overt prejudice and racial bigotry—was the order of the day. That the white majority was inherently special and superior to other races was society's unquestioned assumption. Numerous explicit acts reinforced this position.

One expression I learned from adults was this: "Negroes are fine, if they know their place." Though that place was seldom specified, it was universally understood that "their" place and "ours" were not the same location. In the town of Irving, Texas, where I went to high school, boys would sometimes drive late at night to the African American community of Bear Creek and throw rocks at houses, only to flee when lights came on. Did these activities serve a purpose? Indeed, they were a primeval tactic: The boys were marking their territorial boundaries in much the same way that predators mark boundaries so as not to have them crossed by others. In effect, they were acting out the prejudices passed down from earlier generations. These same boys would boast of their actions, and their behavior would be whispered about among students the next day at school, as if something worthwhile and of significance had been achieved. This same blanket of collective ignorance—under which

I grew up—is still so pervasive in some parts of the country, it hugs the territory like a dense fog in which community members bond through their contempt for non-members.

I have now been studying the pathology of prejudice for decades. Unraveling my racist indoctrination through a vigorous effort to become self-educated was enthrallingly transformative—so much so, that I credit my change of worldview as a major reason I began to write. My personal conversion from casual, unknowing racist to a more tolerant person open to new experiences was so fulfilling and life-changing, I have wanted to share the experience ever since. For more than thirty years, I have been writing books and essays, fiction and nonfiction, extolling the rewards of self-education. Some of the text in this book is from essays I've written and rewritten because this subject has not received enough public attention to affect public policy. That, in fact, is the reason for this book.

As a former peace officer, I want to do what I can to overcome the racism—both implicit and explicit—that is still very much alive today in law enforcement. Too many police departments are not utilizing what is already well-known and established about human behavior; this is a disservice to their men and women in uniform and to the public they are obliged to serve.

The crux of what I've learned is simple: We don't get along well as human beings largely because we grow up not understanding how our minds work—for example, how we are chemically pre-disposed to bond with some people while ostracizing others.[4] We don't appreciate how our brains associate, categorize, and sort—or, in other words, how they stereotype. In fact, our brains prize efficiency, and this stereotyping is simply evidence that they are working according to design. (More on that later.) As a result, mistaken assumptions can set up like concrete. This leads us to apply prejudicial judgments where they are not warranted. We end up putting faith into hunches, which themselves amount to nothing more than abscessed biases. Unfortunately, for most of us who grew up without this fundamental understanding, we may accept our brains' biases as fact—for years, decades, or even for a lifetime, believing ourselves to be bias-free.

But as philosopher Raoul Martinez suggests in his book *Creating Freedom,* having zero bias is not only humanly impossible, but it may not even *be* an ideal:

> **The worst crimes—war, genocide, slavery, the subjugation of women, the destruction of nature—are made possible by mechanisms of control that induce obedience on a mass scale. Few acts are as politically significant as obeying orders and conforming to expectations; political neutrality is unattainable. Despite this, neutrality is generally assumed to be a marker of fairness preferable to bias. However, what counts is the nature of a bias, not bias itself. A truly neutral being does not care if children eat or starve, nor if the environment is preserved or destroyed. A truly neutral being does not care about anything at all.[5]**

Once you begin to understand how our brains record and map our life experiences, it becomes clearer why it is so difficult to change our perceptions: Because our biases consist of snapshot perceptual assumptions intended to capture reality—not as it should be, but as it is. Our unconscious is like software that we have no way to code directly, because we don't have access to its coding language. Changing a bias is not as simple as just changing our minds; it literally takes a rewriting of reality to perceive a change of reality. In other words, our subconscious is amoral, caring only about nailing what is real, not what is right or just. And yet, how many of us were smart enough as children to perceive that most of the adults we encountered were dead wrong when it came to their observations about other people? We may indeed experience dissonance bumps along the way, but how many of us have the intelligence to suddenly "get it" that most everyone we admire is wrong about things so fundamental to our society? For most of us, myself included, it takes years of dissonant experience and the study of myriad subjects to unravel a racist upbringing.

I've had my share of dissonant revelations over the years. When I joined the Marines at age 17, some of the noncommissioned officers were African Americans. But, although it was clear to me at the time that they were exemplary human beings, some much smarter than I, that wasn't yet enough dissonance for a paradigm shift. But another instance in my mid-thirties stands out above all others: Reading Martin Luther King, Jr.'s *Letter from a Birmingham Jail* for a college class assignment. King wrote of unjust laws, which he called "difference made legal," as well as of law that was "just on its face and unjust in application."[6] Few experiences in my memory stand out with greater intensity than my realization that King was right. The truth of his compelling argument struck me like a lightning bolt, followed by a thundering reverberation of just how wrong I had been about understanding the nature and lasting effects of racial prejudice. We will achieve the American Dream— the one that Martin Luther King, Jr. advocated—only when the citizens in all communities and the police trust each other, when all our citizens live under the same umbrella of justice, and when black men are not assumed to be a greater threat to a police officer's safety than those who are white.

I abandoned a career in law enforcement after four years, only to become, just a few years after I left, so captivated by the scientific approach to bias and prejudice that I have since spent another life-time studying it with the intensity of a graduate student. I spent more than four decades in the Alaska oil industry working in the Arctic, with an equal amount of time off at home studying. My unrelenting interest in the behavioral sciences and myriad other subjects has fueled my books and essays about self-education, while my unforgettable experience as a Dallas police officer now serves as the impetus for *Blue Bias*.

I've now been reflecting critically for a half century on my experience as a police officer. I have spent this time intensely interested in the psychology of human behavior—especially the behavior of police officers. That some of the peace officers I know *still* don't comprehend how bias affects their personal behavior alarms me, because it subverts the moral authority under which law enforcement operates in society.

Now, I'm not formally trained in psychology, neuroscience, anthropology, evolutionary biology or primatology—and I was only a police officer in a single major city for one period in the 1960s, but I'm going to tell you some things about these subjects, about police work, and about yourselves that it's highly unlikely you've heard before. And though I may sound like a sociology professor or a psychologist at times, I'm simply an ex-cop with an insatiable interest in the behavior and well-being of peace officers and the public, of which I am now a part.

A friend with 36 years' experience as a police officer and 23 years as a police chief in a fair-sized city reminded me that an officer with only four years' experience is not a rookie, but is also not a veteran. I concur. In fact, he said an officer during this timeframe is something of "a dangerous creature," and again, I agree. But I am a veteran of having spent decades studying the human condition while reflecting on my police experience, and my learning suggests that until we push the boundaries of education much further in the behavioral sciences, the whole administration of law enforcement remains a dangerous vocation.

Some of the things I'm going to say are sure to piss you off. I would just about guarantee it. For example, in the realm of politics, I'm an unapologetic liberal; if you are not, some of the things I say may well encroach on your values. That said, I also value conservative values, in that I acknowledge that life without them would be untenable. I am an ardent believer in the overarching notion that in police work one should strive to maintain a balanced view of liberal and conservative cultural norms, because identifying either too far left or right is destructive; make no mistake, our political orientations—left, right, or middle—each come with their own myopic lenses, which color, shape, confirm, and set our expectations about everything we experience. In effect, our political identity becomes the producer and director of the whats and whys of our life experience.

One way to widen your life experience is by reading the literature of those who care deeply about these issues. And this includes reading about subjects that, because of our tendencies for overspecialization, rarely get a mention in our daily lives, but should—because their significance is vital for achieving just policing and robust community service. It is for this reason, and because most academics excel far more at their research than at sharing it with the public, that I am indeed focusing to a great extent here on the literature of others.

My reflections on the authors whose works I report on here, along with all my statistical references, do still reflect my biases and my life experiences up to the present, but these biases have now been tested and in some cases transformed, and these life experiences now include a daily habit of rigorous academic exploration and questioning. Your life experiences and learning are going to help determine how you respond. If you disagree, and in many cases you most assuredly will, don't shut down: Continue the investigation. Collect your own evidence, including statistics you have confidence in, and I think you will find, if you and I were to try our level best and take the issues we disagree on all the way to metaphysical bedrock, there is *more* than probable cause to believe the truth lies somewhere in middle ground. (This is especially true when it comes to statistics, where most often the problem is not the numbers themselves, but in how they are interpreted.) What matters here is public safety and your safety, along with that of your fellow officers. Your work as a peace officer is made all the harder because the beliefs about racial prejudice by the American public depend in large part on partisan politics, and an egregious misunderstanding of the nature of bias exacerbates our inability to deal objectively and dispassionately with issues concerning race.[7]

Our unabridged system of civil and criminal justice is predicated on the pretense that judgment in law is bias-free. And then, in plain sight, our politicians from both parties appoint judges whose biases are publicly known—and with whom they proceed to attempt to stack the courts—all the while pretending the very bias upon which the selections are made is nonexistent. It's little wonder there is so much confusion about the nature of bias.

Wherever you stand on politics, by better understanding your biological predispositions, you will be able to gain valuable insight into the mysteries of human behavior—a valuable strength, and one that is much needed today. After all, police work is all about self-control, and—as Harvard psychologist Steven Pinker reminds us in his 2011 work *The Better Angels of Our Nature*—"self-control is a muscle that can be strengthened."[8]

Besides, for peace officers, keeping a tight rein on one's emotions and maintaining a sense of reasonable restraint are critical job requirements. If you can't handle me, an ally with provocative ideas, then you don't have much of a chance to keep an even temper on the street when circumstances call for it.

Of course, politics matter in policing, often in ways that are not immediately apparent. So, similarly, it is worth reminding you, whether you are a peace officer or not, to take your political passions to the voting booth. By remaining aware of this parallel responsibility as citizens, peace officers on the street may stay grounded in cadence with their sworn objective.

My personal position concerning law enforcement is that the oath you take to protect and serve is a sacred trust, and that all people, regardless of race, creed, color, or religion, are to be treated with equal dignity.[9] Made still simpler, my political philosophy is that we should police *as if people really matter. All* people—not just those who are affluent, or those with political connections, but everyone, lest we forget why Lady Justice wears a blindfold.

Speaking of which, I have a question I want you to reflect on: Might it be appropriate to consider asking Lady Justice *to remove* her blindfold? She wears a blindfold to ensure that we are all treated equally under the law, but it's clearly not working for too many of our citizens. Maybe a hard look is needed to compensate for being in the dark; just keep this in mind as we proceed, and we will revisit the issue.

One more vital point: Some of the measures needed to attend to social issues of crime and punishment can *only* be addressed politically. Most often, the role of police officers becomes to carry out political agendas via legislated morality—because the enforcement of the law is politics writ large, as our history of unjust laws makes clear.[10] Politicians fear high crime rates, thus they apply pressure to law enforcement officials. Far too often, this process becomes a numbers game, with patrol officers pressured to crack down, make more arrests, write more tickets and issue more summonses, et cetera.

If you are an officer of the law, you may feel you lack control of the politics of this equation. But if you remember nothing else about this observation, remember this: Police officers who arrest innocent people on trumped-up charges simply to play a numbers game are no different than arsonists posing as firemen. Also keep in mind your other role here, as a citizen who votes, and who can employ your knowledge and experience to do so intelligently.

We human beings are primates, but we tend to deny the comparison, because we consider ourselves far superior to (other) animals.[11] Although human conduct is comparatively complex, we do share some fundamental behavioral traits with our simian cousins, especially relating to dominance and hierarchy.[12] To effectively confront and prevent abuses of police power, we must acknowledge this fact and deal with it responsibly.[13] Whether we deny our animal nature because of self-regard, arrogance or self-deception, the result is the same, in that we begin our journey holding a map with the wrong coordinates. When I originally got the idea for this book, in fact, my working title included the words *Primate Peace Officers*. Several friends advised against it because of racial implications. I didn't understand, until I found this reference in former prosecutor and Georgetown Law Professor Paul Butler's *Chokehold*: "Sometimes the association between black men and primates is explicit. Los Angeles police officers referred to cases of 'black-on-black' crime as N.H.I.—no human involved."[14] I changed the title of the book so as not to invoke this despicable example of racism.[15]

This book does not have an anti-police motive or message. To the contrary, I hope to show that by not taking full advantage of what we have learned about human behavior, we are doing our police a disservice and even putting them in harm's way. By putting men and women in police uniforms with badges and guns and sending them to perform jobs without intensive training about how their minds work, we are setting them up to always be biologically at odds with their sworn objectives. The only practical way to guard against this is to arm them with knowledge and to inspire and spark their interest in this subject, so they will be eager to continue learning as science reveals new insights.[16] Along these lines, and especially if you are a peace officer, I encourage you to also read the endnotes. If you can offer advice that helps address the issues in this work, I would like to hear from you.

As Steven Pinker reminds us, psychology is still far from understanding everything that makes us tick, but a little learning about what the field has discovered can go a long way toward making our lives easier.[17] Cultural anthropologist Ernest Becker observed that overspecialization has led to a "general imbecility" when it comes to understanding ourselves.[18] Indeed, we most assuredly need experts in human behavior, but we ourselves also need much more knowledge about how our minds actually work. Our intuitions about the world are simply reflections based on subconscious observations, recorded 24/7 and later fed back to us when we experience something our subconscious recognizes; without understanding how this process works, we may readily embrace our first impressions when we should instead be suspicious of them. Put another way, if we don't understand how easily our minds accept casual observations as facts, we can mistake the actions of one individual to represent the behavior of many, especially when it comes to categorical differences such as race. It has been my experience that pinning a badge on your shirt and a gun on your hip will reveal your core human values to the nth degree.

As any officer soon learns, it is not a stretch to say that too many of our citizens are frighteningly ignorant about facts they should have learned as children. In the 1960s, Paul Goodman became known for a book with the evocative title *Growing Up Absurd*; I understand it was an exploration of why younger generations were feeling out of step.[19] With apologies to the author, however, I invoke it here for the title phrase alone. "Growing up absurd" speaks volumes of how we all grow up: Without the slightest idea how and why we believe what we believe—yet prepared to defend those beliefs fervently, sometimes even to the death. Without adequate knowledge about how our minds work, it is a difficult fate to avoid.

That said, you cannot fully appreciate the uniquely absurd experience of being a law enforcement officer without pinning a badge on your shirt and arming yourself to ride along. With that thought in mind, whether you are a journalist, a recruit, a veteran of the streets, or a civilian, I ask that you pretend for the duration of this book to have enrolled in my big-city police academy, where we will deal with human behavior by arming ourselves with knowledge of its causes—and do a better job of policing as a result.

One more thing: Most everything we do in law enforcement hinges on an assumption that we have enough probable cause to act. So, every time a subject is mentioned in this class that gives you enough probable cause to investigate further, make a note to follow up. (I've helped by providing some starters.) My endnotes also are opportunities to delve further.

WELCOME TO MY
POLICE ACADEMY

*We can choose neither our parents nor time of birth, and it
is not in your power to decide whether there will be a war
or a depression. The instructions contained in our genes, the
pull of gravity, the pollen in the air, the historical period into
which we are born—these and innumerable other conditions
determine what we see, how we feel, what we do. It is not
surprising that we should believe that our fate is primarily
ordained by outside agencies.*

—MIHALY CSIKSZENTMIHALYI, *Flow* [1]

Welcome. Regardless of the specific nature of your interest
in the subject of law enforcement, this class is an attitude
and temperament check like no other—that's a promise—and it
will offer you a big-picture perspective about the training of peace
officers that you will find nowhere else. You are embarking on
an occupation in which the accumulation of stress over time will
change you both physically and mentally, while very likely pushing
your faith in humanity to the breaking point. What I'm offering
you, by means of an advocacy for becoming truly interested in your
profession, is gaining a humanitarian perspective grand enough
in scope and depth to keep you grounded in your objective and

enthusiastic enough about your work to reap the intrinsic rewards that come with providing a truly valuable public service, regardless of the serial disappointments you are going to experience.

There are subjects and instances where my narrative will become more applicable to a general audience, but where practical I will take the position of addressing police recruits because the effect of appreciating one's personal involvement can boost your perspective.

Officers-in-training: These sessions are specifically created to help make sure you are well-suited for this type of work, that you can perform your duties safely for the citizens you serve, for your fellow officers, and for the sakes of yourselves and your families.[2]

Civilians: Consider this a unique ride-along experience. As noted in the Introduction, although I initially wrote this for peace officers, I welcome any citizen, journalist, or critic of police work— or anyone with an interest in better understanding and improving police and community relations—to sit in on this "academy" for a chance to understand the challenges and opportunities involved in improving law enforcement from a humanist perspective. For the purposes of this course, please take the role of a recruit; it's a good way to get some sense of "skin in the game," which is necessary to fully understand what being an officer is really like.

Either way, I'm happy to welcome you to the force. In the first edition of Edwin J. Delattre's inspiring 2011 tome *Character and Cops*, former New York Police commissioner Patrick V. Murphy refers to police work as the "unprofessional profession," because there are so many police departments and agencies, yet so little standardization.[3] But ladies and gentlemen, the only thing keeping you from becoming a professional is you: Your determination, your thirst for knowledge, and your attitude.

The information and knowledge required to be a professional peace officer is readily available if you want it. I know you're all excited for your field training, which will take place after you pass my class. But first we will delve in detail into the psychological aspects of police work that you need to be fully aware of to be successful peace officers. In *The Nobility of Policing*, Michael J. Nila reminds us that as police officers you will be "both blessed and cursed to see more of life in a year than most see in a lifetime," and that you must be prepared "emotionally and spiritually."[4]

Most of the traits desirable for being a good peace officer are pretty much common sense: Accountability, personal responsibility, honesty, ethics, trustworthiness, communication skills, introspection, an analytical mind, capability for abstract thought, compassion, teamwork, and objectivity, with the ability to pay attention to intricate detail. But of course, there is another set of traits that determines temperament, which can both coexist with and impact those above. These include your threshold for boredom, your predilection for anger, and your reaction to risk-seeking behavior.

We will come back to these subjects in detail. But for now, I'll just say this: You either have the temperament for law enforcement, or you don't—and if you don't, there is not much anyone can do to help you. But the subject of bias is a different story, and we will dive deeply into the dynamics there. For now, I will put it like this: Life is a never-ending negotiation between what our subconscious assumes is real and what our conscious self believes *should* be real.

Some of you may have seen the Netflix series *Mindhunter*, created by Joe Penhall, based on the FBI's experience in profiling serial killers, or read the book it's based on, *Mind Hunter*, by John E. Douglas and Mark Olshaker. If you have, then you may have some idea about how hard it was for the FBI to get local law enforcement groups to take the idea of studying the psychology of criminals seriously. Well, what I am asking you to do in this class is similar, except I'm not so much interested in the minds of criminals as I am about what's going on in the minds of peace officers.

Police work puts officers into conflict daily with their biology. Ignoring this reality leads to dire consequences. Police work tends to instill in peace officers an attitude of "You can't tell us anything we don't already know, because we have seen so much of what most people haven't seen," and this mindset can be hard to break.

I was in uniform in 1966 when the Supreme Court handed down its decision in *Miranda v. Arizona*, requiring criminal suspects to be read their rights by the arresting officer. Every day in our detail assembly, we were reminded and warned that we had to Mirandize everyone we arrested, but it took months before there was widespread compliance, because too many of us thought it was ridiculous—and we thought we knew better. Most of us *had* heard the horrific stories from old-timers bragging about the illegal methods they had used to get confessions. This alone should have kicked up some dissonance and caused us to understand the need for the Miranda decision. And yet, that didn't happen. The fact that it didn't should tell us something now. For some officers, the only way they finally got the message was by losing a case in court (because of a failure to have read a prisoner their rights).

Since then, we have learned a lot about human behavior via psychology and neuroscience that we do not take advantage of—especially about the nature of bias, where it is needed most.[5] But there are a lot of things we've known for centuries that we also don't take full advantage of, the first being that, as often as not, things are not as they appear, and to be an effective law enforcement officer requires an open mind—capable of closing, but usually kept slightly ajar. One of the most dramatic lessons I learned many decades ago was during domestic disturbance calls, when I and a partner would separate the individuals involved and take them into separate rooms to get their sides of the story. This would nearly always result in each of us thinking the other person was solely to blame for the incident—that is, until we compared notes, which would nearly always suggest fault on both sides.

One thing we've known for centuries is that we as human beings are exceedingly self-deceptive, that we are not so much wired for seeking the truth of matters as we are for winning arguments, and that we are geniuses when it comes to tuning out things we don't want to hear. And more recently, research has proven it. In fact, we are so attuned to see what we expect that we can literally miss seeing a person in a gorilla suit cross a scene in which we are looking for something else.[6]

There are many aspects of law enforcement that are unique. Police work is what I call a high-sensation occupation. Others in high-sensation occupations include soldiers, emergency room doctors and nurses, EMTs, ambulance drivers, firefighters, members of rescue squads, explosives technicians, and corrections officers. The list is long. But these occupations have one thing in common that is hard to come by elsewhere. They all provide accentuated feelings of being alive, at slot-machine frequency, an experience that for some of us can be addictive. Many books about law enforcement reference the thrill of adrenaline addiction, but few admit how this affliction can lead to violence.

In police work especially, depending on the population and demographics of the community, each shift can have an edge to it. Soon, you develop an emotive anticipation for when the calm will finally give way to sirens and flashing red lights. This is not unlike how daily life must have been for our ancient ancestors, who were frequently on the menus of large predators or under life-threatening attack by warring tribes. Their lives were punctuated by moments of stark terror. You can imagine how such experiences would have helped accentuate the joy and everyday experience of simply being alive, and—in the aftermath—led to exhilaration over having survived. I'm sure you can also appreciate that a society such as ours is still comparatively safer—and therefore in this context more boring—than was early life on the Serengeti Plain.[7]

So, if our species still has the hardware that it did when we were hunter-gatherers—when it was a common and frequent occurrence to feel the rush of chemicals in one's brain that helped one escape certain death—it's not much of a stretch to imagine we might have learned to tweak this process to be pleasurable, now that the costs are not so high. After all, to my knowledge, we are the only species that is prone to scare itself on purpose. Perhaps boredom offers subtle reminders of our mortality or our relative unimportance, while danger gives us back the spotlight of attention we crave, so that our lives have both meaning and the rush of excitement that goes with it.[8]

Look, why do you think they call a specialist when someone is taken hostage? It's because they need expertise. But you don't need credentials to gain knowledge. If you take your career seriously, you are going to be the equivalent of a people scientist, and if you know what you are doing, you may not need to call an expert. Putting self-imposed limits on your career because you lack formal education is absurd. Think of your education—the knowledge you need to perform your duties—not as something you get, but as something you take.[9] Better yet, think of it as if it is evidence, because that's what it is. Domestic conflict that leads to violence is your business like nobody else's. If you are truly interested in your work, nothing can keep you from becoming an expert except your attitude. And remember, our brains are also constructed to reward learning with a pleasurable chemical release.[10] This is beginning to sound exciting, right? Back to adrenaline.

So, getting hooked on the thrill of being alive is simply our biology at work, moving us in the direction of what our body is telling us is pleasurable—precisely because we feel most alive when our lives are threatened. Now, this experience doesn't mean you are a good or bad person, but there is a caveat here. For some individuals, a craving for excitement can cause them to unconsciously escalate circumstances; for peace officers, this can be a career-killer. Many years ago, one of my police sergeants was such an excitement junkie that everyone knew he could escalate any incident into a skirmish if possible. Normally, when a supervisory decision or advice was needed, we were required to call a sergeant. But this supervisor listened to the radio to find out where the chaos was, and he responded to the sound as if it were an opportunity for action. He was so intense and tightly wound that while carrying on a conversation he would often stand on his toes, click his heels and twiddle his thumbs.

Addiction is a complex subject. In his book, *Chasing the Scream*, Johann Hari offers some thoughtful observations on the whole notion of addiction, which he says we misunderstand. According to Hari, "addiction is an adaptation. It's not you—it's the cage you live in."[11] He argues that if we can't bond with others we will find a substitute, and that addiction is primarily a malady induced by loneliness.[12] For the record, I'm not suggesting that police officers are excitement junkies because of loneliness. But Hari's study of the criminality of drug addiction is something I would hope you will find of great interest, because it presents a thoughtful perspective about the whole subject of addiction that you will likely find nowhere else—and as peace officers you are going to be immersed in social circumstances with the malady of addiction at the core.[13]

So, I have good news and not-so-good news. First the not-so-good: Even though you have passed your psychological profile tests, some of you aren't going to make it—and it may prove to be the case that some of you shouldn't. We have learned some things about personality traits that are toxic to police work, but given how incredibly complicated human behavior is, we may never achieve 100-percent effectiveness in selecting only individuals well-suited for law enforcement. But again, if you are not a good fit for this kind of work, it doesn't mean that you are a bad person. Police work takes a very special set of skills. It's easy to see how you might not be a good fit as a surgeon, an engineer, or a computer programmer, but of course not being cut out for these occupations doesn't mean you are a bad person either.

One's age and maturity can also make a significant difference in whether one is ready to be a peace officer. Speaking only for myself, I suspect I was too young at age 23 to begin. When we dig in more to the subjects of psychology and neuroscience, you will learn that our frontal cortex does not in most cases fully mature until around age 25 (and for some of us I suspect it is even later), so it's entirely possible to start too early and flunk out or burn out, only to return at a later age and fit right in.[14]

It's also important to your future that you keep in mind one of the very unfortunate realities about work in America. Our system of merit and education sets us up to become qualified in—and, in a sense, grandfathered for life into—careers that not only are we unsuited for and may be miserable performing, but into which we are trapped economically. So, you need to be honest with yourself from the beginning about how you feel about law enforcement. Should you become fully qualified for work in law enforcement but come to loathe the effort, you will in effect be golden-handcuffed— and your misery will likely be exceeded only by that of those with the misfortune to encounter you on official business.

The good news is that police work can be a rewarding experience like no other. Your directive, which has required your sworn oath, is that you are duty-bound to "protect and serve" the citizens of this community: Protect, not abuse; serve, not malign; respect, not mistreat. Are you on board so far? If so, that's a good sign, because I assure you that, although you may grow tired of me reminding you of your oath, I'm not about to hold back on doing so.

Over a lifetime career in law enforcement, you are going to meet hundreds—maybe thousands—of people who will detest your presence and curse you, including many who would even try to kill you if given the chance. At times you are going to be left feeling that you are performing a thankless job. You will also find subtle but priceless rewards—such as the look in the eyes of a child after you have stopped a man from beating the hell out of their mother.

You will likely grow weary of waving goodbye through steel bars to people who have spent the last hour telling you why you couldn't arrest them. You are going to be incredulous at the misinformation the public assumes to be true about your job and what they think you should be doing, compared to what you *are* doing. Simply put, you are going to have a ringside view of human behavior at its best and at its worst—and mostly the latter.

I'm going to challenge you far beyond your expectations about the duties of peace officers. You are not Wyatt Earp, and this is not 1876 in Dodge City, Kansas. You are entering a profession in desperate need of cutting-edge knowledge of human behavior. Our society is maxed out on social angst about how to properly enforce the law. The humiliating errors being made in this enterprise are everyday headline news, and when we push back against public opinion as individual officers or police departments, we lose credibility about our intent.

Do not be fooled into thinking that, since you are not doctorate-level scientists, you don't need to concern yourself with what they know. You need the applicable knowledge more than they do:

They are safe somewhere in a classroom or a lab, but *you* are on the street, where what you do really matters.

If you doubt what I'm saying, I want you to reflect on how you would feel if your actions resulted in the death of an innocent citizen, all because you weren't up to speed on the knowledge required for this job. I'm not suggesting that peace officers need to be social workers, but they are socially engaged as few people are. You aren't psychologists either, but you are constantly using psychology.

Think about it like this: When you climb a ladder, you can see farther; when you know more about human behavior, you can read beyond the petty conflicts you are called on to defuse. In the way frontier scouts used to deduce enemy movements from reading the hoofprints left by their horses, if you understand human behavior beyond superficial appearances, you can deal with problems instead of being confused by symptoms.

If you don't dig deep into your new discipline, you are going to misread situations that you have been called to mediate, and you may miss the real reason your presence is needed. Seeing a woman standing before you silently with two black eyes and a bloody nose, you may make assumptions based on your own background or on the nature of the original call; you may find yourself perplexed or frustrated with what she does or does not say; you may find yourself equally swayed by the man's appearance and words. But if you understand there is such a thing as a culture of misogyny, you may begin to see things yet another way—or at least start to consider other possibilities. Now, granted, knowing this may do nothing more than make an arrest, but if you can't read such incidents realistically—and to some extent understand why they happen—their sheer repetition will very likely eat away your patience and tolerance, and you can become overly cynical.

This happened to me. I became thoroughly disgusted and fed up with behavior that I didn't understand and couldn't relate to, so I abandoned a career in law enforcement. I think the tipping point for me was when I arrived at a residence on Thanksgiving to find a woman with a gun in her hand who admitted to having just killed her husband over the correct temperature to cook a turkey. I wish I had known then what I'm sharing with you now.

Philosophy professor Edwin J. Delattre quotes the late novelist Tom Wolfe's observation that "cynicism is 'a cowardly form of superiority,' because it implies that I do not have to try my best, on the false grounds that nobody else tries."[15] If only there had been someone to point this out to me.

Use your angst over your fellow man's aberrant behavior as probable cause to dig deep and gain the rewards that natural learning provides, and police work will be more like a calling than a job. If you can't generate a continuous and self-reinforcing sense of curiosity about your work, consider finding other employment. Indeed, to stick with this line of work without becoming disillusioned over the long haul, you will need enough of a vested interest in your subject matter to achieve a critical mass of knowledge, so that adding to it is self-reinforcing and thus becomes its own reward.

We've got lots of ground to cover, and I'm going to suggest a lot of additional reading. While it's not mandatory, I promise you—if you really care about your future and your ability to conduct yourself in such a manner that your grandchildren would be proud of your career in law enforcement—studying this material will increase your chances of being effective, and you will have a whole library through which to compare your experiences with those of others. This will enable you to relate without the need to vent frustration by other means. You can't make good sense of what is happening (or what has happened) without understanding the context of what may have influenced that behavior. And speaking of making sense, when you come upon unfamiliar words, phrases, or ideas in your readings, treat them like empty shell casings on the floor of a homicide scene you are called upon to investigate: These are clues. And once you place them in evidence, they become part of your arsenal of intellectual ordnance.

One more thing: To be good at this job requires more of a commitment than simply the motivation required to earn a paycheck. If you aren't truly interested in human behavior—your own and that of the public you intend to serve—then you are likely to fall short of whatever your potential might be as a successful peace officer.[16] The authors of *Counseling Cops* put it like this: "Police work is an identity, not just a job. It can be all consuming in a way that few other professions are."[17]

I can't overemphasize the importance of your mindset in the way you view yourselves and your role in this line of work. Attitude is everything. You literally have the power to take the life of any person you view as a threat to your safety. So, unless you are what I will characterize as being intuitively and responsibly conscientious, I would prefer that you not be set loose in my community. That said, I don't want to see you hurt or killed in the line of duty because you are too hesitant to act when a situation calls for it.

Now, I hope you aren't discouraged by what I've said so far. Retired police chief Dean Crisp, who has followed up his 30 years in law enforcement with a new career as a continuing education instructor, author, and speaker, says the question boils down to the way we see ourselves in the job: As warriors or as guardians.[18] How you see yourself makes all the difference in the world. Guardian, protector, golem, or hero—the one you choose becomes a mindset that underlies the expectations with which you begin each day's work. As cultural anthropologist Ernest Becker put it, we greatly underestimate the human need to be heroic.[19] So, as a peace officer, when you think of yourself primarily as a guardian or as a protector, you can imagine yourself performing bold, heroic deeds, if you wish, but your employment is not predicated on your being a hero.[20] Your job is simply to enforce the law, to protect and serve the members of your community, and to do so safely and with honor and dignity. Given the enormous responsibility of your profession, your reason for choosing it deserves at least this much introspection and reflection.

As a sworn peace officer, you are by oath charged with internalizing a "blue bias" to protect and serve the citizens of your community, but there are so many paths to get off track and misunderstand what that is supposed to be that to get it right takes something akin to obsession. You will learn in this class that you are the architects, the producers, and the directors of your emotions. You, and you alone, are responsible for your actions as law enforcement officers. If you mistake a cell phone for a firearm and you kill an unarmed individual, it's not your sergeant, lieutenant, captain, or chief who must answer; it's not your college professors who may be convicted of murder or manslaughter; it's you. The same principle applies if you mistake a gun for a cell phone and it costs you your life. You are on the spot here. Your actions and behavior will be put to the test, day in and day out. Putting on your uniform means you are hereafter vested in and responsible for developing your own blue bias: To protect and serve the members of your community—and the protecting part includes your own personal safety and the safety of your fellow officers.

I've saved the best news for last. Psychologist Mihaly Csikszentmihalyi has spent decades studying what he characterizes as *flow*. Flow is an experience predicated on optimal interest and optimal learning.[21] In the flow state, one becomes detached from the perceptional motion of time; hours can pass that seem like moments.[22] And the great news for officers truly interested in their jobs is that police work—when predicated by an understanding of how brains work—is prime territory for flow. Flow is analogous to a Mercedes firing on all 12 cylinders in perfect harmony.[23] What could be more satisfying?

Want to start to experience some flow for yourself? Let's begin by taking a brief look at who we are as a people and a species.

THE ROOTS OF BIAS:
TRIBALISM & CULTURES
OF HONOR

Now, you can't be effective peace officers if you do not have a historical awareness of freedom, oppression, bigotry, racism, and peace. The same goes for an understanding of how we internalize our history and culture. Far too much of what is learned in our institutions of higher learning stays in academia for decades before it becomes common social currency, if it ever does.[1] My generation, and most generations after, unfortunately left the subject to experts—and the result is much too much uncertainty about things that are complicated but not that hard to understand.[2]

The first thing to understand is that, for all humans, the way our brains help us make sense of the world is through simplistic categorization. Fundamental comprehension depends upon bias. From the time we are infants, we learn to apply bias to sort the familiar from the unfamiliar, and by doing so, to distinguish one thing from another. In the 1970s and 1980s, sociologist and college professor Morris Massey developed a presentation intended to help teach the general public about how we assume the biases of our respective cultures as we grow up.[3] The fact that Massey directed his work at the public and not to his peers was an unusual and stunning acknowledgement that the public was a critical audience for such work.

Massey applied Austrian zoologist and Nobel Laureate Konrad Lorenz's theory of imprinting to children, arguing that at about the time we reach ten years of age, we have locked in the value lens with which we thereafter view the world. Massey left academia and spent his career presenting his theory and observations to corporations; in doing so, his reputation and work were diminished in academia and largely ignored. But by teaching the general public about the nature of bias, he accomplished something profoundly important and largely missing from public education.

It is imperative we gain a big-picture understanding of how we internalize our cultural upbringing and the fact that we likely share a worldview with others of similar age and experience who grew up in the same regions during the same time. Every generation assumes their group hung the moon, and all the others are just left to wonder how they got it up there, so to speak. To better understand ourselves, we must realize that time, place, and perspective contain lasting impressions; that when we look out upon the world we do not see straight-up reality, but instead what we have learned to see; and that if we do not revise our internalized assumptions with extraordinary efforts based on science and not on folk culture, we can never be as objective as the circumstances of our lives require. That's why Morris Massey titled his video presentation *What You Are is Where You Were When*.[4]

Speaking of time, place and perspective, let's go back—way back. For 99 percent of our time on the planet, mankind has lived in small groups rarely larger than 300 members.[5] This evolutionary experience left its mark on our psyche. Simply put, we are wired for trusting folks close to home and to be wary of strangers. Cognitive psychologist and Yale University professor Paul Bloom reminds us just how early such traits start in his exploration of the development of morality in infants in his book *Just Babies: The Origins of Good and Evil.*[6] He also explores how they may continue to influence us: "We are by nature indifferent, even hostile, to strangers; we are prone toward parochialism and bigotry. Some of our instinctive emotional responses, most notably disgust, spur us to do terrible things, including acts of genocide."[7] In fact, he notes, "for most of human history, nobody saw anything wrong with racism."[8]

All over the world, the evidence is glaring that we are a tribalistic species.[9] Moreover, and of extreme importance to you, is the fact that we have an innate dislike for thieves, cheaters, and in political and economic terms what we characterize as *free riders*—or anyone who manipulates the system to avoid sharing the collective cost.[10] The ethos of tribalism can become an obsession that what is going on in one's head should be the same in everyone else's head. Many of you are going to work in neighborhoods where there are large numbers of people who speak different languages and celebrate customs that may seem strange to you, and even to one another. Minor differences can become major conflicts, and that's when your presence will be needed.[11] As peace officers, your job is to keep the peace, not to take sides. Moreover, you will have your own tribal inclinations to contend with, as we shall see.

Tribalism, of course, leads us to in-group/out-group associations, which open the gateway to bigotry and prejudice.[12] It's the bedrock of human relations. Reflecting about tribalism should be a part of your daily duty as sworn officers of the law, a form of mental housekeeping. In-group versus out-group conflicts are something you will be called on to mitigate, and over time you are very likely to become frustrated because making progress in this arena can seem hopeless.

People need to belong, to have a sense of being valued, which is why gangs form in the absence of a strong family culture. The presence of a gang is simply evidence that a vacuum of honor and respect has been filled, albeit destructively. It doesn't take very long for peace officers to begin to feel what it's like being a minority—because we *are* a minority. The trick is not to develop an us-versus-them mindset, as if we are the good guys and everyone else isn't. It's harder than it sounds, ladies and gentlemen, especially because you have a silent partner in your brain that is likely reinforcing that mindset. I'll introduce you to that partner soon enough; first, let's review some basic types of us-versus-them tactics and dynamics you are likely to see.[13]

Stigma/Labeling

As noted, from birth, our brains learn to group and sort, group and sort, until the objects we see begin to make sense; having done so, we can be said to have applied a bias. That is *not* to say that "my bias is okay, because everyone is biased." This would be explicitly the wrong assumption. To the contrary, to understand the everyday role of bias is to realize one doesn't have to be an avowed and conscious bigot to have subconsciously categorized another group of people as being different from oneself or one's group in some way. However, *if that bias results in negative treatment of others*, the underlying assumption needs to be addressed.

When it comes to labeling and stigmatizing, too often we forget this point. To be stigmatized is to be stereotyped and labeled by having one's identity co-opted and degraded. Examples may include Native Americans being labeled as "savages," women being labeled as "hysterical," or yes, even police being labeled as "pigs." Stigmatizing is a means of demarcating boundaries.[14]

Why it matters: When women and minority groups are stigmatized by police officers, they cannot effectively be served with the protection intended by your oath. It's that simple—and that hard. Once your subconscious has internalized someone as worthy of a derogatory label, you are apt to begin making assumptions of their unworthiness based on too little information.

Now for a brief overview of some of the most common types of stigmatizing/labeling you are likely to see, including racism, misogyny and other close cousins. (We will revisit these in more depth in later sections.)

Misogyny

I'm going to step up on my sociology soapbox as an insatiably curious layman now, for what will become clear as damned good reasons, and I'm going to read you a quote from Jack Holland, who passed away in 2004 shortly after finishing *A Brief History of Misogyny: The World's Oldest Prejudice:*

> **What history teaches us about misogyny can be summed up in four words: pervasive, persistent, pernicious and protean....No other prejudice has proven so durable or shares those other characteristics to anything like the same extent. No race has suffered such prejudicial treatment over so long a period of time; no group of individuals, however they might be characterized, has been discriminated against on such a global scale. Nor has any prejudice manifested itself under so many different guises, appearing sometimes**

**with the sanction of society at the level of social and
political discrimination, and at other times emerging
in the tormented mind of a psychopath with no sanction other than that of his own hate-filled fantasies.**[15]

Modern society is still viscerally dysfunctional about gender.
The tentacles and roots of misogyny live in the bone marrow of our
species. They are so deeply buried beneath written history that we
take many of their assumptions as straight-up reality. It's as if the
world were created in a cultural temperament so entrenched with
this smoldering strain of scorn that it need not be discussed, ever,
because it simply represents the way things are, the way they were
meant to be, the way things must be. That the gender that is physically weaker would bear an unrelenting burden of submissiveness
seems like a no-brainer, based on what we know about strength and
primate behavior.[16]

Why it matters: As peace officers you are going to have an
up-close and personal future deeply involved in settling domestic
disturbances in which the dynamics of gender inequality are going
to be glaring. Until you understand our historical traditions and
the deep-seated beliefs about the roles of men and women in our
culture, you can't be reasonably objective when you face gender
issues, which you surely will, over a multitude of domestic disturbance calls.[17]

One more thing to always keep in mind: Domestic violence
calls are dangerous and unpredictable. In her book, *No Visible
Bruises*, Rachel Louise Snyder reminds us that the most dangerous
place in America for women is in the home and that every minute
of every day twenty people are assaulted by their partners.[18] She
also advises us that her experience in "ride-alongs" with officers
has taught her that the ideological culture of any given police

department regarding domestic violence is what makes the difference in problem solving.[19]

LGBTQ Discrimination

For centuries, our species has been so uncomfortable with what have been considered exceptional differences that a significant percentage have felt compelled to hide the very existence of their biological identity. I find it hard to imagine a greater psychological torment than feeling that you were born in the wrong body or learning that your sexual orientation is regarded by those you love as wrong or aberrant. That people who deal with these identity crises personally must also contend with a public who ridicules, torments, and abuses them is a most unfortunate reality.

Hopefully I don't have to explain to you the disgraceful history of gay-bashing that has taken place globally and which continues today in many parts of the world. In the 1960s, when I was in uniform, we tolerated gay citizens—but, I'm sad to say, we still generally treated them with something I would characterize as begrudging contempt. We were socially ignorant, but ignorance is never an acceptable excuse for what often amounts to disenfranchisement.

LGBTQ citizens are now in most places in America protected by law. In fact, sexual orientation issues have become so politicized and moral progress so rapid, one must check constantly for the latest legislative remedies. I would argue, however, that peace officers can address this seemingly complex issue simply enough, by remembering that "protect and serve" applies to everyone.

Unfortunately, dealing with people who are fearful of gay citizens is something that you will likely need to continue addressing throughout your career.[20] Awakening cultures to the reality of human biological variety has been and continues to be an arduous journey, and you have lots of probable cause here for further study. For example, why is homophobia so prevalent when fear of gays is biologically irrational? As psychology professor Paul Bloom points out, the existence of gay males actually gives other men a relative biological advantage with women. He winds up his argument provocatively, noting: "Male homosexuals should inspire gratitude, not disapproval. Women should be the only ones bothered by male homosexuals, just as men should be the only ones bothered by female homosexuals."[21] Understanding the history of LGBTQ culture, as well as the irrational persistence of homophobia, is important for peace officers, because you are likely to frequently encounter bigotry and prejudice by people who can't be objective enough to see the civil rights and basic human rights issues at play. In my day, in Dallas, police officers were openly homophobic—myself included, I am sorry to say.

In his insightful book, *Covering: The Hidden Assault on Our Civil Rights*, legal scholar Kenji Yoshino describes "covering" as a societal demand that pushes all of us to conform to public mores—so, for example, blacks act white or gays act straight to accommodate public sentiment.[22] Yoshino writes:

> **This covering demand is the civil rights issue of our time. It hurts not only our most vulnerable citizens but our most valuable commitments. For if we believe a commitment against racism is about equal respect for all races, we are not fulfilling that commitment if we protect only racial minorities who conform to historically white norms.**[23]

Racism

From the beginning of our collective American history, the rationale for slavery was the assumption that people whose skin was dark were inferior, biologically and intellectually. All racism that has followed, whether based on biology or culture, has simply been a replaying or retelling of this myth, representing a wide range of ingenious new ways to validate the original assumption. It's the same battle, the same argument in a thousand guises. It's as if we take a few steps forward toward the realization that there are no superior races, and then we back up a few paces and find new ways to re-argue the original prejudicial assumptions. For every new barrier that's knocked down, a new one appears.

The cause is within, asserts R. Douglas Fields, a neuroscientist and senior investigator at the National Institutes of Health in Bethesda, Maryland:

> **Racial prejudice is wired into the human brain. Stereotyping of people as members of outcast groups is also wired into the human brain, but by somewhat separate circuits. [Prejudice is our emotional response toward another group of people based on erroneous preconceptions. Stereotypes are conceptual categorizations of people that we group in our mind according to superficial characteristics]. The human brain instantly sorts people into different groups along racial lines. This may be difficult to accept, but the latest neuroimaging evidence supports this surprising conclusion.**[24, 25]

There may be those who take issue with Fields on his declaration, but I can't say I'm surprised. Over the last few decades,
neuroscientists have established that people tend to recognize faces
of their own race better than those of other races.[26]

Fields expands on this finding:

> **There can be no patriotism without a foreign adver-
> sary, no maternal bonding without seeing other babies
> differently. Ironically, the same trigger to form tribes,
> the human herding instinct, while the cause of so
> much mass violence, is also the reason for human
> coexistence and progress.**[27]

Here we are entering deep political territory, folks—so, if your
feathers begin to ruffle, just keep in mind that oath to protect and
serve. Having grown up in the South, I knew when President Barack
Obama was elected in 2008 that there would be a racist backlash.
White supremacists awoke from their dormancy, because their
reasons to hate were suddenly front and center with a new iconic
symbol—in the White House, of all places.[28] But, with respect to
President Obama, I greatly underestimated how wide and deep
the racial hatred would run, working its way into so many vehe-
ment assertions, even to the point of denying that he was born in
America.

Those who are well-acquainted with American history appreciate the insidious effects of racism, from legal disenfranchisement,
to forced assimilation, to apocalyptic, savage treatment such as
the literal genocide of Native Americans or the forced bondage of
African Americans during slavery. Our history reveals thousands
of events every bit as evil as the actions of the Nazis during World
War II, and although many of the citizens in poor communities

and Indian reservations are unaware of this history, they still bear the psychological legacy of disrespect handed down through generations in many sophisticated guises. If you think I'm exaggerating, read W. Fitzhugh Brundage's *Lynching in the New South*,[29] and *An Indigenous People's History of the United States*, by Roxanne Dunbar-Ortiz.[30] You will find horrifying examples of African Americans and Native Americans being treated with bigotry, hatred, and brutality to an extent that begs comparison to the darkest periods in human history.

Generations of dehumanization take generations to heal. If you think that slavery ended with the Civil War, read Douglas A. Blackmon's *Slavery by Another Name*.[31] Blackmon's examination of post-Civil War history in the South documents the horrific abuse of black men for three-quarters of a century after the war. Shamefully, his detailed accounts implicate law enforcement as well, detailing how agencies in the South imprisoned black men for the sole purpose of forced labor for hire—placing police in the role of overseers.

Simply put, racism is more real than race. Until we deal with this reality and admit its pervasive existence, we will never get beyond it as a people.

All the books I recommend here help to emphasize the complexity of racism, but one has a unique focus in that it addresses progressives who think they "get" racism, but don't—with a message both incisive and profound. *White Fragility: Why It's So Hard for White People to Talk About Racism*, by Robin DiAngelo, presents an exceptionally lucid argument, which effectively makes the case of its subtitle.[32] DiAngelo also has an outstanding video on C-Span's *Book TV*.[33] If you watch her video and read her book, I am hopeful you too may experience a thunderbolt epiphany: The realization that, given our socialization, unless you have studied the subject of racism intently, any objection you raise is likely itself to be the product of a racist society you didn't think yourself a part of. And, most provocatively of all, this may be true no matter your race.

As associate professor of criminology at the University of South Florida Lorie A. Fridell writes in her book, *Producing Bias-Free Policing*, "This fact—that women can have biases against women, Blacks can have biases against Blacks, poor individuals can have biases against poor individuals, and so forth—is frequently lost in the conversation about bias in policing."[34]

This is why, in my view, DiAngelo focuses on white progressives. DiAngelo says the way we are taught to define racism makes it impossible to understand it.[35] I infer that she believes "white progressives cause the most damage daily to people of color."[36] And she argues "that nothing in mainstream U.S. culture gives us the information we need to have a nuanced understanding of arguably the most complex and enduring social dynamic of the last several hundred years."[37] People who deny a racial bias are "demonstrating a profound lack of self-awareness,"[38] says DiAngelo, who also asserts that people who claim to treat everyone the same are really telling us that they "don't understand socialization."[39]

Racism, DiAngelo argues, is not an event but a "system and a structure." And in America, law enforcement is the enforcer and arbitrator of this system.[40] What she says about progressives and aversive racism is especially applicable in law enforcement, because peace officers often don't understand the very subtle nature of racism and bias:

> **Aversive racism is a manifestation of racism that well-intentioned people who see themselves as educated and progressive are more likely to exhibit. It exists under the surface of consciousness because it conflicts with consciously held beliefs of racial equality**

and justice. Aversive racism is a subtle but insidious form, as aversive racists enact racism in ways that allow them to maintain a positive self-image.[41]

The complexity of racism makes it seemingly invincible to redress; it reminds me of building sandcastles on a beach that are obliterated with each new tide, so the construction must begin again. In this manner, there are never enough words to make things right, and every attempt to explain the workings of racism begs another example.

In the 1977 American science-fiction movie classic *Close Encounters of the Third Kind*, you may remember how the aliens telepathically convey a message which causes humans who hear it to become consumed with an overwhelming need to create a simulation of the information they've "received." The subliminal communication turns out to be the image of a mountain in Wyoming, where they have been invited to attend a first formal meeting with the extraterrestrials.

Bias works in similar fashion. If your life experience has recorded thousands of incidents (across multiple media) in which it appears that black men are more dangerous than white men, then when real life poses a similar scenario, your brain is likely to prompt you with an image just as powerful as that *Close Encounters* mountain message.

And since we are naturally masters of rationalization, if this image does not match our conscious beliefs—if it would, for example, present a reality that we feel is politically incorrect—rest assured, we are skilled enough at rationalization that we can pull a reason out of our hat that sounds plausible.

As noted, our brains are bias organs, and their aim is accuracy, not a right or wrong sense of morality, and they record and make inferences sloppily and haphazardly. That we fill our gray matter with mistaken assumptions should have enabled us, with what has been learned in the past half century about human behavior, to make the appropriate course correction by now. Without bias we would not have survived. But remaining unaware of how bias works for the peace officers in this country is both unacceptable and dangerous.

In *21 Lessons for the 21st Century*, Israeli professor of history at Hebrew University Yuval Noah Harari puts it like this: "Most of the injustices in the contemporary world result from large-scale structural biases rather than from individual prejudices, and our hunter-gatherer brains did not evolve to detect structural biases. We are all complicit in at least some such biases, and we just don't have the time and energy to discover them all."[42] Heads up here, folks: Not having the time and energy is no excuse for peace officers. You are not exempt. When in doubt, you must assume you are likely being influenced by unconscious bias, as is everyone else—and you must do all you can to keep the playing field level by reminding yourself that bias is an inevitable function of life experience; when it becomes an obstacle to justice, it can and must be mitigated, and you have the power to do that.

HISTORY LESSONS

How does history affect bias, and what is the history of bias? Let's start with applying this question to the matter of men versus women.

History & Gender

For thousands of years, men had the right to kill their wives and daughters, and in some cultures this practice continues.[1] From the days of Plato and Aristotle in ancient Greece and Rome, through the Middle Ages and Enlightenment, to today, misogyny lives and breathes as if its ubiquity is a self-evident necessity of human survival.

The Christian Bible is a manual for misogynous tradition, and even the teachings of Buddhism, thought to be the pinnacle of egalitarianism, assume a hierarchy of gender with a measure of male superiority.[2]

Millions of females of our species have been raped, bludgeoned, executed, and murdered on emotional whim, all under a banner of righteousness. In the Middle Ages, clergy put women on pedestals and then condemned them to Hell, burning alive at the stake untold thousands suspected of being witches.[3] Then as now, the Original Sin, via the temptation of Eve and her alleged fall in the Garden of Eden, served as a virtuous demerit for women in the same manner that Jews have been stigmatized for having been the accused persecutors of Christ. If you think the fallout of such medieval thinking is not still present, you can't be paying attention.[4] And if you think subjects like this are beyond the pale of policing, I assure you, experience will convince you otherwise.

Even the notion in Christianity that only a virgin was worthy of giving birth to the son of God has ramifications about the behavior of women that are incalculable when it comes to the negative judgments that follow for simply being a female. In keeping with this ethos, women have been, and still are, held to standards that do not apply to men. A man who is aggressive and ambitious is a leader; a woman with the same attributes is a bitch or a shrew. A man who is promiscuous is a ladies' man or a stud; a woman, a slut or a whore.

In some Middle Eastern cultures, women are so subordinate to men that if they are raped, they assume the guilt for the offense.[5] If their behavior is deemed dishonorable to their male relatives, they may be put to death. You may encounter this attitude among people from many cultures and subcultures who adhere to fundamentalist views, including American-born citizens as well as some immigrants.

For most of our species' existence on the planet, women have been regarded as little more than property. Today, the residue of this tradition persists, as you are going to witness up close and personal when called to domestic disturbances. You are also likely to discover, as renowned social psychologist and Florida State University professor of psychology Roy Baumeister has observed,

"Husbands who batter their wives do so to establish their power in the family. Batterers are often men whose wives outclass or outrank them in some way, such as earning more money or having a better education."[6]

Women now maintain the right to refuse consent to sexual relations, but many people have been taught to assume women lose the right over their own bodies in matters concerning abortion. Readily-available contraceptives have resulted in some patriarchal convulsions, because the autonomy they allow women is a threat to men's powers of forced submission. The very idea that women might engage in sexual relations for sheer pleasure, as men have from the beginning, fractures the social hierarchy. Genuine gender equality frightens misogynists. All you must do to appreciate how the roles of gender have changed dramatically over time is to revisit the history of the 1960s.

Read *A Strange Stirring* by noted historian Stephanie Coontz, and even if you were an adult in the '60s—as I was—you may still be shocked by how much difference there is today in the way women are treated by men and by other women. And if you are young enough to be in this class, you will be surprised by how oppressive things were for women and girls only a half century ago; after all, women didn't get the right to vote until 1920.[7] A woman was first elected to Congress in 1916, and to the Senate in 1932. And it was not until the Equal Credit Opportunity Act of 1974 that women could get a credit card without a cosigner.

In the 1960s, when the discussion came up about women joining the force as patrol officers, the idea was considered so absurd that I don't even recall in those days having had occasion to take the issue seriously. And then, when significant numbers of women did first begin to become police officers, the issue of physical strength was always brought up as a reason they could not do the job.

But we are not hiring wrestlers and boxers; we are hiring peace officers. And, for every person in uniform, the likelihood that he or she will meet someone of superior strength is an everyday occurrence. In most cases, competent, well-trained police officers of any gender or stature should be capable of thwarting violence before it becomes physical.

History & Race

Like gender, racial differences have also been used to justify the treatment of people as property. As with gender equality, the fight for racial equality in the United States remains a young and ongoing struggle. But our history with racial bias runs deep—all the way back to colonial days, when this country's very existence was secured with the help of chattel slaves.[8]

On my bookshelf at home, I keep a June 2014 copy of *The Atlantic* magazine with these words always visible: "250 years of slavery. 90 years of Jim Crow. 60 years of separate but equal. 35 years of state-sanctioned redlining. Until we reckon with the compounding moral debts of our ancestors, America will never be whole." The magazine article is titled "The Case for Reparations," and was written by journalist and national correspondent for *The Atlantic* Ta-Nehisi Coates.[9] I look at this succinct summary of history occasionally to remind myself that those in our ranks who claim we now have a level racial playing field in this country don't know what they are talking about, just like when they talk about gender equality.

Most of the rules and laws we live by were legislated by a white majority with the power to encode whiteness into the backdrop of what we experience as cultural reality. And it is not a stretch to say that pluralism and multiculturalism threaten white racists. White Americans will soon be a demographic minority, and this inevitable occurrence is upping the existential angst of lots of people who fear a minority status, especially people who have grown up assuming their privileged lifestyle represents a just status quo. Add politicians who use dog-whistle language to convey their racist contempt to a bigoted constituency, and you have increased the difficulty of peace officers' jobs substantially. That so many of our so-called angry white men can't be made aware of the privileges they have derived from sharing their skin color with those in power is a tragic misfortune.

Which is why professor of sociology at Stony Brook University, Michael Kimmel, in his 2013 book *Angry White Men*, says, "[W]hite men are the beneficiaries of the single greatest affirmative action program in world history. It's called world history."[10] Women and minorities, he continues, are not the enemies of white men; instead:

> **Our enemy is an ideology of masculinity that we have inherited from our fathers, and their fathers before them, an ideology that promises unparalleled acquisition coupled with a tragically impoverished emotional intelligence. We have accepted an ideology of masculinity that leaves us feeling empty and alone when we do it right, and even worse when we feel we're doing it wrong. Worst of all, though, is when we feel we've done it right and still do not get the rewards to which we believe we are entitled. Then we must blame somebody. Somebody else.[11]**

We have a long way to go. This is evidenced by many facts—including, for example, that black men are still followed and detained by police officers and store clerks to a far greater extent than are whites.[12] Black men are stopped and frisked much more frequently than white men; they receive harsher prison sentences; they are more likely to be sentenced to death.[13] And they are more likely to be shot by police officers, whether those officers are white or black.[14] Why? What do you think the statistics suggest? Innumerable studies show that a higher percentage of African American and Latino men are incarcerated, stopped and frisked, receive longer prison sentences for the same crimes as whites, earn less money for similar employment, or have a smaller net worth than do whites. I want you to make it a habit to keep up with these findings yourselves.[15] In most cases, you can simply ask your cell phone, albeit with the caveat to double-check your sources as always, because determining the veracity of online data is continuously getting harder.

Stopping cars for any reason possible, especially in locations considered high-crime areas, has long been a policy of many urban police departments, but there is social cost of trust in doing so. As the authors of *Pulled Over* describe:

> **Investigatory stops erode individual liberty, undermine democratic equality, and divide local communities by income, race, and ethnicity. They target those who are mainly racial or ethnic minorities for intrusive surveillance and leave others, who are mainly white, free from this intrusion. To be white is to be honored as an equal member of the community and treated fairly: To be African American or Latino is to be disrespected as less than an equal and subject to manipulation by arbitrary inquisitive power.[16]**

The statistics offered above about how black men are treated by law enforcement are routinely disregarded by police departments as being inaccurate, with accusations to the effect that these numbers are the result of cherry-picking. But unless you gather all the fruit on the tree, all such selections are cherry-picked. I offer you these numbers, as well as those to come, not as absolute truth, but as probable cause for further investigation. I do so feeling completely confident that the people whom I have quoted or referenced sincerely believe them to be true. If they are mistaken, then through your actions you may be able to change their perception by proving these conditions no longer apply. But ideology aside, you should be concerned that so many people sincerely believe something you don't that is so important to your work.

You are also going to hear declarations from white citizens and fellow officers to the effect that racism is a dead issue, while evidence to the contrary is ubiquitous and overwhelming—as the amount of reading that I suggest you do makes clear. Bigotry and racism are very much alive, and the stark reality is that, despite a body of knowledge about bias, most people in America and the world grow up without understanding its nature or how it is impacting us individually and as a society.

In 1945, just after the end of World War II, President Harry S. Truman proposed a plan for universal healthcare. There was enough goodwill to have made it happen, had it not been for still-blatant racism in the deep South, where fear on the part of white citizens that universal healthcare would mean sharing doctors and medical facilities with African Americans was enough to defeat the effort.[17] To recognize how many U.S. citizens since then must have died because of lack of adequate medical treatment is a staggering proposition.[18] When people try to pretend that racism is over, I hope you will keep these things in mind and understand that, historically, systemic prejudice in the form of racism is embedded in the bone marrow of our culture. That's why reflection is always preferable to snap judgments.

It's also why we need our literature to help us be objective about matters of race. Consider the book and movie *To Kill a Mockingbird*, which represented a social ideal based on Harper Lee's editor's view of a morally-just society; compare this to *Go Set a Watchman*, an earlier work by Harper Lee when she worked with another editor. *Go Set a Watchman* more closely reflects the racial bias of Lee's father and her community. It's idealism versus reality. This disparity between our ideals and our reality is just as true today as it was in the era in which *To Kill a Mockingbird* was set. Fiction can make the imaginary seem real, or it can make our ideals and our sense of honor seem more real than they are.

If any of you are thinking at this point that I am over-focusing on racism, you have research to do. Not knowing and not understanding the history of bigotry and racism in this country is analogous to going through life with a GPS that's a few thousand yards out of sync. Consider a trip to Montgomery, Alabama to visit the National Memorial for Peace and Justice (informally known as the "National Lynching Memorial"), and I guarantee your skepticism will dissolve.[19]

To further understand racism in its historical perspective, read American University history professor Ibram X. Kendi's *Stamped from the Beginning: The Definitive History of Racist Ideas in America* (2016).[20] When I first saw Professor Kendi on C-Span's *Book TV*, I almost stopped watching, because he seemed so young (he was born in 1982). I almost let an age bias make up my mind for me, which would have been a big mistake.

Professor Kendi explains the dynamics of racism as well as anyone I've come across in recent years, and his book is a masterpiece. Kendi details how so many justifications of racism depend on the notion that black people are in some manner inferior.[21] In other words, the racist implication is that it's never the circumstances people are forced to endure, but always their behavior that is the cause of their unequal treatment. If the only place they could buy a home was because of legal redlining, then they shouldn't have been poor to begin with; if they couldn't get a job that paid enough, then they didn't study or work hard enough. Such a focus always puts a burden of proof on black people, he points out, instead of targeting discriminatory policies. Thus, well-meaning people engage in racist ideology to solve the problem of racism. Put another way, if we focus on problems of racism as evidence of the inferiority of black people and not as discriminatory practices inherent in racism, we will never fully address the disparities.

In *How To Be An Antiracist*, Professor Kendi provides a history of the ideological phases he has personally experienced in dealing with racism from having internalized the cultural racist ideology in the community where he grew up, and for a time, having himself experienced a hatred of white people.[22] Kendi observes, "Going after White people instead of racist power prolongs the policies harming Black life. In the end, anti-White racist ideas, in taking some or all of the focus off racist power, becomes anti-Black. In the end, hating White people becomes hating Black people."[23] He writes:

> **We are surrounded by racial inequality, as visible as the law, as hidden as our private thoughts. The question for each of us is: What side of history will we stand on? A racist is someone who is supporting a racist policy by their actions or inactions or expressing a racist idea. An antiracist is someone who is supporting an antiracist policy by their actions or expressing an antiracist idea.[24]**

Critics of antiracist efforts routinely misrepresent the movement. In *The Madness of Crowds*, a book about gender, race and identity, British journalist Douglas Murray demonstrates this mischaracterization in discussing the actions of activists, whom he describes as believing that they are continuing the work of Martin Luther King, Jr.'s goal of ending racism. He writes, "In pursuit of anti-racism these people turn race from one of many important issues into something which is more important than anything else. At the very moment when the issue of race might at long last have been put to rest, they have decided once again to make it the most important issue of all."[25] Given the cerebral complexity of bias, this statement is an egregious misunderstanding of the nature of human psychology and systemic racism. The notion that a historical or an ideological turning point can put an end to racism is to completely misread the human biological and psychological basis in which systemic implicit bias persists, and until we deal with hidden bias at this level, all such rhetoric in my view is a waste of time and a further insult to injury.[26]

The psychological dynamics of racism and racial prejudice have been known for decades. In the 1950s, Gordon Allport wrote, "Not every overblown generalization is a prejudice.[27] Some are simply *misconceptions*, wherein we organize wrong information." Further, he said, "Prejudgments become prejudices only if they are not reversible when exposed to new knowledge. A prejudice, unlike a simple misconception, is actively resistant to all evidence that would unseat it."[28] Allport also reminds us that "defeated intellectually, prejudice lingers emotionally." And he warns us that "the easiest idea to sell to anyone is that he [or she] is better than someone else," that "patriotism may be a mask for bigotry," and that "extreme bigots are almost always super-patriots."[29]

Ta-Nehisi Coates' take on the subject appears in his 2015 book *Between Me and the World*, which is a letter to his son.[30] He writes that, "Americans believe in the reality of 'race' as a defined, indu-bitable feature of the natural world. Racism—the need to ascribe bone-deep features to people and then humiliate, reduce, and destroy them—inevitably follows from this inalterable condition."[31] Taking our notion of American exceptionalism seriously, Coates proposes that we adopt exceptional moral standards to defeat and eradicate this condition. I concur, and I fervently hope you do as well.

Cultures of Honor

How many of you here are from the South? A little over a third? How many of you are of Scottish descent? Only one, I see. How many of you have heard the term "culture of honor?" Okay, most of you. A few years ago, social scientists Richard E. Nisbett and Dov Cohen published *Culture of Honor: The Psychology of Violence in the South*,[32] which made the case that violence in U.S. Southern states is more likely to result from simple acts of disrespect than in the North because of a "culture of honor" among the generations of men and women from Scottish and Irish herding cultures who settled there. Because herding cultures had to be hyper-alert to pre-dation, the argument goes, an ethos of very aggressive behavior was necessary to mitigate losses of their animals—by demonstrating they were not people to be messed with. "A key aspect of the culture of honor is the importance placed on the insult and the necessity to respond to it," Nisbett and Cohen write. They continue with:

> **An insult implies that the target is weak enough to be bullied. Since a reputation for strength is of the essence in the culture of honor, the individual who insults someone must be forced to retract; if the insti-gator refuses, he must be punished—with violence or**

**even death. A particularly important kind of insult is
one directed at female members of a man's family.**[33]

Here we have a clear example of how traditions about gender
become police matters. Reading this, I can instantly recall many
instances of aggravated assault because someone said something
offensive or insulting to someone's wife, sister, mother, aunt, girlfriend, or grandmother.[34]

The culture of honor favors a posture of intensive self-regard
and extreme vigilance, not to mention paranoia, as to one's status
and one's sensitivity to shame and notions of self-worth; in seeking
a reflection of one's own worth in the eyes of others, the stage is
set for hierarchy, gang colors, violence, a felt need for all things
familiar, and a strict interpretation of what those things are with an
unwritten yet well-understood code of conduct. In *Honor Bound*,
University of Oklahoma psychology professor Ryan P. Brown
provides a list of the 50 states in order of their rank in terms of
honor-culture influence.[35] Brown reminds us that "honor cultures
tend to be heavily armed," and further, in "a small town, everyone
knows your name, and everyone knows your shame"; therefore,
trivial altercations in such cultures frequently lead to homicide.[36]

In *Southern Honor*, the late noted historian Bertram Wyatt-
Brown further illustrates the point: "The eyes witnessed honor and
looked down in deference or shame. Thus, a steady gaze from a
slave signaled impudence."[37] People who have grown up in cultures
of honor will likely be able to relate to my description and the
notion that, in such communities, men take their reputations very
seriously. In *The Better Angels of Our Nature*, Steven Pinker put
it this way: "Honor is a bubble that can be inflated by some parts
of human nature, such as the drive for prestige and the entrench-
ment of norms, and popped by others, such as a sense of humor."[38]

Of course, this is not an issue limited to the American South. As Pinker says, "Herders all over the world cultivate a hair trigger for violent retaliation."[39]

In any culture of honor, keep this in mind: When confronting men in the company of other men, if you cross a line of disrespect, they may very well feel they must retaliate simply to save face—and a few days in jail may seem to them much less of a cost than the loss of respect from their peers. Things can easily get out of control when dealing with people who have a strong code of honor. Of course, the notion of honor is a bedrock issue for police officers, and this goes double again for peace officers who have grown up having internalized a Southern-style code of honor, as I certainly did. Perhaps an enlarged amygdala may contribute.[40] I'm guessing that many of you have seen documentaries and movies depicting police officers so hypersensitive to insult that the least little annoyance results in them going ballistic.[41] Law enforcement is no place for people with badges and guns and a deep-seated sense of honor who can't abide insults without becoming violent.

One positive aspect of the Southern honor code is that Southerners are routinely more courteous than Northerners, because there is danger in rudeness—and this includes rudeness by peace officers. I've read numerous accounts of encounters by police officers in Northern communities that come across as being exceptionally rude and disrespectful. Police officers in the South, even those who bear a racial bias, are by comparison more respectful.

My training officer was from back East somewhere, and he had a really pronounced—what in the South was referred to as a Yankee—accent, made worse because he had developed the habit of questioning everyone he encountered as if they were a suspect undergoing interrogation. He was a big man, which I always figured is why he got away with this so often without complaints.

In John Wayne's last movie, *The Shootist*, his character—the ailing gunman J. B. Books—explains the code of the West to an impressionable wannabe, played by Ron Howard: "I won't be wronged, I won't be insulted, I won't be laid a hand on. I don't do these things to other people; I require the same from them."[42] This succinct characterization sums up the unspoken premise of honor in nearly all Western movies: It's the archetype for the Hollywood version of honor, which later became characterized as "macho."

I grew up internalizing this ethos of honor. When I was a child, somehow my father heard that I had been bullied at grade school, so he took me there, had me point out the boy, and stood there while I punched him. The boy, who was older and bigger than me, was so intimidated by the presence of my father that he didn't fight back. Another time, as we exited a drive-in movie theater, a driver honked his horn and yelled something at my father; I remember we followed the car home, and my father jumped out of the car and pummeled the man.

Fortunately, when I was in uniform as a police officer, I did not take insults directed at me personally; instead, I let my uniform absorb them. I hope you can do the same. To help keep your emotions in check, keep this observation from British philosopher and best-selling author Alain de Botton in mind: "Belittling others is no pastime for those convinced of their own standing. There is terror behind haughtiness."[43]

Respect, especially in poor communities, can be hard to come by—and yet, it is an issue of critical importance. In *Homo Deus: A Brief History of Tomorrow*, Yuval Noah Harari characterizes modernity as a deal under which "humans agree to give up meaning in exchange for power," and calls credit "a manifestation of trust." But what if the citizens in the neighborhoods you patrol come up short on meaning and credit both? Respect is a very sensitive issue amid poverty, and you must be careful in showing respect so that you don't come across as mocking or patronizing. And don't assume that because people are poor that they aren't smart. Our ancient forager ancestors were some of the sharpest people on the planet— that's how we got here—and living and surviving in communities where poverty is the norm is not easy.[44] Some of us here might not make it under similar conditions.

Many of us who grew up in the South were taught to have a low tolerance for disrespect, and our list of disrespectful actions we will not tolerate tends to grow as we get older—unless we are aware, as I am making you aware, and unless you aspire to address the issue before it becomes a problem. Now, add to this a few years of work in an area with lots of police action, and add the ratcheting up of daily stress and resentment from being treated disrespectfully (which comes with the job), and those of us hypersensitive to insult can become walking time bombs ready to go off at any moment—even at a minor slight.

You cannot protect and serve if you lose your self-control because of a dirty look or a snide remark. Self-control is the prize for winning the contest between your limbic system and your frontal cortex, a subject we will soon explore.[45] The thing about stress is that you don't have to experience bad situations to experience it (your imagination will work just fine), so when you are at home thinking about work you can still feel the frustration and the hormonal release just by reliving your daily experience.[46] And, two more important points here: The first is that you need to keep in mind that humor can be aggression via ridicule. Fully understanding this can help you maintain your self-control by foregoing the opportunity to laugh at someone when it is really an act of dishonor, and by refusing to lose your temper when humor is being applied to push *your* buttons.[47] The icons and symbols that any culture deems sacred represent a line for some people—so much so that crossing it requires a violent response to preserve their honor. So, if you have people of different ethnicities than your own in the community where you are working, familiarize yourself with their customs pertaining to respect, self-respect and common sense. And also attend to the reverse, for, as philosopher Sam Keen notes in *Faces of the Enemy*, "Whatever a society considers bad, wrong, taboo, profane, dirty, desecrated, inhumane, impure, will make up the epithets assigned to the enemy."[48] Therefore, in some communities, peace officers are called swine. Don't allow yourself to be upset about it when it happens to you. One more decisive point: Everything mentioned about cultures of honor applies to gangs—on steroids.

In *Moral Tribes: Emotion, Reason, and the Gap Between Us and Them*, Harvard psychology professor Joshua Greene offers analogous lessons for all of us who face a metaphorical herding ethos in our occupations (especially apt for peace officers): Consult (but don't trust) our instincts; rights are nonnegotiable; let facts speak for themselves; be aware that we are prone to make assumptions that amount to biased fairness; we share common values; and be prepared to give as well as take.[49]

Here is probable cause for you to study further: Cultures of honor cultivate an environment where insult is often answered with aggression, ranging from ridicule to violence. In what ways do you find yourself, personally or professionally, becoming hypersensitive to insult? Ask yourself this frequently. And keep in mind that in many neighborhoods where respect is considered a hard-won badge of honor there will be young men who will consider jail much more agreeable than allowing you to get away with insulting and demeaning them in front of their friends without resistance. Now, turn this back around and think about what your acceptance level of disrespect is going to be. How are you going to react to insult?

THE ROOTS OF
POLICE RACISM

All over the country, white people still swear that racial prejudice is a thing of the past, and yet myriad statistics show racial
bias is very much alive and firmly established in the present.[1] Many
people sincerely believe that because they don't harbor a conscious
negative racial bias, they obviously don't have one. Yet, in police
departments all over this country, minorities are shown to have
been overpoliced compared to the public at large. There are poor
communities in this country where a police presence resembles an
occupational wartime force.[2] Are the peace officers really the "good
guys" in a world gone bad, or has law enforcement fallen short of its
ideal to protect and to serve?

Paul Butler's insightful book *Chokehold: Policing Black Men*
is an exceptionally accurate depiction of the systemic historical
oppression black men have long experienced, from traditional law
enforcement to the present day. Butler uses the term "chokehold"
metaphorically to capture the totality of systematic oppression, and
I can't find fault with any of his positions.[3]

Now, I'm going to introduce you to someone whose work I hope you will pay a lot of attention to in the future. Norm Stamper retired as police chief of Seattle in 2000. In 1966, the same year I began as a police officer in Dallas, Stamper joined the force in San Diego. Unlike me, though, he stayed with it. Stamper worked his way up through the ranks to become the Seattle Police Chief in 1994, finally retiring the year after the World Trade Center (WTO) riots of November 1999, in which his officers used tear gas on protestors. At the time, he defended their actions as necessary to protocol, but five years later he changed his mind.[4]

Stamper is now an unapologetic police reformer. He is the author of two books, *Breaking Rank* and *To Protect and Serve*, both of which are shockingly candid and unsparing in assigning and accepting blame for the dark side of policing.[5] *To Protect and Serve* is insightful, incredibly thoughtful, and the most decisively prescriptive book I've found thus far on fixing what is broken in policing today. Stamper addresses racism and misogyny in-depth in a personal and historical context, and he elaborates on law enforcement's resistance and reluctance to deal with these subjects effectively. Given the talking points we usually encounter with the subject of police behavior, Norm Stamper's honesty is startling, refreshing, much needed, and appreciated. Keep his name in mind, as we will frequently revisit his work.

Howard Rahtz, a retired Cincinnati police captain, also adds unvarnished historical context in his book, *Understanding Police Use of Force*:

> **The history of police racism, from police-sanctioned violence against blacks to neglect of crime problems in black communities, is one of the most shameful chapters in American police history. Police, after all, were**

the enforcers of Jim Crow laws. Police officers in the north and south were prominent in sometimes brutally breaking up the civil rights marches of the 1960s, and police officers arrested Rosa Parks for refusing to give up her bus seat to a white man. Most of the civil disorder of the last century stemmed from confrontations between police and African-American citizens.[6]

How did policing go wrong? Just posing this question reflects an egregious lack of knowledge. The history of law enforcement in America is too exceptionally dark to be ignored if we are sincere about attempting positive reform in the present. If you are at this point feeling exasperated because it seems that I'm declaring that all police officers are racists, that is certainly not my intention—but we all live in a society where implicit racism is still a systemic part of our culture. And if you are feeling now that I am spending too much time focusing on the past, then my response is that you still don't grasp the gravity of the existential roots of racial disparities in this country, and any effort to be truly objective in the present can't ignore the past without starting off on the wrong foot.

Our Recent Racist Past

I wish I could skip what I'm about to tell you, but to do that would render this just another disingenuous effort to put the best face on a dishonorable past. A half century ago in the city of Dallas, white police officers frequently used the N-word openly. Two friends of mine, now both deceased, then shared an apartment and purchased a color television. The way they decided to settle the ownership of the television when they would eventually go their separate ways was that the first one to shoot a N_____ would get to keep the television.

To place you in the time period, my Dallas service began three years after President John F. Kennedy was killed there. In *Dallas 1963*, historian Steven Davis describes the city then as the United States' "center for resistance" for those opposed to civil rights advances. Indeed, in the wake of the assassination, it gained the nickname "City of Hate."[7] On occasion, I have asked officers who were on the force during that time what they remembered, but I stopped when it became clear it was a sore subject. My father had friends in the District Attorney's office, and I recall that he was approached about being on the jury for the Jack Ruby murder trial of Lee Harvey Oswald.[8]

In those years, we had a law on the books about suspicious behavior, whereby people who were stopped late at night in what was characterized as a high-crime area (as if any place were exempt) could be locked up overnight for investigation if they had tools in their vehicle that could be useful in a burglary, just in case it was found the next morning that burglaries had been committed in the area. This was an equal-opportunity law that could work against whites and minorities both, but as you might imagine, it was used disproportionately on minorities. The result was that people arrested for investigation of burglary would be stopped again. This time, because of having been arrested before, they could be treated as known burglars and were much easier to get past the jail sergeant. This kind of policy surely should have been unconstitutional.[9] How many lives were ruined I don't know, but my guess is that in some regions of the country similar practices still apply. In some, I suspect they may be worse today than ever because of the recent antagonistic political rhetoric about policing.

And when it came to the injustices bound to overt racism, this was only the tip of the iceberg. Sometimes white officers—and even some black officers—pretended to have the civil authority to issue divorces and other legal decrees when attempting to resolve domestic disturbances. I suspect most people being treated in such a manner knew it was a disingenuous and disrespectful ruse, and yet I suspect some citizens believed that the police had such authority.

In those days, it was commonly known that there were white officers who would stop any vehicle occupied by a black man and a white woman. If they couldn't come up with a reason to put at least the man in jail, they would write down the information from the man's driver's license (if he was in fact driving). Then the officers would let them go, write the man a traffic ticket for some made-up offense using a slightly different mailing address, and then report that the person had refused to sign the ticket. Consequently, the next time the man was stopped, he would be arrested for tickets that he had no way of knowing he had, because he hadn't gotten a notice in the mail.

Now, this practice was common knowledge among police officers in those days, and the most likely reaction to hearing about such incidents was to laugh. Think about that. Let this historical reality sink in a bit, and then think about the insistence still today that racism is a thing of the past.

In some black neighborhoods, a few South Dallas officers on late-night shifts would shoot dogs for sport—not just stray dogs, but dogs in yards or on porches, even. Whenever I heard of the shootings back then, I was so incensed that I made calls as a citizen reporting them, but nothing ever came of these that I know of. Several times I worked with partners, some of them senior, who wanted to shoot dogs and cats—and I would not allow it, regardless of their seniority. And, regarding dogs, K9 units in those days were known to let their dogs bite suspects when it wasn't at all necessary; it was needed for training, they claimed. I strongly suspect that this still occurs. No doubt, I expect much of what I've just told you comes as a shock, and it should. Do I think such behaviors can still be found in some law enforcement agencies in various parts of the country? It would be naïve to assume that they don't. Do I think it's rare? I sure hope so, but the outcry over *Black Lives Matter* suggests a different perception among the affected community.

It is not my position that most white police officers are overtly racist, but that both black and white officers are likely to harbor a subconsciously-assumed bias, seeing black men as representing more of a threat to them than white men. This should not be that hard to appreciate, given police statistics nationwide regarding arrest and police shooting incidents involving black men compared to those involving white men, especially in cases in which they were shown to have been unarmed. The evidence is irrefutable.[10]

In-Groups, Out-Groups & Tribal Tendencies

Now, as if this cycle of racial bias and negative stereotyping were not enough, we also must contend with the fact that we human beings are a tribal species, evolutionarily rigged for an in-group versus out-group worldview. This divisive delineation of *us* and *them* is literally in our genes; the tribal instinct is how we construct an us, while the ability to readily identify a *them* helps us bond.[11] We are innately wary of outsiders and strange customs, and yet, at the same time, we are profoundly social creatures, eager to form groups based on similarities and appearances.

Scientists who study human behavior have demonstrated this in many ways. For instance, people given different-colored hats on entering a room will show signs of bonding by hat color in a matter of minutes.[12] But you don't need to be a scientist to understand this.[13] What's your favorite sports team? Just consider our propensity to take sides in professional team sports, where the players aren't even from the regions they represent. Another part of being tribal is that we have an innate sense of fairness.[14] This can easily lead to an aversion to people who do not appear to pull their own weight or behave as we expect.

How does all this apply to being a peace officer? Given time, as I pointed out in the section on cultures of honor, officers may begin to feel like members of a minority—because you are. You are also in a special position in society of being always on the lookout for enemies, cheaters, and especially criminals. But if you assume a persona as "one of the good guys," versus everyone else as the "bad guys," you have ceded too much control to your subconscious, and you will miss opportunities to be more effectively and mindfully aware. For example, if you remember that gang members—by nature of their association—are trying desperately to matter as human beings, you will have a leg up in relating to them as human beings.

Ironically, and unfortunately, our increased interconnections through technology encourage polarization. As anthropologist Jack Weatherford pointed out more than two decades ago: "The communications industry has retribalized the world."[15] And thus, we are constantly made aware of our cultural differences, which make echo chambers seem like a refuge.

Our group identity is reinforced and reassured when we can collectively define and identify outsiders, and so, when given the opportunity—on the Internet or in real life—we naturally seek the shelter of group consensus. But assuming an "us and them" association of "the good guys versus everyone else" is an unacceptable occupational hazard for law enforcement officers, because thoughts lead to actions. Psychologist Roy Baumeister gives us this fair warning:

The stronger the tendency to see one's own group as good—and this tendency is often surprisingly strong—the more likely one is to regard one's rivals and enemies as evil. Such views may then be used to provide easy justification for treating one's enemies harshly, because there is no point in being patient, tolerant, and understanding when one is dealing with evil.[16]

For reasons I hope are obvious, our tribal tendencies, as humans and as officers, need to be a focal point of continuous introspection for law enforcement.

One of life's most underappreciated and underutilized lessons, and one that you must master to be effective, is that things very often are not as they appear. We pay an enormous social price for not constantly heeding such wisdom. Until you understand the deep-seated nature of racial bias and the enormous intellectual and emotional effort it takes to overcome it, you will be doomed to experience failed social interactions, resulting in communal strife and possibly even lawsuits aimed at your police department.

I don't know if a lifetime of subconscious assumptions can ever be completely overwritten, but I do know from personal experience that a strong effort to deconstruct one's own racial bias can be psychologically transforming—and that this is something you need to do up front to be an effective peace officer. To me, it's clear that the future of police-public relations depends upon a sincere effort to overcome our ignorant assumptions based on our biology. Human biological predispositions are something we should learn about as early in life as possible so as not to grow up thinking we are the odd person out. We human beings need to know that there are others who see the world pretty much as we do and others who don't even come close to the way we view things.

It's damned important, however, not to underestimate how much determination is required to objectively understand the nature and debilitating social effects of racial prejudice. As I alluded to earlier, your day-to-day experience in law enforcement is going to work against you, as your intuition will be convinced that it knows more than you do about reality as it seeks to keep you safe from ills, real or imagined. Moreover, it's crucial to understand that when children grow up internalizing prejudicial views that are not successfully challenged, their bigotry can prevail and remain socially corrosive for most of a century.

Things Are Not as They Appear

As I write this in 2019, American demographics are changing at the fastest pace in our history. Soon, white Americans will become a minority; signs of discontent lamenting this reality are already evidenced by a rise in hate groups. The irony that the overturned tables of racial discrimination are causing discontent among some in white America recalls the truism that what goes around comes around. Of course, the sentinel-aware brains that are firing up about the issue do not give a damn about fairness or morality. Our brain's lightning-quick impulse is not a fault but a feature, which exists to keep us safe from harm and embarrassment. Unfortunately, in the brain's rush to nail what is real, it makes lots of mistakes, often leading us to be guided by mistaken assumptions that will be hard to change without an intensive effort. If we allow ourselves to react uncritically, we are at fault.

And so, it comes down to this: Most of you have grown up being familiar with our minds being analogous to a computer, but that's way off the mark. As we will begin to review in the next chapter, we have a chemical factory in our heads, and being aware of our chemosensory predilections is helpful when you are charged with resolving conflict.

If you don't have enough understanding of how our minds work, you will likely experience a form of existential angst from being involved in so much apparently nonsensical human behavior. In other words, if you can't understand and thus explain the seemingly irrational behaviors you encounter, your bewilderment will be a continuous source of smoldering anxiety.

There is a persistent myth in police work that seasoned officers learn to detect intuitively when they are being lied to and when people are purposely trying to deceive them. Of course, there are techniques you can study that can be helpful in this regard. But far too often what happens is that officers fall victim to their own personal prejudices, while remaining completely unaware that they have any, and so it's possible to go through an entire career making the same mistaken assumptions, all the while convinced that you have special, experience-based savvy.

All you must do to confirm this is spend some time studying the wealth of false confessions in which wrongful convictions have been overturned by DNA evidence, then read the transcripts of the investigating officers or listen to them being interviewed.[17] Here you will find documented the rabid convictions of investigators absolutely convinced that they have a person of guilt in their presence. This belief is so strong that, for many, even DNA evidence proving they were wrong will not change their opinion that they convicted the right person.[18]

One night, working the evening shift in East Dallas, the dispatcher reported an armed robbery in progress at a 7/11 store, giving a description I don't exactly recall, but let's just say, for example, it was "a white male about 5'9", about 180 pounds, wearing a checkered shirt." I spotted a person matching that description near the location of the robbery who seemed exceptionally nervous and took him to jail for questioning. On arrival, there were four or five other squads with persons also matching the description. Every one of them was nervous. But then, who wouldn't be? If I recall correctly, the very nature of our multiple arrests meant we were required to let everyone go, because doubt was a glaring issue. Is the notion that things are not as they first appear starting to take hold? As we learn more about the nature of how our minds work, this will continue to become clearer.

As the scientists whose work we discuss here would be the first to remind us, the existence of human biological predilections is a hellishly-complicated subject, and all academic findings, including theirs, are a work in progress. That said, to make progress in furthering human relations at all levels, locally and globally, we do need to acknowledge the things we do know about human behavior:

- We are an innately tribal species, and we need to be constantly aware of our in-group versus out-group preferences to maintain some sense of objectivity when addressing our differences.

- We are also a self-deceiving species, better predisposed to try to win arguments than to choose to be objective.

- Perhaps most importantly, our character is much more subject to context than most of us realize. In other words, the circumstances we encounter have more of a bearing on how we react than how we *believe we would react if asked.*

Of course, for every embarrassing incident where police officers are shown to be misbehaving or breaking the law, there are literally thousands of situations where police officers are doing the right thing, saying the right thing, and in effect, for many victims or near-victims, saving the day—sometimes even saving lives—and providing community services. When my father passed away in 2002, the police department in Cedar Hill, Texas, without being asked, escorted our vehicles in the funeral procession and posted an officer at my parents' home during the funeral. But—and it's hard to overstate the case—10,000 virtuous deeds are obliterated by one YouTube video of a person who is not resisting arrest being beaten by officers whose autonomic nervous systems are running on automatic pilot.

It may often seem that public opinion makes policing much harder than it should be. But indeed, our whole lives are much harder than they need to be, for the simple reason that most of us have grown up without a reasonably good understanding of how our minds work, how we come to see the world the way we do, and why we intuitively ignore evidence that runs contrary to our adult worldview. In the epilogue of his book *The Body Keeps the Score*, Boston psychiatrist Bessel van der Kolk says, "We are on the verge of becoming a trauma-conscious society."[19] But I think before that is possible, we will need a much better understanding by the public about how our minds work. (And, if you have read thus far, this explanation has hopefully added to your perspective.)

To make accurate predictions about the weather, we need to understand the dynamics of climate. To gain insight into global geography, we need to understand something about plate tectonics. And yet, nearly every spokesperson, author, politician, media pundit, neighbor, friend, family member—and it seems nearly everyone on the planet, aside from social scientists—neglects to learn how our thought processes function before feeling like they have the knowledge and wisdom necessary to make accurate judgments and predictions about human behavior.

Most people are aware that we have an enormous subconscious database of knowledge and inferred observations recorded beneath our awareness. And most people, I suspect, are even aware that it is from this smoldering experiential data our motivation arises. But very few of us pay any attention to what has been learned about human behavior in the past half century and its implications, ignoring revelations about how our minds work, while we go about acting as if what we see when we look out upon the world is straight-up reality. Moreover, most of us have been taught all our lives that we are primarily rational creatures with a sense of character over which we have firm control, when nothing could be further from the truth.

We are an emotionally-driven species, and our behavior is highly subjective. I've always found it deeply disappointing that our behavior as individuals can be reliably predicted by changing the context, and yet this is something that too many of us never acknowledge.[20] And if others know this about us and we don't, are we not overtly vulnerable to manipulation?

Given what you are learning from this book, is it any wonder that the subject of bias is so misunderstood? It's hard to overstate the case. It's almost as if we are educationally mis-calibrated to not notice one of the most profound aspects of our existence. Even among well-educated people who are very familiar with the dynamics of human behavior, there is a tendency to tip one's hat at the reality of bias and then go back to business as usual. My hope is that by now you have a better appreciation of why police work requires extraordinary talent and commitment. And now, it's time to discover what behavioral scientists can teach us.

THE ELEPHANT ON YOUR BEAT: OUR ORGANIC CEREBRAL ARCHITECTURE

Is it necessary for police officers to be informed about the neural pathways, the glands, the other structures, all those behavior-governing chemicals in their brains? Probably not. But officers who have a solid theoretical and practical foundation of how fear works in their bodies, and who are repeatedly, prudently exposed in their training to realistic, fear-inducing situations, will become increasingly adept at (1) recognizing when their bodies are telling them, Hey, I'm scared here!, and (2) developing personal mastery over how they respond to the fear.

—NORM STAMPER, in *To Protect and Serve*[1]

As mentioned, while I didn't stick with law enforcement, I did become insatiably interested in human behavior, and especially in how it applies to the behavior of peace officers. What I have learned is that taking a course, reading a few books, watching videos, and attending seminars and a few training classes are simply not enough to change entrenched behavior, or even to awaken from the baffling existential nature of bias. We let ourselves off the hook far too easily by accepting what we assume is adequate preparation for a job that requires far more knowledge than we possess. In the introduction to his earlier book *Breaking Rank*, Stamper mentions Einstein's notion of doing the same thing over and over while expecting a different result; this applies here precisely, because we spend too much time discussing human antics and too little studying how our brains function, and how we adopt our beliefs and biases to set the course for everything we say and do.[2]

To have a significant effect on our bodily functions under stress, or on our unconscious biases, it's not a stretch to say that making real progress damned near requires one's desire to change to become an *obsession*. This is what *Blue Bias* is about. If you are not seriously interested in becoming a peace officer or in understanding the behavioral dynamics at work in this discipline, you may want to skim or skip some of the chapters ahead—but if you are truly interested, please don't.

Just knowing and fully appreciating the vacuum of our knowledge in such critical subjects is enough to keep one's unfamiliarity near the front page of awareness, where it belongs. This awareness is needed if we are to improve our behavioral responses, especially under extreme duress. If changing one's seemingly automatic behavior while being stressed is not a constant concern, the chances for having a positive effect in altering it are nil.

Our unconscious emotional self is located, in part, in our limbic system. This emotional self is so formidable that psychologist Jonathan Haidt, professor of moral psychology at New York University, uses the metaphor of an elephant to capture its dominant nature.[3] A rider on the elephant represents the relatively limited power of our conscious reasoning self (frontal cortex) in comparison to the vastness of our subconscious. So, metaphorically, reason is our rider on the back of an elephant. The size differential should give you an appreciation about the difficulty the rider is going to encounter when the going gets tough and our emotional subconscious is excited to the point of rampage.

When in conversation or reading text, notice how quickly your elephant is apt to jump to conclusions that amount to instantaneous emotional validation before you've had a chance to fully digest the subject at hand. You see, our elephant never sleeps. But make no mistake, police officers must become extraordinary elephant trainers, and if we aren't, or if we ever give up trying to be, we need to find another line of work.

Your silent partner is a hyperalert subset of your limbic system, always milliseconds ahead of your rider in making snap judgments—always alert, always reading the present, always interpreting and hastening connections in your brain. This watchman-driver part of your emotional elephant is always manically attentive, working to keep you safe and free from embarrassment. Your silent partner's vigilance is so acute and so determined to keep you free of harm or humiliation that it will form judgments in milliseconds based on very little information.[4] Consequently, your silent partner is prone to making errors in judgment, which, in the case of peace officers, can be fatal.

By now you may realize that, while our decisions can indeed mimic computation, our brains are more closely comparable to glands than to computers. In effect, we have a veritable chemical factory in our heads that regulates our lives through the constant release of human-manufactured hormones that give our lives context and meaning. We live in a chemosensory world, and what follows is a brief examination of the organic brain matter that serves as the physical architecture for the biologically human-manufactured chemicals that make our behavior possible and our lives meaningful.

We are influenced biologically by olfactory senses we are completely unaware of at a conscious level. (This is just another reminder that we are animals—complicated animals, if you prefer to see it that way, but still animals.)[5]

As for how much this impacts police officers, just look to the book *Understanding Human Behavior for Effective Police Work*, where Harold E. Russell, a Tucson Police Department staff psychologist, and Allan Beigel, a professor of psychiatry at the University of Arizona College of Medicine, describe the profession as the "brotherhood of biochemistry."[6] We are going to look at some of the regions of the brain where action takes place that peace officers should be especially aware of. Our ability to affect these chemical processes may be marginal, but awareness is the first step. Much innovative research is underway in this field.

In *September University*, I argue that if the brain rewards of volitional learning could be bottled, the result would likely be considered so powerful as to be considered an illegal substance.[7] Being curious and acting on it is not only immensely satisfying, but it is the reason we are still alive. We are so biologically predisposed to gain rewards from learning that once one's knowledge achieves a critical mass, adding knowledge produces a self-reinforcing endorphin rush.

Let me refer you to *Behave: The Biology of Humans at Our Best and Worst*, by professor of biology and neurological sciences at Stanford University Robert M. Sapolsky.[8] I consider this book to be required reading. My advice is to read it, put it aside for a time, and then read it again. Keep it close by for reference, until your familiarity with the subjects discussed makes you eager to discover news of further research in these disciplines. Sapolsky is all about putting our behavior in biological context, while appreciating the incredible complexity of our conduct.

Professor Sapolsky has a unique and very thoughtful way of explaining human behavior, and from time to time he has fascinating lectures available to the public on YouTube, Ted.com, and C-Span.[9] Sapolsky notes that if we see the glint of metal in a suspect's hand, we are more likely to assume it's a gun if the person is male, and especially so if the person is another race.[10] But why? Well, when we strain to find the behavioral cause of a police officer mistaking a cell phone for a gun, Sapolsky says we need to know what was going on in their head one second before they acted, and perhaps a month before as well. Their childhood experience, and even their prenatal experience via their mother's pregnancy may be relevant, and then we must consider evolutionary experience, all the way back in time to when we lived in small groups as hunter-gatherers. Of course, we don't do this as a matter of criminal investigation. And, once you delve into these subjects, you will quickly conclude that some of these matters are so involved that the right answers to your questions will never be found. The point is, when we try to explain these things away simply, they are just not black and white. Police work is a veritable field of gray.

How many of you have heard the terms "framing," and "priming" or "anchoring" used to describe the way we respond psychologically to social situations?[11] No hands in the air? Well, it may be psychology jargon, but there is nothing mysterious here. This comes about as close to common sense as anything in the field: "Framing" has to do with establishing context, and "priming," or "anchoring," is our tendency to focus on the last example we've been asked to consider—whether or not it is related—before we act on something else. For example, if I give you an enormous number to consider, and then I ask you to estimate something unrelated requiring an answer in the form of a number, the estimate you come up with is likely to be higher because of my having primed or anchored the situation with that first number. The prime or anchor produces a sort of starting point in our thought processes. Imagine how much more effective you might be at diffusing conflict and disturbances if you studied the language of resolution in the context of framing, anchoring and priming.[12] What if you could bring calm to incidents involving heated conflict simply by choosing words that reframe and diffuse the situation?

In a U.S. Department of Justice analysis of shootings by Philadelphia police officers between 2007 and 2013, writes neuroscientist and Northeastern University professor Lisa Feldman Barrett, 15 percent of those shot were unarmed; in half of *those* cases, an officer misidentified a nonthreatening object or movement as a weapon.

"Many factors may contribute to these tragedies, ranging from carelessness to racial bias," she writes, "but it is also possible that some of the shooters actually perceive a weapon when none is present due to *affective realism in a high-pressure and dangerous context.*" (The emphasis is mine.) "The human brain is wired for this sort of delusion, in part, because moment-to-moment interoception [the work of your silent partner to give you that inner sensation or hunch] infuses us with affect, which we then use as evidence about the world."[13] Simply put, we see what we expect to see, because our life experience has conditioned us to do so. In fact, we are so used to seeing and hearing what we expect to hear and see that when we hear a song sung or a poem read by someone other than the first person we heard perform it, it likely won't sound right. Our subconscious is more comfortable with the familiar, because it intuits that being familiar is instrumental in keeping us safe and secure.

Back to Sapolsky. Another way to think of our past is that all the things Sapolsky mentions have contributed to the totality of what and who we are today, all of us. So, when we are in uniform on the street, we are influenced by our past, the context of what's occurring in this instant, how we feel, and how we relate to the future. This may sound like such common sense that you think it need not be discussed, but I'm confident that with some years of rewarding experience under your belt you will appreciate that such thoughtfulness goes with the job. Just try it. After all, if you aren't open to new and weird experiences, how are you going to cope in a job that presents you daily with them, including some that will test the limits of your ability to endure disgusting behavior?

Once again, human motivation is incredibly complex. Aside from sleeping when we are tired, or eating when we are hungry, we aren't very good at guessing the real reasons for our actions from one moment to the next, let alone knowing why others are acting. Our assumptions are, as often as not, based upon sparse information, and worse still, we are egregiously self-deceptive.[14] This is especially dangerous for peace officers, because your self-deception in believing what you want to believe (despite facts to the contrary) comes at the public's expense.

Our actions are heavily influenced by context. Change the context, and our response is likely to change as well. One thing we know for certain from research is that we human beings are experts at rationalizing our behavior when asked why we have done this or that. We are prone to make up something on the spot that has nothing whatsoever to do with our actions, but which may sound plausible in our own minds as a reasonable explanation because we are experiencing confirmation bias.[15] So it's hard to overemphasize the importance of understanding this behavioral trait in police work when dealing with suspects and witnesses. After-the-fact explanations that make sense can stop an investigation that should be just getting underway, while someone's admission of being clueless about what happened can result in suspicions of guilt.

We are not born blank slates. Our genes have predispositions that are turned on and off by our life experiences.[16] Amazingly, we are born with wiring that remains incomplete and continues making connections until we draw our last breath. And yet, as individuals, we are emotionally stamped by our cultural imprint. Although any number of things seem innate in our makeup as human beings, many aspects of our biology are more apparent than real. We interface and interact with the world to replicate the reality of what we have learned through our individual life experiences. Lisa Feldman Barrett writes:

> **Emotions are not temporary deviations from rationality. They are not alien faces that invade you without your consent. They are not tsunamis that leave destruction in their wake. They are not even your reactions to the world. They are your constructions of the world. Instances of emotion are no more out of control than thoughts or perception or beliefs or memories. The fact is, you construct many perceptions and experiences and you perform many actions, some that you control a lot and some that you don't.**[17]

Your silent partner encompasses all your life experiences, your health, your emotional baggage, and the way you are feeling at any given moment. Your silent partner is forever looking out for you, to keep you safe not only from physical harm, but free from embarrassment, and free from being uncomfortable in social situations. But your silent partner has millions of records to sort through in the blink of an eye. And though you can usually trust your silent partner, you must be very much aware that your twitchy silent partner can at any time revert to a sense of being on the Serengeti Plain, so to speak, where life-threatening occurrences were all too frequent and decisions had to be made in milliseconds. This is why training and the confidence it inspires are so important, because when you really do know what you are doing, you are less likely to overreact.

So, your silent partner is your elephant's sentinel intuition writ large; it's the equivalent of your security central headquarters—a system always scanning the horizon for possible harm or embarrassment. This is the part of your elephant that speaks to you via feelings without words, the part that prompts you to fill in the lines and cross the T's and dot the I's you can't see consciously, but which you infer. Oftentimes, your silent partner experiences confusion when in unfamiliar territory, so, if simulation is called for because comparison is the only way you can assess the situation you find yourself in, then simulation of something similar is what you will get. And thus, simulation can instantaneously turn a cellphone into a weapon because of a streetlight flashing, reminiscent of earlier observations of a gleaming light from a gun barrel. When your safety calls for a guess, a guess you will get. Your silent partner constructs emotions in concert with previously-learned emotion, and this process is repeated endlessly all the way back to the beginning of you.

Your silent partner is unconcerned about what is or isn't moral. That's your rider's territory. So, consider this: How many times do you think your rider has witnessed instances where police officers have been involved in shootouts with criminals in movies and television shows? Your silent partner doesn't stop to ask whether this situation is real or just something observed on the big screen. What do you suppose your silent partner assumes about the fact that our streets are full of people with primitive emotions and armed with modern weapons? Most police officers spend their entire career without ever firing a shot. Contrast this with police training, where you move through buildings with pop-up photos, some of unarmed civilians and some with people aiming a gun at you with the intention to shoot. Do you think your silent partner may be influenced simply by the frequency of occurrence? Something else to consider: Lisa Feldman Barrett argues that our emotions as individuals are unique, and yet we are pretty good, based on experience, at sensing what is on people's minds by the expressions on their faces.[18] Though this remains unsettled business in academia, there is still lots of support for Paul Elman's Facial Action Coding System (FACS) which has long been assumed to be a reliable method of interpreting facial expressions.[19] But next time you go through target practice with photos of people poised to shoot you, ask your instructors if the expressions on these shooter's faces are congruent with what would be considered a facial expression of aggression with intent to kill.[20] If they don't know, you might politely call their attention to the latest research that shows intent is relevant.[21] Your silent partner makes snap judgments in milliseconds, and we don't know what he or she knows, but we should consider ourselves duty-bound to offer them the best versions of reality that our training departments can produce.[22]

Presumably you can see right away how various issues could impact your judgment about whether to pull a trigger when you are confronted. What you see in front of you in such situations is, in effect, a culmination of your life experience, edited and incessantly tweaked over and over, so that in the present moment, you are fully prepared to do what is necessary to stay alive, to stay safe, and to save face. Moreover, when you are face to face with a suspicious person in a dark alley, your silent partner will be projecting based on experience—real or imagined, from the cinema or from your past—because your silent partner is only interested in interpreting what's happening now.

Further, the way our elephant feels is influenced by the status of the flesh. In other words, our physical health plays a key role in what our silent partner tries to infer or convey. Feeling ill or having had a dreadful day as a police officer can result in a simple error in judgment with dire consequences.

One day, on a disturbance call in Dallas many years ago (I don't recall the nature of the call except that it involved a man with a knife), I arrived with my partner, and a man started down an apartment's outside stairwell with what looked like a knife in his hand. My partner, who was senior to me, unholstered his gun and aimed it at the man. I climbed the stairs and met the gentleman before he got to the bottom. Again, I don't remember why the man had a knife, but I clearly remember not being very alarmed myself, and that he gave me the knife without resisting. He looked inoffensive, and he was in fact harmless. But although it was obvious to me that he was not a threat to us, my partner was agitated that I had gotten in his line of fire and kept him from shooting. Technically from a police tactical point of view, my partner was right, in that I had taken an unnecessary risk. I perceived that the individual was not a threat and he wasn't. But what was disappointing to me was that my partner had just learned that the man was not a threat, and still his main issue was that I had been in his way and kept him from shooting.

So, are any of you discouraged by what I've said so far? No hands in the air? Are you beginning to understand the complexity of the field you are entering? When you see policework represented in the colors of black and white, take this as your reminder that elephants are gray, not black-and-white.

Limbic System

Bringing together what we have learned so far: The stomping grounds of your elephant and the headquarters for your silent partner are part of an overarching system that operates as a sort of regional headquarters for your emotions.

In 1952, neuroscientist Paul D. Maclean coined the term limbic system while putting the concept in an evolutionary sense by referring to it as a triune brain, or three brains in one: The reptilian cortex, the paleomammalian complex, and the neomammalian complex.[23] Now, this is metaphorical oversimplification, but it helps in putting the matter in perspective. All you need to be concerned about here is that this is about learning to control your emotions when everyone around you seems to be unable to control theirs.

The functions of our brain that take place beneath our conscious awareness are breathtaking in scope and complexity. How many of you believe the notion that we have free will? I expect most hands are in the air, for now. But I will ask that question again before we are through.

Amygdala

Your amygdala is an almond-shaped structure in your brain's limbic system located close to the hippocampus just under the cortex: It's in the temporal lobe, and it makes up a big part of your super-intuitive ride-along companion. Stimulating the amygdala can result in an outburst of aggression.[24] In a tenth of a second, the amygdala can activate upon seeing the face of a stranger and make a distinction based on race and the degree of danger the person represents. The amygdala has a lot to do with mediating aggression. The amygdala is the hot spot for fear and anxiety; as such, this brain organ is always hyperalert for signs of danger, causing a reaction that occurs milliseconds before your conscious awareness even kicks in. This means your silent partner is making assumptions before you are even aware that anything is taking place, such as intuitive reactions to faces of other races.[25]

Post-traumatic stress disorder (PTSD) is evidence of an overactive amygdala. Amygdala anxiety plays a role in our decision-making process by intuiting a sense of fairness in our favor, in effect, looking out for our interests. The amygdala's vigilance is what makes it useful as our personal sentry, our lifeguard, or bodyguard, always poised to act instantaneously or alert the frontal cortex of danger. The amygdala is your silent partner's sentinel awareness center, always ready to set off an alarm in your cerebral apparatus—where it will send messages to other regions of your brain to do what is necessary to keep you safe.

But your amygdala also processes information that comes from your cortex, meaning it is supersensitive to your well-being. For example, say you are interrogating a suspect, and your amygdala is awakened by what the rider has heard via the cortex, which amounts to a threat; when this is the case, your silent partner will send a feeling to your frontal cortex that will be interpreted as danger.

American journalist and filmmaker Sebastian Junger spent 15 months embedded with a U.S. Army platoon in eastern Afghanistan. In his account, titled simply *War*, he chronicles the feel of war in an uncommonly-revealing examination of the psychological costs of combat.[26] Junger shows the effects of battle fatigue on the psyches of individuals who, after spending so much time in what can only be described as full-throttle stress, get hooked on adrenaline rushes of the intensity that only war can satisfy.[27] Yet, on another level, they learn to hate the very thing from which they derive purpose.

The movie *The Hurt Locker* offers a clear demonstration of this phenomenon. Or, as neuroscientist and professor of psychiatry and behavioral sciences at Emory University Gregory Berns puts it in his book *Iconoclast*, "So while it is true that time heals all wounds, as far as the brain goes, scars remain."[28]

In *War is a Force That Gives Us Meaning*, former war correspondent and university lecturer Chris Hedges says, "the rush of battle is a potent and often lethal addiction," because "war is a drug."[29] War, as Hedges points out, tends to simplify things as being black and white, right versus wrong, often obscuring the fact that it is anything but. I think the same is true in police work, in how peace officers get hooked on the accentuated feelings of being alive in the face of danger. If war is a drug for soldiers predicated on an adrenaline rush, then surely in some instances the risk associated in dealing with criminals is a drug for peace officers. Hedges points out that war is our most powerful way to achieve meaning.[30] And it may be that the residue of crime also gives us the dark side of meaning.

From my experiences as a Marine and as a police officer, I can understand what it's like to feel the reward of adrenaline rushes, so I can readily appreciate how veterans of extreme combat become psychological casualties, regardless of whose side is said to have won a war. Veterans of extreme combat experience a time warp in which the recent past is too painful to remember, while the future is degraded for the simple reason that they may not have one. This leaves an exaggerated present, where hyper-vigilance is necessary just to stay alive. After a time, combat becomes vital to keep memories of the recent past in the past and the prospect of no future at bay, even though engaging in combat presents an elevated risk. And thus, one enters an addictive cycle of needing the very thing one needs to escape.[31]

Ernest Becker also pointed out, as have many others, that we humans can only bear so much reality.[32] Posttraumatic stress disorder, or PTSD, would appear to be an overdose of reality. PTSD is an example of what happens when the security that we assume comes from the sanctuary of our culture is overwritten with a foreboding and unrelenting expectation of chaos, and once the psychological refuge is gone, it's hard to recover.[33] The tragic result is that the present suicide rate of American servicemen and women now rivals the number of casualties in actual combat.[34] Another caveat about military training is that personnel trained to view the enemy as the "other," as something less than human, will likely need a lot of training and supervision to ensure that they do not bring this mindset to your local neighborhoods as police officers. If you are a veteran of extensive combat training and actual combat experience, you have some serious probable cause here.

Now, you are not soldiers or neuroscientists; you are police officers. But like neuroscientists, you need to know something about what is going on in your heads to meet your objectives. And if you are careful—very careful—your silent partner won't jeopardize your career and become a threat to public safety. In recent years a lot has been learned about human behavior that is still not being used in a practical sense.[35] You can change that by becoming so interested in your profession that you will constantly be alert for current information to add to your knowledge and experience. As psychologist Mihaly Csikszentmihalyi points out, "To keep enjoying something, you need to optimally increase its complexity." Human behavior offers an inexhaustible field of exploration, and as Csikszentmihalyi observes, "Enjoyment appears at the boundary between boredom and anxiety, when the challenges are just balanced with the person's capacity to act."[36]

I expect that before today you may have found it unusual to hear someone suggest that peace officers should keep one ear tuned to the science of human behavior, and that you should look upon colleges and universities as important resources. I hope I have made this point clear enough so that you can appreciate the seriousness of the matter. As you will soon see, your police experience will very likely cause your amygdala to increase in size, and when this happens you are also likely to experience a spillover into feelings of disgust.

Insular Cortex

You can think of the insular cortex as your headquarters for disgust.[37] Primatologist Frans de Waal notes that disgust has become the "Cinderella of emotions" because of the attention it is getting in psychology.[38] My take is that this is good news because understanding the nature of disgust is vitally important and this part of your brain is going to get a workout in police work. Witnessing human behavior at its worst will become routine. The trick is not to become so overcome with disgust that you succumb to bitterness and burnout, because it's easy to do. Your frontal cortex (your elephant rider) needs to become astute at offering perspective under disgusting circumstances. Something to keep in mind is how a career in law enforcement is likely to affect your worldview about the nature of human beings, and how you can learn how to address that so that you don't become disillusioned, jaded and callous. Philosophy professor Edwin J. Delattre says:

> **Burnout is not a cause, but rather a description of failure. Clinical studies treat burnout as "the debilitating malaise that affects people in the helping professions ... like police officers, who initially have**

high expectations of personal contribution" but whose expectations, either of themselves or of their work, go basically unsatisfied.[39]

It is thought the insular cortex likely developed in response to being poisoned or sickened by tainted or spoiled food during periods when this was frequently a matter of life and death. This brain region may also be activated when identifying people whom we see as "others." For example, we human beings are a clever, multitalented species in that we can turn our political foes into icons that have the same metaphoric value as food poisoning.[40] Any human being can become associated with disgust simply by being mentioned repeatedly in a negative context until one becomes disgusted at being reminded of them; this technique is frequently used to disparage political candidates.

In their book *Objection: Disgust, Morality, and the Law*, University of Miami professor of psychology Debra Lieberman and professor of legal studies at the University of Central Florida Carlton Patrick put it like this: "From courtrooms to novels to the media to everyday conversation, criminals are frequently described in disgust-inducing terms: vile, slime, scum, dirt bags, pieces of garbage, pieces of shit. They are associated with dirt, refuse, reptiles, insects, and excrement."[41]

As peace officers we are also quite capable of using metaphors to associate people we encounter under negative circumstances with disgust.[42] So you are going to have to work extra hard to keep this region from becoming overcrowded. I'm guessing I am likely the first person to also recommend that peace officers become intimately acquainted with the nature of metaphors and how we use these language tools to make sense of everyday existence, and how a simple change in metaphor can dramatically change the context and approaches we use to solve problems and the attitudes of the people involved. But keep in mind that your insular cortex is quite capable of taking metaphors to capture disgust *quite* literally. Metaphors frame our discussions and set the tone and the response parameters for what is being presented. It shouldn't be surprising that war metaphors can make violence appear to be the only solution to a problem. So, if you find yourself needing to be articulate while mediating a dispute, avoid war and battle metaphors.[43] In *The Origins of Creativity*, renowned American biologist, theorist, and naturalist E. O. Wilson said, "Without metaphors, we would be savages." This is an important observation to keep in mind, especially if you are charged with keeping the peace.[44]

In *Philosophy in the Flesh*, linguists George Lakoff and Mark Johnson say that:

> **Conscious thought is the tip of an enormous iceberg. It is a rule of thumb among cognitive scientists that unconscious thought is 95 percent of all thought— and that may be a serious underestimate. Moreover, the 95 percent below the surface of conscious awareness shapes and structures all conscious thought. If the cognitive unconscious were not there doing this shaping, there would be no conscious thought.[45]**

These language scientists contend that metaphors are our primary means of navigating abstract thought, and that metaphors provide the very grounding for our moral system of right and wrong.[46]

So as peace officers, how could you not be interested in this subject? We use a moral accounting system: A moral mapping in which *up* is good, while *down* is bad, *warm* is better than *cold*, *big* is better than *small*—the list is endless.[47] Metaphors provide us with a system of power relationships comprising what is considered a natural moral order, and nowhere do you more need a sentinel authority to stand guard than at the door to your insular cortex, because once we have allowed ourselves to stereotype and stigmatize individuals, groups, or races of people as belonging to a category of disgust, we have set our prejudice in our insular cortex in concrete, where it will take a jackhammer of dissonance to free it. As professor of psychiatry Gregory Berns reminds us, "Categories are death to imagination. So, the solution is to seek out environments in which you have no experience. The environments may have nothing to do with the individual's area of expertise. It doesn't matter. Because the same systems in the brain carry out both perception and imagination, there will be a crosswalk."[48] In other words, once we assign something to a category, we have in effect put it away, as in being out of sight, out of mind. Or, in many cases, categorizing something may result in not considering exceptions to what you have up to now assumed to be the rules, and it's time to apply some imagination. Recall my comments about our political orientations in the Introduction. If we categorize our political opposition as being "the other" as an equivalence of disgust, we essentially tune them out and relegate them to a status of having nothing to say worthy of our attention. In other words, our polarization is set, and yet, you are going to be serving a public in which half or more of the citizens you encounter are going to see the world very differently than you do, which calls for some empathy if you can rescue it from your gray matter. Both liberal and conservative values are necessary for a fully-functional democratic society, and ignoring or disparaging either side as being unworthy of consideration is a recipe for failure and a virtual guarantee that justice will remain beyond our reach.

Anterior Cingulate Cortex

You can think of the anterior cingulate cortex as Empathy Central.[49] It helps regulate your blood pressure and your emotional relations with others. Empathy is a critical sentiment in law enforcement. Norm Stamper argues that police officials and critics alike are likely to agree about the empathetic ability of peace officers in being able to put yourself in another person's shoes.[50] I suspect that this region of our brain can be influenced through continuous effort. My personal experience suggests that we can be taught to care and empathize with others through the actual practice of doing so. As for what research says, the jury is still out on this topic—as it is, for that matter, on all these cerebral science subjects—but the future is promising.[51]

In the suggested reading, you will find the real-life reasons that you can and should connect with people with whom you may never have had a reason to believe you needed to meet. In learning to personally relate to others, you can develop some damned good reasons to protect and serve people you previously felt no connection with at all. And make no mistake, if you cannot somehow relate emotionally to some members of the community you serve, they will know. Norm Stamper suggests that empathy should be a job requirement for police candidates, requiring proof that they can express empathy backed up by past examples.[52] So, we bring this issue to the thoughtful and careful attention of our frontal cortex.

Frontal Cortex

The frontal cortex (the primary headquarters of your elephant rider) is the last part of our brain to reach maturity.[53] This is something to keep in mind when dealing with children, especially adolescents, because we find them in adult circumstances while they are still immature, and yet, we have great difficulty relating to the fact that they don't act like adults.[54] The frontal cortex acts in the personification of an adult, the reasoning and focus center of the rider charged with controlling your elephant. Our frontal cortex is what makes us so very differently able from our fellow primates. Your frontal cortex is incredibly complicated, but that's okay; your job is not to understand it so much *per se* as to arm it with unforgettable information about how to keep your elephant under control. The more your rider learns, the better the chances are that he or she can do so.

Hippocampus

Wear-and-tear alert here, folks. The hippocampus is a horseshoe-shaped cerebral organ located above your brain stem, and it is integral to the function of your emotions, your long-term memory storage and your spatial navigation.[55] Extreme cortisol stress to the hippocampus can result in memory impairment. If you spend a lifetime career as a peace officer, your hippocampus is going to get a workout. Too much cortisol because of continuous conflict can impair bone formation and result in damage that can cause interference in the hippocampus's ability in comparing similar experiences.[56] For peace officers, this can spell confusion and affect your judgment, because of an inability to distinguish among separate volatile incidents. The hippocampus mediates learning and fear. Robert M. Sapolsky notes:

> **The hippocampus decides whether a factoid is worth filing away, depending on whether the amygdala has gotten worked up over it. Moreover, the coupling can**

rescale. Suppose someone robs you at gunpoint in an alley in a bad part of town. Afterward, depending on the circumstance, the gun can be the cue and the alley the context; or the alley is the cue, and the bad part of town the context.[57]

So, clearly, this is a heads-up about the importance of your ability to manage the stress that comes with the job. If you reach the point that you are getting your cues and signals mixed up about what is and isn't dangerous, you are vulnerable to making egregious errors in judgment.

Moreover, it's important to realize the complexity of how your memory functions. In his book *Aware*, professor of psychiatry at the UCLS Medical Center Daniel J. Siegel observes:

When we have an experience, we *encode* the firing of neural networks at the present moment, which then alters the connections in the brain in the forms— strengthening synapses, altering epigenetic regulation, laying down the interconnecting myelin sheath. These changed connects are the structural basis for memory *storage.* At a later time, an internal or external cue similar in some ways to the initial encoding experience can trigger the firing of those stored neural connections, and then we have memory retrieval.[58]

Siegel reminds us that when retrieved bits of information are recalled and enter consciousness, they are not tagged as coming from the past. So, what we learn about the role of the hippocampus helps us to realize why it is vital that we are aware of the complexity of being aware. The seriousness of this dilemma is simple to understand, but it's much harder to address, because Siegel's observation suggests that incidents you have encountered in the past can seem to be happening all over again in the present: This could result in the kind of confusion that could cost you your life, or cause you to unnecessarily take the life of another.

BRAIN CHEMISTRY

The chemical concoctions our bodies manufacture provide us with meaningful experiences. These processes are incredibly complicated, but you don't need to be a neuroscientist to appreciate their role in behavior.

Dopamine

Here is your reward potion. Dopamine is an organic chemical that we humans self-manufacture, and it helps control and regulate our brain's reward center.[1] You need to fully appreciate how this works, because it can get you fired—or worse—killed.

I will get back to this in detail, because you need to fully understand what's going on in your heads and how certain things you do become such rewarding experiences that you may learn to crave them without being aware that you are doing so. Dopamine is a neurotransmitter synthesized in multiple brain regions and is experienced by us as a reward chemical.[2] Dopamine is triggered simply by the anticipation of obtaining a reward, and acts of anticipating getting even—such as by engaging in acts of revenge, can produce the chemical.[3] The effects of dopamine are more linked to anticipation of a reward than the actual reward itself, and as such the anticipation can become a key link to learning.[4] Thus, intermittent reinforcement can be more powerful than regimented reward, which helps explain the appeal of slot machines.

As Robert M. Sapolsky puts it, "(N)othing fuels dopamine release like the 'maybe' of intermittent reinforcement."[5] And so, the pursuit or chase can become more important than the reward; dopamine fuels such goal-directed behavior, binding the value of the reward to the pursuit itself.[6] And thus, a particular kind of call for the police can signal the feeling that excitement is due, because your reward is forthcoming—so the existential question you need to constantly ask yourself is: "Am I becoming prone to overtly just taking actions, rather than addressing the reason I have been called, in order to reap the rewards I am accustomed to expecting?"[7] You should also be aware that the rewards of dopamine depend in part on there being a reasonable chance for success.[8] And prolonged stress can cause a depletion of dopamine.[9] People who may be described as adrenaline junkies may have difficulty maintaining adequate levels of dopamine, prompting them to seek new stimuli.[10] And there are alternative stimuli. For example, the rewards of learning can truly be exhilarating. When all your knowledge about a subject begins to achieve critical mass, adding a fact or an idea can cause a dopamine-driven kaleidoscopic reorganization that is both exhilarating and enthralling. On this I speak from experience.[11]

Oxytocin

Oxytocin is a hormone that plays a significant role in our social relations, including bonding and relating to others, and it has some social effects that can move us toward in-group bonding at the expense of out-groups.[12] We are only now beginning to appreciate the role of oxytocin in our sociality. This hormone may be a key to understanding our tribal nature, which both bonds us and sets limits on our exposure to otherness. If we perceive an exposure is extreme, oxytocin begins to take over and negatively influences our emotional response to cultural differences. This discovery should maintain our attention and awareness: The very hormones that aid mothers and fathers in bonding with children and enable adults bonding with one another and with groups can also act as a toxin against others.[13]

As Csikszentmihalyi observes, "The larger the group with which one identifies, the closer to ultimate reality one gets. Only the person who sees the entire planet as her world can recognize a toxic substance as poison no matter where it is dumped."[14] The same principle applies to justice and the notion that a crime committed against one is a crime committed against all.

Testosterone

Here we have a hormone that is a subject of much misunderstanding.[15] Testosterone is a male hormone and an anabolic steroid that plays a vital role in dominance.[16] Instead of literally making us more aggressive, it renders us capable of doing what needs to be done. If aggression is called for, aggression we will get, if it is in keeping with our temperament. It is generally assumed that a spike in testosterone automatically means increased aggression, but this is an oversimplification in that testosterone helps us do what we are already inclined to do.[17] If it is in our nature to become physically aggressive, then this hormone will aid in our becoming so, but if we are predisposed to reason our way toward a resolution to a conflict at hand, then this hormone will also help us in that function. Testosterone is a chip-on-the-shoulder supply of chemi-cals battle-ready to challenge dominance when an occasion arises. And occasion is a key word here, because the appearance of an attractive woman in the company of men can cause a spike in tes-tosterone. So, think about how many times as police officers, both male and female, that you will find yourselves in situations that cause your body to literally man up, so to speak.

Testosterone rises in young adulthood and begins to subside with age, and it's important to keep in mind always that it's a read-iness aid, and not something that causes us to act against our will. (So, you can't rough someone up and claim your testosterone made you do it.) Another point important for you to understand as peace officers is that violence is less a result of too little self-esteem and more likely to be the result of too much.[18]

Here is something to think about that I haven't researched in great depth but that might be something for you to be on the lookout for: What might be the hormonal effects of peace officers in groups when in the presence of many other officers? What is the likelihood that a group of alpha males and alpha females will cause an unusual spike in testosterone, so that if you respond to a conflict as a group, not only will you be set for combat, but you will likely take your cues from those most inclined by temperament to become physical?[19]

Something else that's important to consider for future reference is that sexuality and aggression are both responsive to testosterone. The degree to which we respond to the release of testosterone into the bloodstream depends upon the number and distribution of receptors we possess as individuals. Once you are on the street for a few months, I would be very interested in hearing from you if you think that your job has caused you to feel different both mentally and physically. Do your friends and family members think that you have changed? Do you feel naturally more aggressive than your "old self"?

Serotonin

Here is another misunderstood human-manufactured chemical.[20] Serotonin is a monoamine neurotransmitter found in blood plate-lets and in the gastrointestinal tract. Serotonin levels are dependent on good nutrition and the availability of protein. Low levels of serotonin cause hyperactive reactions to stress, while elevated levels dampen fear, diminish aggression, and are associated with dominance.[21] In other words, just as testosterone levels are elevated in alpha males and alpha females, serotonin seems to make a differ-ence in establishing and maintaining dominance.

Cortisol

Cortisol is a steroidal hormone that enables us to deal effectively with stress, and thus it is often referred to as a stress hormone.[22] Also, higher levels of testosterone can mean lower levels of the stress hormone cortisol.[23] We release cortisol in response to fearful situations. Cortisol can be good or bad depending on circum-stances; extreme stress causes the hypothalamus to send hormones to the pituitary gland, which prompts the adrenal gland to let loose with cortisol and adrenaline and supply muscles with oxygen and energy, while raising blood pressure and speeding up the heart rate.[24] It's like pressing the gas pedal to the floor. Police officers may experience this level of all-out stress as a matter of routine, but with slot machine irregularity. What we need to guard against is letting cortisol levels get too high and staying there, because the wear and tear on the body takes a toll.[25] Recall the example of cultures of honor discussed earlier and the fact that increased cortisol and testosterone result in an instantaneous response to insult.[26]

The Rage Circuit

Rage is something all police officers witness, and it helps to have some understanding about what causes it, because sometimes rage is preventable in both ourselves and in the people we encounter. In *Why We Snap: Understanding the Rage Circuit in Your Brain*, neuroscientist R. Douglas Fields outlines nine triggers that explain not only instances of our rage, but also our heroics, some which involve examples of superhuman strength. Fields uses the mnemonic LIFEMORTS to recall them quickly.[27] LIFEMORTS encompasses: Threats to Life or Limb, Insults, Family issues, one's Environment, Mate (or spouse) issues, Order in society, Resource issues, Tribal and identity matters, and finally, being Stopped—as in being restrained or oppressed.[28] Fields writes that:

> **Recognizing the nine triggers of rage and understanding the compounding circumstances that press on them helps us comprehend how someone can snap and commit a violent crime, but it does not excuse the actions any more than understanding that a bank robber commits his crime for financial gain, [and] it does help illuminate why these perplexing crimes occur. Acting on that understanding could help prevent them.[29]**

Indeed, a deep understanding of our proclivities for losing our self-control could help tremendously in keeping peace officers from appearing in embarrassing online videos.

Five of Field's triggers are problematic in law enforcement, especially because increasing exposure to stress can set these rage points to a hair-trigger status.[30] As peace officers you will frequently find yourself in situations threatening Life and Limb; being subject to perceived Insults is a given (recall cultures of honor); establishing Order is the very nature of your job; your Tribe in blue speaks for itself; while being Stopped from performing your duties as a peace officer is both unthinkable and unacceptable in law enforcement. Your response to any request for a police presence is an assumption and assurance that dominance has arrived, and once on the scene you are expected to prevail in enforcing the law.

Jaak Panksepp, an Estonian-born neuroscientist and psychobiologist who died in 2017, coined the term "affective neuroscience" to describe his field: The study of the neural mechanisms behind emotion. His research caught the public imagination in the early 1990s, when news articles came out about his work "tickling" rats. But his work was no laughing matter, having since influenced the understanding of autism, depression, and mental illness.

Through his work studying emotion among a range of mammals, from rats to humans, Panksepp identified "subcortical circuits" we appear to share in common, which provoke similar emotions across species when our brains are electrically stimulated. Of particular interest to us is his description of what he called the RAGE neurocircuits: "The general locations of these circuits have been identified by localized electrical stimulation of the brain. … The more we understand about these circuits, the more we will understand the fundamental nature of anger itself."[31]

Similarly, the more we understand about the nature of hypervigilance and prolonged exposure to stress, the better chance we have of controlling behavior: Ours and others'. For, not only can these RAGE circuits be stimulated, Panksepp noted—they can be suppressed. "Will such knowledge help us deal better with human violence, a most serious social problem?" he wrote. "(N)ew possibilities for biological control are bound to emerge," including non-pharmacological interventions such as meditation.[32]

THE TAX OF HYPERVIGILANCE

So far, we have reviewed a bit of history as well as some basic biology. We've even taken a tour through the limbic system, learning about the amygdala, the frontal cortex, the anterior cingulate cortex, and the hippocampus along the way. You need to have a reasonable appreciation of how these organs function and a deep appreciation for how hormones influence us, while also understanding how the chemical cocktail of testosterone, oxytocin, and adrenaline affects behavior. Biologically, we are armed to cope with stress by using the chemical factory in our heads to shut down the bodily functions we don't need now and to give more power to the organs we do need, to fight, flee, or cope. The trouble is, when we tax our system by ramping up and setting off all the alarms, all too often our system incurs damage because our other organs won't be functioning as they should.[1]

In his book *Emotional Survival for Law Enforcement*, Kevin M. Gilmartin, a behavioral scientist and retired peace officer, describes the experience of sustained hypervigilance as an emotional roller coaster that taxes the autonomic nervous system, which regulates pulse, respiration, body temperature and blood pressure.[2]

Police work, at times, can be akin to an emotional black hole. I'm still prone to memory flashbacks of a shooting in the West Dallas projects, in which a woman was shot through a screen door with a shotgun loaded with birdshot. The blast implanted part of the screen in her face, blinding her and turning her face into a bloody pulp. Before I arrived on the scene, she had painted the walls red with blood feeling her way around the apartment; all the while, her hysterical toddlers were screaming at the top of their lungs, running in circles, not knowing what to do to help their mother.

Top this off with a train wreck in West Dallas where I found part of a human brain parked on the locomotive engine, as if a passerby had placed it there for safekeeping. Images like this are hard to shake and they have a habit of popping up unexpectedly.

Over time, the health effects can become debilitating, if not life-threatening, so learning to handle your stress is a big part of your job. In *Breaking Rank*, Norm Stamper reminds us that police work is among the most "emotionally dangerous occupations in the country."[3]

Dealing with Your Daily Doses of Stress

As a peace officer, it goes without saying that stress is routine: It's business as usual, and as such, it's your home territory, so you are expected to help others deal effectively with it while keeping your own under control. However, in too many law enforcement organizations, a macho culture tends to downplay the attention required to deal effectively with stress. In fact, only a few decades ago, your doctor would have likely also scoffed at the notion that stress could result in damaging one's health—because the chemistry of stress was still a mystery.

I'm sure you have heard the notion that there is such a thing as good stress and bad stress. In the simplest sense, we like challenges that are not so difficult that we are overwhelmed by them; then there is the stress that taxes our mental and physical ability to cope. If we don't learn to deal with it over time, it effectively causes our health to suffer, compromising our immune systems and even shortening our lives. Unfortunately, police work involves lots of the bad kinds of stress, where we shut down some of our bodily functions to cope with something urgent. The long-term health effects can be costly.

For the first few years, the routine stress for many new officers is exhilarating: It's what makes this work exciting; it's a source of much enthusiasm for the work and the oft-heard exclamation that police work "gets in your blood." But over time, it's easy to become jaded and even fed up with the infantile behavior one witnesses daily. Encountering so much emotional and adrenaline-soaked conflict inevitably causes both mental and physical changes in the men and women who work as peace officers, and it's almost a given that many officers will become exceptionally cynical and bitter. When we encounter police officers that seem a bit stressed, it's helpful to keep this in mind.

Also keep in mind that being a police officer today requires not only much more knowledge and dedication than ever before, but also a continued dedication to self-awareness and self-discipline. And, while expecting perfection in temperament is simply unrealistic, holding yourself and your colleagues accountable is necessary—for your own sake and for the safety of the public you serve.

How can you accomplish this seemingly impossible task? Having been a police officer, as well as having spent so many years reflecting on my experience as a private citizen, there is no better behavioral guide in my view for peace officers than simply following the golden rule. Treat citizens the way you would want to be treated if the situation were reversed. Every time you find yourself in a dilemma about your objectives in keeping the peace and enforcing the law, all you need to do to put your bubble back in the center of the level is to *imagine your role as that of a citizen instead of a police officer*. A gentle reminder of this on occasion might be worthwhile.

One of the physical changes police work will have on your body is that it will increase the size of your amygdala.[4] Instead of thinking of the amygdala as part of a ride-along in our brain (as we have done), psychiatrist Bessel van der Kolk likens the amygdala to a smoke detector and our frontal cortex to a watchtower. In *The Body Keeps the Score*, he advises:

> **Effectively dealing with stress depends upon achieving a balance between the smoke detector and the watchtower. If you want to manage your emotions better, your brain gives you two options: You can learn to regulate them from the top down or from the bottom up. Knowing the difference is central for understanding and treating traumatic stress. Top-down regulation involves strengthening the capacity of the watchtower to monitor your body's sensations; mindfulness meditation and yoga can help with this. Bottom-up regulation involves recalibrating the autonomic nervous system, (which, as we have seen, originates in the brain stem). We can access the ANS through breath, movement, or touch. Breathing is one of the few body functions under both conscious and autonomic control.[5]**

Kevin M. Gilmartin's book *Emotional Survival for Law Enforcement* is an exceptionally enlightening overview of the emotional journey so many peace officers experience: Starting out loaded with enthusiasm and zeal, and ending up jaded, bitter, often divorced, alienated from non-police friends and family—and in extreme cases, suicidal.[6] As Edgar Sandoval and Ashley Southall write in the *New York Times*, "More police officers commit suicide every year than are killed in the line of duty; since 2014, in New York City, an average of five officers have died each year by suicide."[7]

I can relate to the gradual cynicism that sets in when the daily witnessing of the worst in human behavior begins to erode one's enthusiasm for work. Once you become very much aware of what is going on in your city, the place may become tainted, so to speak—no longer seeming like somewhere you want to live or raise a family. After we moved to Alaska in the early 1970s, I was interviewed for the *Dallas Times Herald* by a reporter who was interested in why so many people had moved from Texas to Alaska. I mentioned my police experience in Dallas and something to the effect that I didn't think the area was a good place to raise a family. The piece made the front page. Still, after all these years I can drive through most areas in Dallas and experience a flood of memories: An arrest on this corner, a shooting or stabbing on that street, et cetera. After talking to a young man on Elm Street one evening, I drove around the block only to find him dead on the sidewalk from a gunshot wound. Now every major city is alike in that so many criminal acts are occurring at any given moment, and for most residents, ignorance is bliss. Not so for police officers.

I don't recall the nature of the call or the arrest, but one of my most heart-wrenching memories was holding a little girl in my arms. She was two, maybe three years old; her mother was in hand-cuffs a few feet away. The girl held her arms out toward her mother, sobbing and crying, "Mommy!" This child with cigarette burns all over her arms and legs still wanted to go to the person who had burned her: Her mother. The haunting thing about this incident is to wonder what kind of person a child treated like this would grow up to be. It's exceptionally hard not to become jaded, cynical, and callous when one's gray matter becomes crowded with memories that indict our species.

Too many such occurrences in one's city changes the geography until, wherever one is, one can only drive so far before one of these instances will automatically resurface in your memory.

You pull up in front of a house on a possible attempted suicide call. Walking toward the front door, you hear a shot. You burst through the door that isn't locked, and there sits a young man in a wooden rocking chair facing the door; the chair is rocking, and blood is spurting from his head in perfect synchronization with the rhythm of the chair. This one still replays in my head, even after so many years. In time, these kinds of incidents reach a critical numerical mass, and at least for me, the city no longer feels like a place you would want to live. It's no different than any other major city, but here you are much too familiar with what is going on: Too damn much crime and chaos, too much evil.

Gilmartin discusses the appeal of the hypervigilant state police officers experience. He writes, "Very few careers create hypervigilance in the workforce. Very few careers have workers who begin their careers with such enthusiasm."[8] In this short but profoundly pertinent book, Gilmartin takes you through the progression that begins with excitement and exhilaration, but then slowly but surely veers off track, heading downhill and resulting in officers becoming jaded *en masse* from the wear and tear of careers that end in bitterness, or worse.[9] Life for peace officers—both men and women—who don't have the support and understanding of what is occurring to them both mentally and physically from living through on-and-off hypervigilance (of red lights, sirens, adrenaline, and myriad, dangerous incidents) too often progresses to psychological withdrawal and the existential loneliness of a fractured identity. Another way to experience exhilaration, from my experience, is to achieve a critical mass of knowledge, so that the intellectual rewards from learning give you the adrenaline rush *without* the red lights and siren. The confidence that comes with this kind of learning should further enable you to keep your head when those all about you are losing theirs—and, given time you will likely be promoted to a supervisory level.

Alpha Males and Alpha Females

If recruitment ads for police officers were more accurate, they would say, "Alpha males and Alpha females required." Peace officers are by design alpha roles; whether you are male or female, this is simply the nature of your job. In law enforcement, to resolve conflicts, we regularly assign men and women to jobs in which they are expected to exhibit dominance.

Asserting dominance means being in a position in which one's increased level of stress hormones goes with the territory, and this in turn incurs an emotional and physiological tax. Peace officers often go from one conflict or domestic disturbance to another for days on end, encountering some people very glad to see them—and too many others who have the opposite attitude. But dominance does not mean out-of-control force or anger. Citizens call the police to have someone take charge of situations that have gotten out of control—not to make them even more uncontrolled. Simply put: 911 calls are requests for what I would call *thoughtful* dominance.

However, as you are now aware, being in an alpha position does over time greatly influence the chemical and hormonal reactions in your body. Your amygdala will likely grow larger, and it may become overactive. As a result, your aggressiveness may begin to show itself in hair-trigger temper tantrums. Based on your experience of having to put up with so much B.S. that you feel you are due a break, you may develop that "internalized sense of entitlement" characterized by Keven M. Gilmartin as "one of the most damaging traits to law enforcement."[10]

It's easy to see how an alpha posture can get out of hand. I'm sure you have seen film clips of police officers seeming to go ballistic with very little provocation. If not, check out the subject on YouTube.[11] Simply stated: Your duties as police officers and your biological predispositions are going to be at odds. Listen to this very carefully—and, please write this down: This aspect of your career requires *intensive* elephant training.

Comedian Adam Conover of *Adam Ruins Everything* has a YouTube video declaring that the theory that alpha-males exist is B.S.—that the scientist who first coined the term "alpha wolf," for instance, discovered he made a mistake in judging the evidence. But Adam over-simplified. For, as ethologist Marc Bekoff later noted, "social dominance is real, but has been widely misunderstood and misused."[12] I propose this test: Go into the jungle in the Eastern Democratic Republic of Congo or the mountain region of Rwanda and challenge the local silverback gorilla about his being in charge as being "so much B.S." You will be disabused of your conclusion. In fact, more research has identified the biological and brain connections that can drive such behavior.

The dynamics of alpha male and alpha female hierarchies in apes and wolves are intricate and far more sophisticated than first appearances suggest, but to suggest this means that no hierarchy exists at all is foolish. Alpha domination is multifaceted, and this is an important and profound lesson for peace officers. Of course, we do not live in bands like mountain gorillas, but we do share the biological chemistry and predilections of our primate kin. And what science has found is that, although physical strength is a key attribute for alpha males and alpha females, it is not an absolute requirement. In addition to obvious need for strength, effective alpha dominance requires tact, and the enthusiastic cooperation of others, because subordinates often have much more power than is immediately apparent. And this should be a wakeup call for peace officers: Working in a job that demands always taking charge in conflicts requires much more finesse than brute force, and failing to understand this can end your career.

Like our primate cousins, we too live in hierarchies, in part because they provide order. In *Mama's Last Hug*, primatologist Frans de Waal expresses his bewilderment that in academia, admitting that we live in hierarchies is still taboo. He says that every time he receives a new social psychology textbook, he searches the index for the terms "*power* and *dominance*" but rarely finds them.[13] Earning a living by resolving conflict on a daily basis in a culture whose behavioral predispositions rely on subconscious attention to hierarchal manners that we don't even acknowledge as existing is challenging to say the least.

Body Language

Think prehistory here, class: For thousands of generations before our species learned how to use spoken language, we still had methods of communication—gestures, grunts, pointing and the like—but more than that, we had to learn to interpret a stranger's intentions simply from the way they carried themselves, their posture, facial expressions and their stance. Now we still pay attention to these things, but our penchant for words has moved them off the front page of our awareness. We subconsciously observe the body language of everyone around us, and we intuit feelings that we may not even be fully aware of, and yet the communication between individuals in many cases is analogous to questions asked and answered.[14] For example, a stranger may approach us whose body language is that of an alpha male, and we intuitively acknowledge such with our own body language, without even realizing we have done so. Our silent partner sees to this kind of behavioral posture without even letting us in on it.

My educated guess is that the body language that we mostly process subconsciously today was our first and preferred language thousands of years ago, until gradually, over generations, spoken language took its place. So, body language is something we still understand at some level (at least our silent partner is tuned in), and yet, it's likely that there will be lots of opportunity for misunderstanding the actions of others, especially if our silent partner is biased.

I highly recommend that you study the subject of body language. Learning to read body language fluently is a way of syncing your elephant, your silent partner, and your rider so that you have a chance to see instantly what others feel but can't quite articulate.

In *September University*, a book I wrote a few years ago, I put it this way:

> **(L)et's say that beneath the software of the latest state-of-the-art operating system for computers is an old, fully functional MS-DOS program. This program contains critical and crucial information for the well-being of the computer, but it is so overridden by the new fancy program codes that no one pays much attention to it anymore. Worse, no one really knows how to read the data. Even so, this information is vital**

to the very stability of the system, and overlooking its importance portends danger for computing. This is perfectly analogous to human behavior regarding mirror neurons and the fact that we so readily relate to others beneath consciousness.[15] When we are all sitting around a conference table, unconsciously mirroring one another's body language, what we are seeing is the old MS-DOS program attending to our relating as it has done for thousands of years. Chances are, we like the folks we are imitating, and we are saying so with our actions, even if we no longer recall consciously that that is indeed what we are doing. We are, so to speak, aware, yet unaware, of our awareness.[16]

When we were having meetings in the oil industry at Alaska's Prudhoe Bay, on occasion I used to say, "Freeze: Nobody move," at which time I would point out how many in the group were relating to others or were seemingly distancing themselves from others, according to their body language. At future meetings, group members who'd been made aware started sharing knowing looks with me as we saw similar body language in progress.

So, this means when you find yourself on the street in uniform among a crowd of citizens it might be helpful for you to realize—even as the others may not—that your old MS-DOS systems are communicating, and you need to know what they're saying, because it could be crucial to figuring out what is to come and what actions you need to take.

Body language has a lot to do with status and dominance—and the latter is your turf by edict of law. You are not allowed to lose in matters where the law is to be enforced and where force is required to accomplish it. But peace officers must maintain the upper hand in recognizing subtle attempts at dominance. That we do this anyway, beneath consciousness and by responding in kind, or by submissive or aggressive behavior, makes it all that much more important that you understand what is going on.[17] Maybe delving this deeply into otherwise subconscious behavior sort of takes the fun out of spontaneous conduct, but your knowledge about the nature of dominance could save the day.

Eye contact, for example, is governed by dominance, which is why civilians venturing through strange neighborhoods can come to serious harm simply for looking at someone too long. It's usually the case that when two people lock in eye contact that the submissive person looks away first.[18] So, if you approach an individual as a peace officer and you can't maintain eye contact, it should be a warning you should consider that you may be dealing with someone who thinks they are dominating you, and it appears that, at least thus far, they are.[19]

There will be times when you confront individuals where you will want to gain and maintain an upper hand, but it would be unwise to push your dominance to the breaking point in consideration of the other party's sense of status and honor.

Contagious Aggression

As Robert M. Sapolsky makes clear: We don't hate violence *per se* in our culture, we just hate the wrong kind of violence.[20] Because we glorify the "right" kind of violence as a major focus of our entertainment, we expect that peace officers will frequently be participants in the *good* type of violence. But for some officers, when their participation level and frequency of violent actions begin to feel routine, they can become oblivious when they enter the territory of the wrong kind of behavior. So, it's back to that debilitating assumption of entitlement. There are biological reasons why we enjoy seeing Dirty Harry exact revenge for senseless crimes.[21] But unfortunately, it's too easy to get off track and completely out of control, especially when we are working in groups.[22]

What is happening when we witness an officer beating on someone who is clearly no longer resisting? Emotion has taken over, their elephant is on the rampage, and the incident is running on instinct, being driven by hormones. Thoughtfulness and control at this point have been overridden by biological impulse: When more than one police officer is involved, they may even begin to take their cues from one another as the emotion takes on a life of its own. Officers with enlarged and hyperactive amygdalas arrive on a scene brimming with testosterone, and thus they interpret the slightest acts of resistance on the parts of the citizens they are confronting as overt hostility. You are seeing this play out when you watch YouTube videos in which, if the orders the officers give are not followed immediately, they instantaneously begin to apply physical force.

Again, our biology makes it clear that we human beings are animals. Without enough self-awareness or open acknowledgment of this, we can be depended upon to act instinctively; until we own up to our predilections, nothing is going to change.

Many primates are hyperaware of hierarchy and dominance; after observing them for a brief time, it's usually easy to determine who is dominant and who is subordinate.[23] We may not dwell on these things consciously, but we sense intuitively who is and is not dominant in almost all social situations. This is easily practiced or demonstrated by randomly examining body language in group settings, as mentioned. And, as renowned German psychologist Erich Fromm observed many years ago, it's when we deny our animal nature that it can manifest in its worst forms, but he didn't mean this the way it seems at first blush. Fromm argued that we would be better off syncing with our animal inclinations than our human dispositions because the latter are more aggressive.[24] Our brains developed over eons, driven by experience without the benefit of language. To deal with the silent partner's communication that we are not consciously privy to, we must bring it to the surface by interpreting what we are seeing. Thousands of years ago, before the development of language, when a group of hunters downed a beast of prey that had still not succumbed to their blows, how do you suppose they communicated what needed to be done? Or another way to put this in perspective is to realize that when we meet strangers, it's likely that our silent partners are involved in interactions determining status and dominance that happen in milliseconds, before we are aware of how we feel about what is occurring, even while intuitively and bodily we are already acting out our parts in the encounter.

Next we are going to watch a film from 1991 of the Los Angeles police beating the daylights out of Rodney King. I'm sure most of you have seen it before, but this time you are never going to forget it. King was struck some 40 times, while unable to resist, except in trying to avoid being hit. So, there are 30 of you in this class, and we have this film set up to slow-motion stop after each blow (even if the blows happened simultaneously).[25] We will draw names from a hat, and half of you will take turns sitting up front here facing your class members. After each blow, those of you in the audience will ask the cadet facing you a simple question: "He is not resisting; why are you still hitting him?" Each time, the cadet responding will need to phrase a response to the question in terms not used precisely before. If you do not add something original, your classmates will remind you to rephrase.

We will continue with this exercise until we have drawn all the names and half of you will have been asked the question 40 times.

The drawing of names will cause you some apprehension that you may be called on, and hopefully the process will register as a significantly emotional experience, one that at least is worthy of a lasting memory. This exercise will take most of the day and may last into the following day, as it will require hundreds of original answers. So, after this, I trust that in the future, when you feel the adrenaline rush of excitement, when you and your fellow officers must arrest a suspect who is not resisting, you will not need to be reminded not to strike the suspect based on a cue from the officer on your left or right, and that you may even recall the difficulty of answering hundreds of times. It is my intent to ensure that you will never need to be reminded again of the dangers of emotionally-aggressive contagious behavior, in situations like Eric Garner warning 11 times that he couldn't breathe. Perhaps after this exceedingly thoughtful experience you will be more likely to hear him *beyond* the contagious excitement of the moment.[26] Because, as psychologist and Stanford University professor emeritus Philip Zimbardo reminds us, equally at fault in the above scenarios are the good cops who remain silent while their buddies are engaged in brutality.[27]

We don't have enough research in this type of exercise to judge the level of success with this method of training, but I do believe it will be unforgettable. Time will tell if it is in any way effective, but I think we must try until we get it right. Now, if you think this is a waste of time or that you need not be too concerned about this subject, I have an alternate exercise when you leave here today and get someplace quiet. I want you to take out your cell phone and do a YouTube search for "police brutality." Use your imagination with some key word searches, and then spend some time watching peace officers having career-ending meltdowns, some wound so tightly they must, metaphorically at least, have amygdalas the size of grapefruits.[28] Ask yourself if you want to show up there someday and become a viral video star as the entire world watches the drama of your career-ending conduct, and as attorneys file lawsuits that will result in a six-figure payout by your former city or police department.

In *To Protect and Serve,* Norm Stamper advises the reader to "Queue up YouTube's Top 10: Worst Police Beatings Caught on Tape." He also points out that "theoretically the entire list can be replaced by ten new entries at any time."[29] Moreover, it should be self-evident by now that a group of police officers beating on a subject who is not fighting back are clearly not doing it because they are afraid.

In the 1960s in Dallas, police used chokeholds routinely. I don't recall their use injuring anyone, but I'm not at all sure it would have been made public in those days if it had. I do know that it was exasperating watching the video of Eric Garner telling the officer choking him that he couldn't breathe.[30] The fact that Garner was not resisting is the point seemingly lost on many peace officers.[31] I'm fully aware that there are times when the force necessary to stay alive may be lethal. What I find hard to accept, though, is the relentlessness of examples on the evening news of officers degrading the reputations of their respective departments because they are using unnecessary force driven solely by adrenaline. In his book *Conformity,* Cass R. Sunstein points out that all it takes in many cases to turn an action that's out of control around is the voice of a single dissenter.[32]

One afternoon when I was off duty in Dallas (in my private car and in civilian clothes), I was a few blocks from my home when I saw a man running toward me. He turned a corner and ran into a service station. Then, behind him a good 50 yards were two men wearing suits chasing him, but they were too far behind to see where he went when he turned the corner. I pulled to the side of the road and confronted the two men, showing them my identification as a police officer. They identified themselves as FBI agents and said they were chasing an AWOL Marine wanted for armed robbery. I said I knew where he was, and we entered the service station. We went our separate ways searching for the suspect, and then I heard a Marine Corps war whoop coming from the restroom and entered to find the suspect, who was a very big man, thrashing the FBI agents. I put a chokehold on the fugitive, and then the FBI agents—who routinely investigated police officers for excessive force—suddenly stood back in a crouched position and began to pummel the suspect Floyd Mayweather-style, as if he were a speedbag.

Now, exceptional force was certainly called for, but the punching did little to restrain the subject enough that we could get handcuffs on him. I wound up receiving a letter of commendation from then-FBI Director J. Edgar Hoover, sent to my chief of police in Dallas.[33] But the lasting lesson for me is that losing objective control of a situation because of an adrenaline rush knows no boundaries in law enforcement—and may even be rewarded.

Check out the YouTube video at U.C. Davis dated April 2016 in which police officers pepper-spray a group of restrained protestors sitting on the ground arm-in-arm and ask yourself where the authority comes from that authorizes such a punishment. Then try to get your mind around the damage this does to the public image of the objectivity of police officers nationwide. Nothing shouts "unprofessional" louder than videos of police officers using fists and clubs to hit people who are not resisting.

On YouTube, you will also find some excellent short lectures by police officers who have discovered on their own the value of what I am trying to get across in this presentation.[34] It's not just that you need to learn to keep your head about you when those about you are losing theirs, but you also need to be able to help calm down your fellow peace officers when their emotions have taken over.

Any questions? No hands in the air? Good.

INFLUENCING YOUR
LIMBIC SYSTEM

As it turns out, your silent partner is part of what is acknowl-edged by scientists as a radar-like detection system that operates beneath conscious awareness. (I think of it as an entity working on our behalf, like a security company.) To describe this, neuroscientist Stephen W. Porges introduced the term *neuroception*. In his polyvagal theory, Porges hypothesizes that the neuroception of our autonomic nervous system works to keep us safe, first by detecting threats, and next by providing the best response possible, physically and mentally.[1] That response is hierarchical in that it may include strategies from any of the various stages in our evolution, from our ancient reptilian defense mechanism of shutting down and playing dead, which Porges notes is still intact, to our mammalian response, more commonly known as "fight or flight," which is more recent, and in most cases more effective.

Porges maintains that the human nervous system retains a hierarchical triad of neural circuits, or responses to danger, from its evolutionary past: Social engagement; fight or flight; and freeze—or system shutdown.[2]

Social engagement assesses risk and safety through eye contact, facial expressions, and the sounds and prosodic nature of the
human voice. Porges describes these observations as a preamble to a
social bond—or the opposite.[3] Does the person you are encountering during a police incident look like a friend or foe; do they sound
like a threat; are there background sounds that signal danger?

If the answer to the final few of those questions is yes, depending upon the severity of the threat, the "fight or flight" response
kicks in—with increased heart rate, increased oxygen intake,
and an adrenaline rush with an immediate infusion of cortisol
making you biologically ready and physically able to fight or to
flee (as appropriate). If, on the other hand, your silent partner is
stumped about what to do next, you may experience the involuntary biological response of shutting down, reminiscent of a reptile
playing dead.

This system—"fight or flight" or "system shutdown"—is well
known in law enforcement and in the military. Of course, the
autonomic nervous system is involuntary, meaning that we have
no control over it—at least not of the shutting-down part. What is
less well-known and understood in law enforcement are the subtleties of neuroception, like precisely how it works or how we might
influence our nervous system so as not to be so readily subject to
an involuntary response, especially a shutdown. We may have more
influence on our fight-or-flight response than has been assumed.
And any one of us could make discoveries in this area, because, as
Porges frequently makes clear, the polyvagal theory is a work in
progress.[4]

As noted, our silent partner is constantly scanning the environment to assess risks.[5] But how does it know what presents a danger
and what does not? Porges hypothesizes that we have evolved to
share some responses in common with other vertebrates:

Due to our phylogenetic history, the rumble of low-frequency sounds shifts our attention from social interactions to potential dangers in the environment. This reaction is shared with other vertebrates, including reptiles and amphibians. In contrast, high-pitched screams from another mammal (not just from our children, but also from dogs and cats, for example) elicit a sense of urgent concern or empathy as a response to the perceived pain or injury of a targeted other. In humans, high-frequency screams shift our attention from the social group or object of focus to the specific individual who is screaming. Shrill music in the range of human voice, however, elicits visceral and emotional states that are associated with either impending doom or a sense of urgency.[6]

So, like a submarine pinging the water with sonar for the presence of enemy subs, our silent partner is constantly looking for danger of any kind using sight and sound, and as Porges points out, we have a face-heart connection in that we can readily perceive a threat from the face of another.[7]

Finally, it's important to keep in mind that although our shutdown system is an obsolete evolutionary holdover, and shutting it down may or may not get the desired result of saving your life, the more dire the emergency, the more ancient the evolutionary response. And we have no conscious control over it. So, that means when your autonomic nervous system senses that you are overwhelmed, you are apt to freeze or faint. Think of all the times you have heard of other people freezing during emergency situations and thought, "Well, I wouldn't have chosen to do that." But that's just it. This is not a matter of choice.

This kind of instantaneous response has been necessary to our survival. If our bodies could never take appropriate actions when threatened without having to think things over, it's not likely that you would be paying attention to this now, because our species would likely not have survived. Evolution works for obvious ingenious reasons (some not so easy to perceive, until you give them serious thought). The fact that the left hemisphere of our brain controls the right side of our bodies, for example, makes perfect sense if you imagine trying to escape being chewed on one side by a predator; control from the side not experiencing trauma improves the odds of escape.[8] Nonetheless, standing in frozen paralysis is rarely as beneficial in our modern life as it might have been to an early reptile.

So how do we gain the ability to influence our silent partner by hacking its reptilian response? Since neuroception takes place beneath conscious awareness, the only direct access we have is through controlled breathing. Psychiatrist Bessel van der Kolk explains that, "When you deliberately take a few slow deep breaths, you will notice the effects of the parasympathetic brake on your arousal. The more you stay focused on your breathing, the more you will benefit, particularly if you pay attention until the very end of the out breath and then wait a moment before you inhale again."[9]

In other words, to influence your silent partner, breathe. Since you don't know how to talk to your neuroception directly, you need to concentrate on concentrating, so to speak. Participate in the situation you find yourself in; remain aware of the uncertainty you are facing as an act of social engagement and observe the context: Is it day or night; are you confronting a man or woman; if they are of another race, do you know the history of bias in this regard; what is the reputation of the neighborhood? If you are aware of the typical stereotypical boobytraps likely to cause you to project and turn the cell phone glitter into a gun, you have a much better chance of seeing what is really there instead of jumping to a conclusion; you have assumed a posture of mindfulness. So, when you answer a call that portends the possibility of violence: Breathe, think, see. Don't project. You are in this situation by choice, and you can choose to call upon all your faculties and knowledge to help you through it.

A call to mindfulness is powerful. Many years ago, working for Arco in offshore drilling operations in Nome, Alaska, I was with several others waiting at the airport for our helicopter's arrival from the rig. Our security man was a retired Army sergeant. As our helicopter came into sight, a small aircraft appeared from another direction, and it looked like they were going to collide in midair. Our security man said, "Get ready to remember what you are about to see." The aircrafts dodged one another successfully, but I will never forget how the suggestion to remember what we were watching—which appeared to be a catastrophe in the making—seemed to shift the gears of my perception, allowing greater clarity.

Another story: I've made more than 600 trips in and out of the Arctic aboard jet aircraft, so I soon learned that air turbulence makes my hands sweat. It took me a while, but I figured out that if I held my hands under the air blower in the overhead, cooling them stopped the sweating and in the process eased my anxiety. I effectively reverse-engineered my sympathetic nervous system, slowing down my propensity to move into "fight or flight" actions prematurely.

You can do it, too. For peace officers, this is about keeping your cool under fire; by doing your best to help your rider influence your silent partner—you can keep that elephant from raging or playing dead. I expect that revelations in this field of science are going to continue to reveal methods to gain greater control of ourselves in emergency situations.

Extensive training, as our military demonstrates, enables us to become accustomed to dangerous situations while keeping our emotions under control. But this subject is so easily confused. On YouTube you can find all sorts of videos from medical professionals who claim they can help you calm or hijack your autonomic nervous system. I've watched a slew of them, and most are not very helpful to law enforcement. Your objective in emergency situations is clarity. You may indeed need to engage in fight-or-flight mode. You may find yourself in a gunfight, and you may need to take cover. Your objective is to avoid shooting someone holding an object that is not a weapon as well as to shoot when it is, and you could otherwise lose your life.

I was working on December 8, 1968—I don't recall out of which Dallas station or substation—and I vividly remember participating in a frenzied multiple-station search for the suspect who killed Officer Floyd Knight at the 7-11 Store at 810 North Edgefield in Oak Cliff.[10] Floyd Knight was a member of what we called "Holloway's Raiders," a shotgun squad formed to thwart a rash of armed robberies.[11] Knight was behind a one-way mirror in the 7-11 store when a man pulled a gun on the clerk on duty and—for reasons lost forever—he either didn't see the suspect, who had forced the clerk into the back room where Knight was posted, or he was too slow to react. From what the clerk said, maybe Knight was caught by surprise: Either he didn't have his shotgun in his hand, or he forgot to take the safety off his newly-acquired .45 automatic pistol. For whatever reason, hesitation cost Floyd Knight his life.[12] I've often wondered if maybe he just could not bring himself to shoot another person, but what we know doesn't support that conclusion.

In his book, *On Killing*, Lt. Col. Dave Grossman calls our attention to the fact that most species, including our own, have an innate distaste and reluctance for killing their own kind, and that it is only recently in America's history of war that most of our servicemen and women have begun to shoot to kill.[13] Grossman attributes this increase in willingness to use deadly force to a history of desensitization through entertainment cinema and classical conditioning.[14]

If you plan to spend your whole work life as a peace officer, I highly recommend Grossman's books and his lectures on YouTube. But I differ with him strenuously about media depictions of police behavior. Grossman accuses the media of wildly and blatantly misrepresenting, for example, the incident in Ferguson, Missouri, in August of 2014, in which a white police officer, Darren Wilson, fatally shot 18-year-old Michael Brown, Jr. I agree that many incidents involving police brutality and excessive force can be attributed to a minority of peace officers, and that media reports on videos of excessive force sometimes misrepresent what happened. But I wonder if Grossman read the DOJ Report on the incident.

For those of you with experience in law enforcement, as I mentioned before, if the statistical data and the incidents of abuse that I have frequently referenced do not seem valid to you because of your work experience, perhaps we can say that at least this implies good intentions on your part, and it may reflect positively on your work, but if you are of a mind to refute all media criticisms sight unseen, you would be well advised to read the Department of Justice (DOJ) Report on the Ferguson, Missouri Police Department of March 4, 2015.[15] And it is exceptionally naïve to think that there aren't still a lot of police departments in America that routinely police like Ferguson did before the incident mentioned above.

The DOJ Ferguson Report found clear and blatant evidence of decades of overt racism, police brutality, racist harassment, unconstitutional arrests, and arbitrary stop-and-frisk searches steeped in racist assumptions, while the safety of the citizens of Ferguson was much less of a priority than seeing them as a source of municipal revenue, for having been arrested for minor infractions become a major impediment to the liberty of the residents of Ferguson.[16]

Grossman also argues that the decrease in the homicide rate nationwide is because of medical advancement, and in that he has a point. But in his book *On Killing*, the word "racism" that appears in the index does not actually address racism; instead, it directs one to a discussion of cultural, emotional, and moral distance, as if this were enough to address a 250-year-old malignancy affecting law enforcement in a nation highly resistant to all attempts at remedy.[17]

In *The Anatomy of Disgust*, University of Michigan law professor William Ian Miller discusses how contempt works as a dynamic of democracy, creating feelings that can be characterized as either upward contempt or downward contempt.[18] Or, as Miller says, "Contempt and humiliation, contempt and shame, go hand in hand."[19] Upward contempt describes contempt experienced by low-ranking individuals toward high-ranking individuals. He suggests that when contempt reaches levels of disgust it subverts democracy by undermining tolerance. The results are dire: When citizens—because of poverty or race—become so associated in the eyes of peace officers with disgust that the innate revulsion to killing one's own kind is overwritten, a disparity results that shows up statistically in the number of black and poor Americans jailed or shot by police officers. This is why I argue that tiptoeing around the blatant social reality of racial bias by talking about cultural distance and emotional distance will never get us to a point of solving the problems of our double standard in policing.[20] When you are facing a situation where the actions you take can make a difference of life and death, consider this: Relegating your opponent to a status other than human always forecloses the possibility of achieving justice.

In their 1997 book *Deadly Force Encounters*, behavioral scientist and law enforcement consultant Alexis Artwohl and writer Loren

W. Christensen discuss how to contain one's arousal state when all hell breaks loose. They describe these physical changes: Pounding heart, rapid shallow breathing, dizziness and a felt need to urinate or defecate.[21] They describe some likely perceptual changes: Tunnel vision, hearing distortion, time distortion, dissociation, the possibility of temporary paralysis, and that you will act according to your training automatically. They advise harnessing the power of fear thus:

> **Once you understand all the physical, cognitive, perceptual, and emotional changes caused by the biochemistry of the high-arousal state, you will not fear them, be confused by them, or be distracted by them. To help control your arousal level, learn the controlled breathing techniques and physical relaxation methods described in this section to help keep your arousal level down and your energy focused.[22]**

But think how the complexity of this subject as well as the mixed messages of those trying to be helpful fog the issue. If you are on the verge of mortal combat, this is not the time to practice yoga. A deep breath you may be able to manage, but not much else unless you have extensive training. I suspect that for some individual officers, training may in fact cause their amygdalas to become hypersensitive, and it just makes things worse. To stay in law enforcement, these officers need a desk job or something that will ensure they stay out of harm's way. But for the clear majority, training does what it is intended to do.

We may never find a one-size-fits-all method in mitigating overreactions in the use of force, and it may very well be that this is a problem for which each of us must find our own solution. For you as peace officers, this can be a matter of life and death. The greatest leverage you have may rest on your dedication to being mindful about what you are about to witness and engage in.[23]

Revisiting and Rethinking Bias

Okay, what have we learned? What can we take with us to the streets to ensure we will meet our objective and be true to our oaths to protect and serve and to assure the safety of everyone concerned? What actions do you take? What questions do you ask? How much probable cause do you have to continue your study of human behavior?

Let's start with revisiting bias, because it is a core issue. You know by now that as human beings, we are all biased about many subjects and issues to varying degrees. You should also know that there is one method of addressing bias that can yield positive results: It is not new but goes all the way back to the 1950s work of Gordon Allport, who advocated repeated exposure to exceptions to stereotypes.[24] In other words, find as many examples as possible that defy the stereotypes. In addition, Allport noted the value of self-insight, saying: "Knowledge of oneself, research shows, tends to be associated with tolerance for others. People who are self-aware, self-critical, are not given to the ponderous habit of passing blame to others for what is their own responsibility. They know their own capabilities and shortcomings."[25] Consider the irony that some of the best advice in addressing bias is not new: We have known for years how difficult it is to be objective about implicit bias, and yet we have failed miserably in applying tactics we know can have positive results.

Here is where we need to recall Lisa Feldman Barrett's argument that not only do we create our own emotions, but we can also revise them. She regards our emotions to be as unique as our fingerprints and says that when we look out upon the world, we are making end-less predictions based on our prior experiences.[26] Barrett's theory remains a controversial subject in academia. Primatologist Frans de Waal recalls a debate between Barrett and Jaak Panksepp in 2016 in which Panksepp was arguing in opposition to Barrett, but he observed that if one were to assume that Panksepp was arguing in favor of emotions and Barrett was talking about feelings, then both sounded correct.[27] Now, I'm not trying to confuse you, I'm just urging you to keep an open mind with the admonition that research on the subject of your feelings and emotions is worthy of your future interest and attention, especially if there is a difference in these two words that are so often used interchangeably.

Barrett suggests that the theory of constructed emotion brings new light to the issue of personal responsibility. "If you grow up in a society full of anger or hate, you can't be blamed for having the associated concepts," Barrett writes, "but as an adult, you can choose to educate yourself and learn additional concepts. It's certainly not an easy task, but it is doable."[28] I know this for certain myself, because I have done it, and I have been trying for decades to inspire others to do so as well.

But as I mentioned earlier, as much as I have become an advocate for ending racial bias, and despite my years of intensive scholarship, my own bias test results still show that I view black men differently than white men. My subconscious seems unchanged by my learn-ing, and I don't have a satisfactory answer as to why I haven't been able to change it. I don't think Lisa Barrett is wrong in her assertion that our emotions are unique and therefore malleable; I just don't know yet how to change my own subconscious. That is why I assert that bias is analogous to human software for which we haven't yet perfected the coding. The same affective realism, which Barrett blames for at least some of those flawed Philadelphia shootings, continues to stream a bias of inferred assumptions from both passive and active observations, but instead of on Netflix, it's happening in our heads. Then again, if I can make racial decisions upfront that are just, have I not already corrected the problem—or at least its conscious manifestation in society? Has my rider already trained my silent partner in matters where racial bias counts—effectively, so to speak, taming my elephant? My question is unanswered, but I hope you will remain interested until you are personally successful at mastering your own emotions and until science helps to provide more satisfactory answers.

Implicit & Explicit Bias

Given the history of law enforcement in America, how and why has it taken so long to take a serious look at the biological dynamics of bias in respect to how our brains function? We've surely had hundreds of thousands of incidents suggesting enough probable cause to suspect prejudice has played a crucial role in the snap judgments made by peace officers. Human culture versus human biology remains the problem central to law enforcement. Fact is: We were designed to make assumptions based on scant evidence. Allport put it thus: "Overcategorization is perhaps the commonest trick of the human mind."[29]

In the 1978 Western *Comes a Horseman*, the character played by the late Richard Farnsworth encounters James Caan's character on horseback, the two men study one another for a few moments, and Farnsworth says to Caan, "I think I've got you figured."[30]

That is what our brains do, all the time, day in and day out. That's how we have stayed alive long enough to live in this moment. And that's what, as peace officers, we must be mindful of and consciously fight.

So far, I have assumed that you have some awareness of the two fundamental kinds of bias: Implicit and explicit. Explicit bias—in the form of racism, for example—is basically quantified hatred, in that a negative value is assigned, openly acknowledged, and expressed. An implicit bias is a belief that is accepted as being real, usually with no conscious understanding that it even reflects a negative assumption or that one even exists.

For example, a few years ago, there was a photo going around of a dozen or so black women dressed in scrubs in a hospital operating room. Implicit bias is why most people who saw the photo assumed they were all nurses instead of the surgeons they were.[31] We warn people that if you had chicken pox as a child, the shingles virus is in your body and may act up under conditions of stress. Similarly, if you grew up in a racist culture, a racial bias still lurks in your subconscious and may reappear given the right circumstances, even though you are consciously opposed to any kind of racial bias. Implicit bias is alive and well beneath our conscious awareness—so firmly ingrained in the background of our culture that it becomes mistaken for reality. Explicit bias forms from the fumes of implicit bias.

A careful examination of recent evidence suggests there is enough probable cause to conclude that there is a decided implicit racial bias in the American judicial system at large.[32] And law enforcement is not the only helping profession so plagued. In her 2015 book *Just Medicine: A Cure for Racial Inequality in American Health Care,* University of Virginia School of Law professor Dayna Bowen Matthew makes a crystal-clear case for how implicit bias impacts the medical profession, resulting in the unnecessary deaths of thousands of people annually due to substandard medical treatment.[33] And, as in the field of law enforcement, the medical profession is mostly made up of people who want to help people.

Results of implicit-association testing (or IAT), however, suggest that these professionals do have biases.[34] Statistics verify the harm being done.[35]

I have taken the Harvard Implicit Bias test on race, gender, and age. Although I consider myself an aggressive advocate for the elimination of negative bias, I scored as having a strong preference for Europeans over African Americans; men over women, with relation to science and liberal arts; and young people over old people, although I am an old person myself.

So, how do we rid ourselves of implicit bias? The answer may lie with each of us individually, though we may each require a different tack, depending on our past life experiences. What works for me might not work for you. In my experience, you must first understand the nature of biases, then identify your own, and finally care enough to do the homework so your brain may overwrite them.

When it comes to topics like bigotry, racism, sexism, misogyny, and double standards in law enforcement, or the treatment of women and minorities, peace officers have extensive probable cause to investigate these matters further. Unless you follow up these leads, you can't satisfy your sworn oath that you will protect and serve the members of the community where you work. Do your own research. Until you explore these questions *because you really want to know the answers*, not much is going to change.

Finally, in law enforcement, we are hung up on the notion of intent: Criminal intent. Since implicit bias is unintentional—there's no conscious intent to cause harm—some argue that we should not be held accountable. That, however, is a sophomoric argument, if the matter of justice is still considered important. As Henry David Thoreau argued, if we are the beneficiaries of an unjust system, we are responsible for correcting the system and making it just.[36] Knowing that an implicit, unconscious bias is causing citizens harm in healthcare or in law enforcement but being unwilling to address the issues involved is morally disingenuous.

Why are we chemically cocktailed to out-group strangers? You don't need a Ph.D. in anthropology to come up with a satisfactory answer. The fossil record of human cultures reveals a much more brutal prehistory than we like to accept, and in that light, the benefit of having evolved to be wary of strangers is not at all hard to understand. The trouble is, that was then, this is now.[37]

Steven Pinker reminds us that as a species we are becoming less aggressive.[38] We have a patch for the ancient biology that interferes with contemporary society: We call it education. We just aren't very good at passing it on, because our archaic system requires that we charge an exorbitant price for it, and thus, although our institutions of higher learning make great discoveries, these are very slow to become mainstream, because the market for college would likely dry up without its economic model.[39] It's important to keep in mind how our ideas about education merge with the reality of how our minds work.

Our brains don't record what *should be* subconsciously; if they did that, they would be derelict in their primordial duty to keep us safe. Our brains keep a record of what *is*, so we can be safe from harm and embarrassment.[40]

You don't need to have a background in neuroscience or anthropology to intuit that thousands of generations of our species have been made possible because our sense of awareness—both conscious and subconscious—has been selected to ensure our continued survival. Our brains work 24/7 to keep us safe from danger and free from surprise and embarrassment.

Although human evolution is ongoing, we nonetheless have the same physical hardware that we had when we were on the menu of large predators.[41] Because surprise can spell danger, our brains are always hyperaware, still making lightning-fast assumptions based on very little information. Subconscious acknowledgment of what our brains accept as being real occurs in milliseconds. Then our conscious mind kicks in with the most plausible explanation it can come up with to put the best face on biases we don't even know we have.[42]

I implore you to read *Everyday Bias: Identifying and Navigating Unconscious Judgments in Our Daily Lives*, by social justice advocate Howard J. Ross, and to watch his presentations on YouTube. Ross covers this subject as well as anyone I've encountered.[43] The first chapter of his book is titled "If You Are Human, You Are Biased." This book is easy to read, clear, to the point, and profoundly important for everyone who eats, sleeps, breathes, and interacts with other people.

Probable cause alert: When looking for suspects with biases based upon mistaken assumptions, each of us can assume with complete confidence that we are suspect number one. We are biased, too, because that's what brains do, and if this were not the case, we would be incapable of learning cause and effect. It's just too bad that we are so sloppy about the process, and that we make big assumptions based on scant evidence.

Memory & Emotions

Another key to understanding racism as it applies to police work is the intersection of memory and emotion. These days, most of us must no longer worry that the snapping of a twig means we are about to be pounced upon by a hungry beast. But our brains still mimic paranoia in their need to ensure survival, and in fact, for peace officers, there are uncommon dangerous elements of risk that are routinely part of your duties. A mistaken assumption about an approaching stranger on a dark night when you are alone in a parked squad car could prove costly; and yet, the stranger might simply be anxious to report a crime or just say hello.

The history of our species' survival has depended upon favoring the familiar and ostracizing those who seemed different. Moreover, it would have been taken as a sign of betrayal to one's tribe not to assume a posture of superiority over people with strange customs. A viable future meant separateness—and survival emphasized this reality—and not to honor such circumstances could be dangerous.

Simply put: In the distant past, in primitive cultures, intuitive prejudice based upon cursory observations was not only morally justified, it was considered a requirement for survival; conformity was, and still is, a means of bonding with one's tribe. Our ancient ancestors, having met strangers and suffered deaths to disease as a result—without any knowledge of how disease spreads—made a negative association with the "other." The hormone oxytocin likely facilitated this stigmatization; as mentioned earlier, the hormone bonds in-group members while simultaneously fostering alienation of non-members.[44]

Our gray matter has stored and haphazardly catalogued millions of bits of data to help us form assumptions about myriad characteristics. Simply stated, we have internalized specific beliefs about age, appearance, race, accents, politics, clothing, tattoos, gender, food, clothing, colors, neighborhoods, furniture, houses, occupations, facial features, body weight, height, sports, hobbies, music, books, movies, and the list goes on. Some of what we have internalized are just nudges toward stereotypical assumptions; some are likely set in stone. When we encounter situations that include the characteristics listed above, we have emotional recollections, which trigger an algorithmic lineup of buried assumptions, each surfacing with biases and intuitions that are dependent upon our life experiences and training. For example, in a police patrol setting, the nature of the call for police, the neighborhood, the time of day, the sex and race of the people you encounter, the way you are feeling—each of these conditions affects your judgment.

A few years ago, I was giving a talk about adult education to a group of senior citizens at a university campus when it occurred to me just how and why we have evolved to so easily recall drama. We have very little difficulty remembering life-threatening events. Tell a child to watch for bears while walking through the woods to school, and in time, without incident, the warning is forgotten. But if that child must climb a tree to escape a bear even once, no more reminders are necessary. When our ancient ancestors lost a tribe member because of a tactical mistake in downing a woolly mammoth, they likely didn't forget that lesson either. The same will apply as you begin to make arrests and figure your way out of tough spots. We absorb and recall drama without strain, and in doing so we lay the groundwork for new millisecond assumptions, and thus, new biases.

We've already made note of the role of the hippocampus. Here is how neuroscientist David Eagleman adds something worth remembering:

> **Nature seems to have invented mechanisms for storing memory more than once. For instance, under normal circumstances your memories of daily events are consolidated (that is, "cemented in") by an area of the brain called the hippocampus. But during frightening situations—such as a car accident or a robbery— another area, the amygdala, also lays down memories along an independent, secondary memory track.**

Amygdala memories have a different quality to them: they are difficult to erase, and they can pop back up in a "flashbulb" fashion—as commonly described by rape victims and war veterans.[45]

Hard-to-erase memories are the key to why we so easily remember drama, especially if it results in trauma.

Thinking about our experiences with literature, movies, and television, where we learn in vivid narrative style what is going on in the lives of others, what groups believe about this and that doctrine: All the biases, prejudices, and bigotry are writ large in these resources. So how do you suppose we can go through life learning about these things and remain unbiased? It's just not possible: We are all biased to a degree. If minorities in our novels, television and movies are always depicted with certain characteristics, we will have a subconscious record on file for immediate recall in the form of feelings that nudge us toward accepting these traits as being real and worthy of consideration; it won't matter all that much whether we are in moral agreement with these feelings, because our gray matter prioritizes its duty to present reality in milliseconds, so we can make judgments on matters of life or death.

In a nutshell, we all have biases about all sorts of subjects and circumstances, and that's a good thing, because we couldn't live without them. We rely on having an enormous record of seemingly accurate snap-judgment assumptions archived beneath our consciousness and available instantaneously: Convictions about every possible kind of cause and effect—especially about people, how they behave, who can be believed and trusted, who can't, and why. For our sentinel awareness, our observations seem to represent straight-up reality. In other words, that's how it looks and how it seems, so that's how it must be.

As we grow up, our brains pay careful attention to millions of things deemed significant but unworthy of being called into our conscious awareness. But just because we aren't knowingly aware of everything going on around us doesn't for a minute mean that our gray matter is not recording it.

If you grew up in a culture with a glaring racial bias and yet think you were unaffected, think again: It just doesn't work that way. Our brains strive persistently to read our peripheral social interactions, soaking up sentiment as effectively as dry sponges absorb water. If, when we are children, the adults in our presence bear a racial prejudice toward a minority, even if they try to hide it, we will read it in their body language. We will record the looks on their faces, their eye-rolling gestures, the tone of their remarks—and emotion helps seal the deal. We will internalize the imprint of a social bias when the adults think we aren't paying attention to their tacitly-shared assumptions about stereotypes. Children are not born prejudiced.[46] However, numerous psychological studies demonstrate that children internalize the subtleties of racism at a very early age.[47]

That explains those research studies in which young black children show a more positive attitude toward white dolls than black dolls.[48] Short though it has been, their life experience already tells them that white dolls are apt to live in better houses, in better neighborhoods, and that they are likely to belong to little girls whose parents have better jobs and more money. Their views are implicit assumptions, having been ever-so-subtly formed by internalizing the prevalent bias of media and their social environment. We should find it hurtful and morally unacceptable that we cannot correct an environment in which young black children prefer white dolls because of what they've learned about living.[49] Beneath their consciousness, they've noted that white is *good* and black is *bad*. And when stereotypical attitudes are learned at an early age, they tend to become more rigid and polarized over time.[50]

Remember again neuroscientist Lisa Feldman Barrett's compelling case that our emotions aren't really something we inherit, but something we create, as unique expressions of our culture.[51] Barrett describes how emotions differ among cultures and how, as individuals, we experience our own signatures of fear, joy, and anger. In our mind's eye, we project the essence of our learning, as if shining a spotlight that contains our personal history of interpreting reality onto everything we envision.[52] In other words, we bring our cultural baggage with us always, and we apply it to every situation we encounter.

Neuroscientist Gregory Berns describes the amygdala as:

> [A] twitchy character with a long memory. Once the amygdala encodes an unpleasant association, it doesn't forget.[53] These memories sometimes resurface at the most inopportune times, and in the worst circumstances, since the amygdala is responsible for traumatic flashbacks. But all is not lost. There are two ways to keep the amygdala in check. One is proactive, preventing or limiting the brain from making unpleasant associations that it will remember. The second is reactive, acknowledging the fact that unpleasantness is unavoidable but need not be paralyzing.[54]

Berns reports on one study that shows that reappraising emotional scenes and replacing negative incidents with positive reactions reinforces the frontal cortex with a decrease in that incident's association with the amygdala.[55]

In this context, try to get your mind around the impressions that have been indelibly etched in our national consciousness throughout the history of American cinema. Take a fresh look at the toxic effects of what I call "amygdala radio"—the talk-radio juggernaut of fear and resentment that takes legitimate issues of discontent and politicizes them by finding someone to blame— someone without political power.

Bias can be positive or negative and as simple as, *"If you see that, it means this."* So, if we are raised in a culture where a demonstrable negative bias directed toward a minority is a common experience, and if the bias expressed stigmatizes the minority as being law-breakers or untrustworthy in general, our brain is storing this information for reference, to avoid unsatisfactory encounters in the future. Now imagine yourself as a police officer working in a community of minorities and having negative and hostile encounters with local citizens for years and years on end. What effect do you suppose that will have on your brain's attempt to capture reality? Never stop thinking about this, and you may become an exceptional police officer; dismiss it as being unimportant and not applicable to you, and your career in law enforcement may end abruptly.

Confirmation Bias

Just like any other human being, peace officers are all born masters of confirmation bias.[56] Regardless of our conscious opinions about equality and justice, when confronted with decisions involving race, most of us will feel an intuitive tug toward our internal record of life experience. If we're interviewing applicants for employment, for example, or asked to approve of a person who wants to date our son, daughter, or other family member, our subconscious take on reality will likely weigh heavily in our decision-making. And if the family member's potential date is of the "wrong" ethnicity or social class, according to our internal database, but saying as much would be considered publicly offensive, no problem. We can easily come up with ingenious alternative reasons to show why this person is *still* not suitable. This is what academics call *confirmation bias.*

Unfortunately, we human beings don't come with an owner's manual, but when it comes to peace officers and our social behavior in matters of dominance and hierarchy, we may know enough to start writing one.[57] If we remain oblivious to the subtle nature of bias, we are allowing our subconscious to call the shots. Whatever we come up with as a rationale, regardless of how prejudicial the judgment might be, we will still perceive it as being completely fair and impartial, even as our bias (masquerading as intuition) offers cautious rationalizations to conceal our deepest and most morally incorrect feelings. Think about how many movies and television shows you've seen, or novels you've read, in which a police officer has a hunch upon which the plot rests. It is natural to assume that this intuitive sense is an exercise of objectivity. While that is sometimes the case, over the career of a peace officer, bad judgment repeated countless times can be the reason innocent people wind up in prison.

Our justifications may result in our not hiring a minority applicant or not giving our approval for someone to date a person we've subconsciously stigmatized, while we remain absolutely convinced of our total objectivity. There are mountains of irrefutable employment data showing statistical proof of an employment bias and persistent racial profiling in law enforcement in America that very few people who manage these processes will admit to. Disparities in the way the judicial system treats minorities—from arrest, to sentencing, and incarceration—scream bias, and yet many people in law enforcement today still deny it. But think about how applying this bias every day must impact police work, and the message should start to come through. There is probable cause to believe bias is pervasive.

Even though I opened the subject with this question, it is in fact impractical and counterproductive to ask people if they harbor a racial bias, just as it can be difficult to spot a confirmation bias without introspection. We can't expect an honest answer, because we can't give one. We don't have direct access to a subconscious record with its millions of bits of data any more than we have access to the neurological programming that enables us to tell up from down, left from right, and hot from cold.

Be alert: Biased information based on years of subtle observations will continue to be fed to us consciously from our subconscious as intuitive implicit feelings or explicit knowledge; these inclinations require very few visible or audible cues to enable us to instantaneously match and confirm our internalized data—while we maintain that we don't have a prejudiced bone in our bodies.

How do you know when you're engaging in confirmation bias? Racial bias becomes especially suspect when we come down hard on a reason for disqualification with more aggressive emphasis than we would apply in similar situations with persons of our own ethnicity or social status. By now I trust it is clearer to you that by not seriously focusing on how our minds work, we are setting ourselves up for misunderstandings that can have devastating results.

USING FORCE
APPROPRIATELY

Sometimes it doesn't seem quite clear enough to many of our citizens that, when enforcing the law, police officers are not in the business of backing down. While it's true that officers might break off from a car chase for the sake of public safety, it's a mistake to assume that police officers will not routinely use whatever force is needed to overcome someone resisting arrest. This is easily demonstrated by incidents in which overwhelming force is used, and in which a score of officers will be called to achieve the arrest of one individual.

Sometimes exceptional force is needed. Spend your career in law enforcement, and it is a given that you are going to come face to face with some of the most despicable and perplexing people on the planet. You are likely to arrest and take into custody thieves, rapists, murderers, con artists, swindlers, psychopaths and sociopaths—some in this list would have no more remorse over killing you than they would over swatting a mosquito—as well as individuals who are innocent or merely suffering the effects of mental illness. Some of these people will break every standard of conduct for civility, and to stop them, nothing you do save overwhelming force is likely to work. But of course, you know this when you sign up and take the oath as a peace officer. It's when you begin to treat ordinary citizens as if they belong in the first category—without provocation or probable cause—that you have lost control of your elephant. Think about this in a community perspective and how much damage a raging elephant can do within an organization that has a monopoly on the use of legitimate lethal force.

Arrests and Confrontation

Your presence and professional appearance mean a lot in how you are treated by those who pose a threat to you. If you are tall and mean-looking with a gruff voice, you will be met by some with willingness and submission, and by others with the opposite response. Keep in mind, too, our lessons on cultures of honor, on rage, on emotion. Of course, you will be trained in felony stops and take-downs until you have these methods down pat, but I agree completely with retired police captain Howard Rahtz, who says peace officers also need the verbal skills of a therapist.[1]

To understand why, pretend for a moment that you have just pulled up at your residence, where you are approached by two police officers. As you get out of your vehicle, one of them tells you that you match the description of a suspect in a criminal case, and you are under arrest. How long do you think it would take you to process this information? You know you are innocent, and now you are going to be seriously inconvenienced—to say the least. My point is, it takes a few moments for most people under such circumstances to get used to the reality of what is happening to them, whether they are guilty or innocent. So, if you are too quick to try to handcuff them without first calmly walking them through what you are about to do, their involuntary reflex reaction, at having put your hands on them, is likely to be, or at least to look like, resistance, and you are going to have a skirmish that very likely could have been avoided. Of course, some people are going to resist violently no matter what you do or say, but in many instances if you calmly and respectfully explain that you are going to need them to turn around so you can handcuff them, and that you would like to proceed without needing to use force, many will comply, and it can save you a lot of time, trouble, possible injury, and court appearances over your actions.[2]

But when you confront people under this kind of circumstance, always be ready for the unexpected. I responded once to a shooting call in South Dallas, and I wound up wrestling a man to the ground who had been shot six times with a .38. He, of course, needed immediate medical assistance, but he resisted because he was experiencing shock.

And here is an aside that's important to always keep in mind. In police work, especially when patrolling heavily-populated areas, you will be so busy with so many incidents, often one right after another, you are going to be left with myriad first impressions that will also serve as lasting impressions. You are going to encounter people who have been hurt, shot, stabbed, or hit by a moving vehicle, and you are going to be so busy, there will be no follow-up. You aren't going to know what happens to them: Did they live or die; what really happened versus what appeared to have happened? The downside is that first impressions are often wrong, but you are going to stack them up in memory like cordwood. The man I mentioned above who had been shot before I arrived? I don't recall who shot him or why, and I still don't have any idea if he lived or died.

Losing Control

If you ever lose control in a crowd situation, you will never forget it,
I can assure you. Working in the West Dallas projects many years
ago, I answered an assault call at a municipal swimming pool with
a partner fresh out of the academy. A young man had allegedly
sexually assaulted a woman at the pool, and she called the police. I
don't recall why, but at the entrance of the pool, a crowd had gathered—and it just kept getting larger and unrulier. My partner and
I arrested the young man and brought him out the front door, at
which time the crowd decided he shouldn't be going to jail. By this
time other squads had arrived, because I had asked my partner to
call for backup while I was questioning the suspect.

As we brought our suspect outside in handcuffs, onlookers
tried to free him, in the process kicking my partner in the groin.
The crowd then exploded into a violent riot, damaging squad cars,
breaking windows and throwing rocks and bottles. A thrown
bottle smashed the windshield of a passing motorist, and a child
was injured. We managed to get our prisoner in the car and left
the scene as the commotion finally subsided like a spring thunder-
storm. Always be aware when you are making an arrest in a crowd
that time is of the essence. Be aware of your surroundings and how
your actions are being interpreted by others at the same time you
are working quickly to keep the peace.

Tools and Equipment

You have several tools that are preferable to use before a maximum
level of force is deemed necessary: Nightstick, mace, stun gun,
beanbag shotgun and a few more—all intended for use to avoid
using your firearm. Most of these tools, as Howard Rahtz points
out, are remnants of the Stone Age.[3]

Now, what I'm going to tell you is not department policy; it is from my own personal experience. When I was on the street, I didn't carry a nightstick or a club of any kind, because I always thought that upon seeing that I was carrying a nonlethal weapon, a suspect resisting arrest might intuit that my gun would not be the first option and think that he could take a chance. But here is the thing: I'm not sure my approach worked better for suspects, or for me. Nor am I countermanding the authority of your supervisors if they require you to carry a nightstick, or a taser, which I believe may have the same psychological effect.[4] I'm just putting this out there as something to ponder. Some police departments have experimented with forbidding nightsticks.[5] At the very least, you have probable cause to pique your interest into the psychology of the tools we choose to use to make arrests.

Training

You are going to attend extensive training courses where you will be schooled in hand-to-hand combat. You will be shown how to breathe so as not to stall your sympathetic nervous system and keep it from misfiring prematurely, so you can avoid an involuntary and inappropriate response under extreme stress. These details matter. And so do the targets you are confronted with during combat.

If you are presented with cardboard pop-ups of people pointing knives or guns at you, and the expressions on the faces of these caricatures do not accurately depict what people look like in an act of violence, you might consider sending them a polite thank you note for the course, and seek out other training.

Neuroscientist Jaak Panksepp has noted that our brains are "predisposed to associate fear with the potentially threatening configuration of anger more readily than with a pleasant face."[6] Real is real, after all, and even though, as Lisa Feldman Barrett has shown us, facial expressions can be unique, we are better at reading faces than we are at discerning the subtleties, such as not everything shiny is a gun. There is some universality to facial expressions. Moreover, your silent partner will decide the likely intentions from the face in front of you in about forty milliseconds. Become accustomed to shooting targets with non-aggressive facial expressions, and what do you think your silent partner will recall when a real-life situation calls for a split-second life-or-death decision?[7]

In his book, *Before You Know It*, Yale University instructor and cognitive psychologist John Bargh recounts studies that revealed some of the mindful and mindless intricacies of racial bias:

> [P]articipants were instructed to assume the role of police officers, and to shoot as soon as they could when a photograph appeared on the screen of a person holding a gun. The person in the photograph was always holding something, and half the time he was unarmed and holding something else entirely, such as a wallet. Half the time the person in the photo was white and the other times they were black. In the control condition, as in several previous studies, white participants were more likely to shoot an unarmed black person than an unarmed white person, and less likely to correctly shoot an armed white individual than an armed black person. But in the implementation condition, where participants first told themselves, "If I see a person, then I will ignore his race!" this bias was significantly reduced.[8]

A probable cause alert is due here, for the simple notion of mindfulness.

You are, after all, training your silent partner what to look for, and keeping things as real as possible makes sense. Also keep in mind that your physical fitness will not only project your ability to rise to the occasions required of you—it may literally help you feel less fear. Studies show that a resting heart rate correlates with decreased fear, which is a profound argument for staying in good physical shape.[9]

In time, if you are working in a highly-populated area, you are likely to become hypervigilant, because the events and incidents you encounter will leave indelible memories, and especially when you encounter situations that seem in some way like previous bad experiences, you are going to be on edge. And truly, police work is rife with experiences stranger than fiction.

Once, I answered a disturbance call in South Dallas, and the man who answered my knock at the door was panicked. He said his girlfriend was locked in the bathroom and was going to kill herself. I called out to her, asking her to open the door. Silence. I kicked the door several times, and when it finally burst open, a woman about eight months pregnant came running toward me with an icepick held high in the air as if she were going to stab me with it. I grabbed her arm, and she dropped the ice pick. Another officer had arrived by then, and we handcuffed her and took her into custody. The image of her coming out of that bathroom toward me is lodged in my memory like the shower scene in the movie *Psycho*. Expecting the unexpected with controlled breathing and with the intention that you are paying special attention to what is happening enables you to see clearly what those without training are likely to miss.[10] In the blink of an eye, things can turn deadly.

Another incident comes to mind. I was on a walking beat with a partner at the State Fair of Texas. (We might have been paid by the Fair as a part-time assignment, but we were both in uniform.) It was night, and the fairgrounds were crowded. My partner and I attempted to break up a fistfight. I wound up on a man's back with my left arm around his neck in a chokehold; with my right arm, I was trying to thwart a man on my back who was trying to take my holstered weapon. My partner was on his back with his gun out, the barrel digging into the man's back, while yelling that he would shoot him if the man succeeded in grabbing my gun. Luckily, some off-duty deputy sheriffs came by and helped us clean up the mess. Things like this can happen anytime. They can begin in a flash and end just as quickly, but they leave memories that will last a lifetime.

I came close to shooting a burglar in a South Dallas bar one night. I was working with a partner with the nickname Red. We had answered a silent alarm call late at night, and when we arrived, we found two doors unlocked—a front and a back. I entered first to find a man hiding in a closet; he wouldn't show me his hands, and I was beginning to think he had a weapon. My revolver was pointed at him, and I was close to squeezing the trigger because he would not respond to my warnings, when Red entered from the other door jacking a shell into the chamber of his shotgun—at which time the man finally showed his hands.

They were empty.

It was a weekend, so we knew the jail downtown was probably crowded, and since we had a table, chairs and lamp light, we decided to do our paperwork at the scene instead of at the crowded and noisy downtown jail. We were parked on another street to avoid being seen, and behold: While doing our paperwork, *another* burglar burst in the door, and now we had two. Then, as we were leaving the downtown jail after booking our two suspects, we got *another* silent alarm call on the same bar, only to catch yet *another* burglar. He had been in the bar the whole time we were there but had wedged himself in a very small drink cabinet, Houdini-style, and was having trouble extracting himself.

As I said, stranger than fiction.

Maximizing Minimum Force

In most arrests, a minimal use of force will get you your desired result. This is where your ability to stay calm and objective will keep you in control. I recall many instances where officers were too quick to use force because their orders were not obeyed instantly or the person they were arresting was over-the-line belligerent; regrettably, I include myself in this recollection, because I have memories that I wish I could go back to and edit.

As our amygdalas become hypersensitive and enlarged due to repeated experiences handling domestic disturbances and conflicts, we must be mindful of how much effort will be required to maintain our self-control. Internally, this means finding a way to give precedence to the ability of our rider over our silent partner's hasty tendencies. Nothing is more instructive here than to put yourself in the shoes of the person you are taking into custody. I used to take it as a matter of pride that I could talk people into handcuffs without a struggle, in cases when I doubted others could have done so. But, upon lots of reflection, I have no doubt that there were times when I was also too quick to anger.

At the organizational level, bodycam videos from routine arrests should be viewed occasionally in the company of other officers, with the aid of behavioral professionals; anything less is inviting trouble. Officers who can't accept this level of scrutiny need to be convinced to do so, reassigned, or regretfully terminated if they can't be reasoned with. If you take your oath to protect and serve as a sacred trust, as it is intended, then you should have no qualms about being held to account.

It is also important that you understand that what your job asks of you clashes with your biological disposition. That you are being monitored by those who understand and sympathize with the difficulty you experience—and who care enough to offer additional training and guidance before you let yourself get out of control and in big trouble—should in some sense be comforting. After all, when you must get physical in a hand-to-hand confrontation, the stakes are always higher than in a typical altercation between two civilians; you are armed with a lethal weapon, and many police officers are murdered with their own weapons.[11] This reality is often overlooked or given little attention when a civilian is killed while resisting arrest, but under no circumstance should you allow your weapon to be taken.

However, when police officers strike a person who is not resisting—and continue to strike them—it means that stress has taken over. Striking people who are not resisting demonstrates lack of control. As fellow officers also subject to the same pressures, we may feel empathy for those who snap and overreact—and we may understand the chemical signals that have contributed to their actions—but that does not mean we can, or ever should, tolerate this overt display of unprofessional behavior, which reflects poorly on us all. Officers who can't control themselves under such circumstances should be given some time off, reassigned, or terminated, so as not to subject citizens to this kind of treatment in the future.

Okay, we are at a critical juncture here: Time for an existential attitude check. So, what should you say to the assertion that black lives matter? Silence? This is not a trick question. Your answer must be, "Yes, black lives do matter." You do not answer with, "All lives matter," because saying that "Black lives matter" is a distressed plea made in the face of vital statistics showing black lives do not seem to matter as much as those of whites, especially when it comes to law enforcement.[12] You have no doubt noticed how some police organizations have taken a hostile approach to the assertion. In my view, this is an egregious misunderstanding of the issue, and to the extent this view remains prevalent, it will ensure abuse, always lying in wait as an easily-sprung booby trap of a public relations disaster. If you perform your duty in compliance with your sworn oath, the result will show that black lives do matter and the very existence of Black Lives Matter as a movement *puts us on notice* that people are paying attention to police behavior.

Optimizing Maximum Force

Asking if some kinds of police training may be reinforcing the wrong lessons is a fair question with ample probable cause. I have long suspected that police training in which one encounters shoot-or-don't-shoot photographs—one after another—or videos of armed villains versus innocent citizens may increase the tendency of some officers to shoot in cases of mistaken identification.

In my four years as a police officer, I fired my weapon once. It was a spur-of-the-moment decision, and at the time I knew I shouldn't do it, but I did it anyway. It was late at night in West Dallas, and I received a call of a break-and-entry in progress at a private residence. I was only a block away from the call. I pulled up in front of the house with my lights off and ran to the door. An old woman met me at the door. She was hysterical, barely able to tell me that someone was trying to get in the house through a back-bedroom window. I ran into the room just as the suspect was stepping through the opening. He saw me and fled. I ran out the front door and chased him. It was very dark, and when it appeared he was going to get away because of his lead, I fired a shot in the air because I wanted to scare him. The old woman was so traumatized that I didn't want to take a chance on him coming back. When you fired a weapon, then as now, reports were required. But after I told the sergeant who arrived on the scene what I had done and why, he chose to let it go without a report.

Fast forward a half century. In February 2015, I caught a burglar in my home. He pointed a handgun at me. I ran to another room, grabbed my shotgun, and caught him exiting my garage, where he kneeled on the ground and again pointed the gun at me. I told him repeatedly that if he didn't drop the gun, I would blow him in half. He finally dropped the weapon, and I called the state troopers on my cell phone; luckily, there was a trooper close by. Now, if someone points a gun at you while you are in uniform, I do not recommend that you try to talk them into putting it down, because it may cost you your life.

But on reflection, despite my excitement, I recall noticing the expression on the intruder's face as he pointed his gun at me (I was only about 15 feet away); it was not in my mind a shooting face.[13] As I remember this incident, my adrenaline rush was so over the top that it was a couple of days before I could feel completely calm and settle down and sleep without awakening frequently.[14]

I can't help thinking that the experience of having to shoot numerous times in a short training exercise may cause in some officers a tendency to shoot more than if one had had different training. I suspect the frequency itself may influence our silent partner. My studies and experiences cause me to think that the training may result in erring on the side of personal safety. In other words, the training will make shooting seem more of an option; it may save your life, but it may also prime you to shoot an innocent person by mistake.

The whole point of your training and your attitude toward the use of deadly force should be to develop the kind of calculated awareness during a highly stressful incident that will help you maintain enough presence of mind to see what is real and *to avoid reacting* based on training that is not actually applicable to the situation you are facing.

MEMO TO MANAGEMENT

TO: Chiefs, Deputy Chiefs, Colonels, Captains, Lieutenants, Sergeants, Corporals, and Training Officers
SUBJECT: Protecting Your Officers' Physical & Mental Welfare

You are alpha males and females who manage subordinate alpha males and females. You are responsible for their safety and the safety of the public citizenry you both serve. And, as you know, your officers are subject to conflicting situations and hostile encounters far above the norm in a peacetime community. Therefore, **they will experience physical and mental changes** because of the adrenaline-soaked experiences they will encounter.

This is to inform you that you must be hyperaware of the health and mental welfare of your officers. Moreover, by nature of their daily exposure to stimuli, **if you fail to make your views explicitly clear** about police behavior and the ethos of protect-and-serve **with zero tolerance for abuse**, then **they will cross the lines** of acceptable behavior—**not out of disregard** for their oath of service, **but simply because their emotions will naturally begin to override their self-control**.

You must never allow any level of abuse of power to become acceptable as business as usual, or the aggressiveness of your officers will in time inch exponentially further and further over the line.

You are no exception to this rule.

This sounds much simpler than it is. But, if it is not always on the front page of your day-to-day awareness, the behavior of your officers will get out of control. Remember, when ducks and geese fly at high altitude in V-formation, the leaders must take frequent breaks and go to the rear of the formation, because breaking the aerial trail is extremely taxing. The same principle applies to peace officers who deal with conflict daily. And please, use the colleges and universities in your area as resources for behavioral studies, and if you can, partner with them to make use of the latest research data possible.

Follow these guidelines or pay the "tax"—in ruffled feathers, excessive cortisol, and lawsuit settlements!!!

Sincerely,
Charles D. Hayes

Although such a memo is rarely actually delivered, management in police and sheriff departments is indeed exceptionally problematic because of the emotional volatility of the work. Cortisol-drenched officers who are emotionally drained from having addressed one conflict after another cannot be expected to be cheerful when reminded by management of things that seem petty and beneath their dignity under the circumstances. Simple clashes of personality in the ranks of law enforcement routinely destroy careers, but instead of being seen as a symptom, they are often thought of simply as the straw that broke the camel's back.

In his book, *Emotional Survival for Law Enforcement*, Kevin M. Gilmartin does an impressive job of discussing the difficulties and the emotional repercussions from line officers that come with managing police agencies.[1] There are no magic bullets, but I suspect the greatest success comes from a dedication to thoughtfulness.

In *Policing the Black Man*, in a chapter by Yale University law professor Tracy Meares and Yale University law and psychology professor Tom Tyler titled "Policing: A Model for the Twenty-first Century," the authors write that:

> **Interviews with police officers suggest that police officers want from their commanders the same sort of fairness that the public wants from them. And, like members of the public, officers often feel that they do not receive their due even in their own station houses. Hence, it is also important to rethink the organization of police forces to give field officers more opportunity to express their views, better explanations of the goals of department policies, more transparent procedures for discipline and promotion, and in general more respectful treatment.[2]**

Let's hope your management heeds this advice.

Blue as the Enemy

Given the amount of existing documented evidence of police abuse and misbehavior, the fact that police officers in America still have prominent levels of public approval shows how badly citizens want to believe in our service, but this may be changing—as we shall soon see. That police officers are routinely given the benefit of the doubt in view of our written history suggests that the public at large still has faith in the aspirations of law enforcement, if not the reality. Obviously, we human beings have a deep-seated psychological need to feel safe, but the history of abusive policing in America is so horrific that it takes existential stamina just to read through it. That's why no amount of complaining by peace officers today that we should simply move on warrants should make us do so, without first thoroughly understanding the historical foundation we are still building on—because anything less than a solid understanding leaves you on shaky ground.

The first chapter of criminal defense attorney Robbin Shipp's book, *Justice While Black,* is titled "Officer Friendly is Not Your Friend," and the rest of her book backs up this claim.[3] It should disturb you that anyone with an ounce of objectivity would believe this to be true, let alone that it *is* true in many circumstances, but if you read her book and you are honest with yourself you cannot help but find her argument compelling. What we need is for our culture to resolve to wage war on ignorant assumptions and learn *en masse* what is already well-known about the nature of bias. We may have a better chance of being hit by a comet than having this happen soon, so police officers need to compensate. We might have an opportunity to inspire enough empathy and goodwill to set some of our negative tribalistic inclinations aside, or at least mitigate them long enough to behave like enlightened adults.

Our Enemies in Blue, by anarchist author Kristian Williams, is a 572-page tome of documented abuse by peace officers, citing myriad instances of police brutality, many that are criminally indefensible.[4] William's book is written from the perspective that policing in America has more to do with preventing democracy, instead of helping to make democracy possible.

Now, since the publisher of this book boasts about being the world's largest and most productive anarchist publishing house, you can easily infer that some of the incidents described in this work contain a fair amount of biased spin. But many of these incidents can't be dismissed out of hand, and because they can't be, works like this are good training material for those entering law enforcement about what *not* to do. And it also offers insight about how the police are viewed by groups that consider them hostile. The selected bibliography in Williams's book alone is worth the cover price.[5] This tome is an excellent guide to putting police work in historical perspective from the standpoint of those who do indeed see us as the enemy. Works like this should not be avoided by police supporters, but studied, because they are bursting with probable cause for investigating irresponsible behavior.

The July 3, 2018 edition of *TheGuardian.com* reported that a police union in South Carolina objected to a novel about police brutality being on a school reading list because it would lead to mistrust of police. The novel, *The Hate U Give*, by Angie Thomas, has received rave reviews from critics. I read it, and in my opinion, instead of objecting, police officers in South Carolina would be well advised to read it themselves to ensure that what Thomas writes about remains fictional; nothing occurs in the novel that hasn't happened in the past, and it should be in our shared interest to keep it from happening in the future.

In his book, *The Beast Side*, D. Watkins has a chapter titled, "Cops are the Terrorists in Our Neighborhood," and he offers some advice for staying alive. He says the cops are afraid of you, so don't startle them or talk loudly, don't move your hands too fast, and don't run. Also: Don't act angry; assure them you are not armed; and never think they won't shoot you.[6]

When you combine the cultural resentment of those who have been historically oppressed by policing and you begin to surface the historical record of abuse, the emotional angst in America could easily shift from smoldering resentment to riot-ready in the blink of an eye. Police trainers and training departments would be well-advised to read the books of their critics, because until you confront the history of policing for the horrific past that it represents, you can't get a realistic sense of the justified anger and resentment still prevalent in many communities in this country.

In 1996, columnist Carl T. Rowan published *The Coming Race War in America*. I was an admirer of Rowan's work, and I read the book shortly after it was published, thinking at the time that, at least in this case, Rowan was a bit over the top. But that was then. Race relations in America have since grown more problematic, especially with a White House occupant whose racism is too palpable to hide, so Rowan's argument deserves another look. Rowan declared that he was not an alarmist and that a coming race war could indeed be avoided but that doing so would require knowing what we are up against and acting accordingly.[7] Rowan was also specifically concerned that the presidential campaign of Pat Buchanan was based, in no small part, on a bigoted and unconcealable racist agenda. In Rowan's view, Buchanan's tone said what his words wouldn't.

The idea that black men in America are more apt to be criminals was to Rowan a notion forged by both implicit and explicit assumptions in news and entertainment media steeped in racial bigotry as well as a reaction against affirmative action. Rowan believed this deep-seated resentment over affirmative action is so pervasive in America that a race war was unlikely to be prevented. "So many hate groups are at large," he said, "that a few of them are bound to try to make good on their threats to make parts of

America, or all of it, the exclusive home of superior Aryan whites. Too much rage has built up in the minds of young blacks who are trapped in the corridors of resentment and hopelessness to assume that they will not strike out with firepower, especially if provoked."[8] And yet, Rowan was even more fearful of the so-called "militias" that have sprung up all over the country; given today's political climate, you as officers of the law need to keep them in mind, because these organizations have members whose blind hatred is barely containable.

Rowan also said:

> **If we Americans are ever to escape the threat of "Armageddon" and the "rivers of blood" that *The Turner Diaries* predicts, we are going to have to make early and massive interventions in the lives of the millions of children who constitute a hopeless underclass.[9] I mean interventions at home, in schools, and in teenage life choices. The education and lifestyle initiatives must be financed in part by government, in part by private institutions, and otherwise carried out by volunteers.[10]**

Compare the threat of racial resentment from decades past to today, and it becomes clear that, although we have clearly made progress in race relations via affirmative action, explicit racism is still alive and well in America, and implicit racism is much more real than was apparent. Rowan felt the first step in averting a race war would lie in muting the cries of hatemongers.[11] Paying close attention to these cries is imperative on our part. Affirmative action has been effective in making it clear that black citizens can do anything as well as white citizens, and as this is made clear by example and is internalized as representing reality, this fact will become the unconscious bias of yet another generation, and slowly but surely a change in perception will produce a glacier-like paradigm shift; a complete change by this standard will likely mean black and white will be viewed equally in another 300 years. Or sooner, if we wake up and use what we know about how our minds work to address racial injustice.

Carol Anderson, in her book aptly titled *White Rage*, offers us some perspective:

> **The truth is, white rage has undermined democracy, warped the Constitution, weakened the nation's ability to compete economically, squandered billions of dollars on baseless incarceration, rendered an entire region, sick, poor, and woefully undereducated, and left cities nothing less than decimated. All this havoc has been wreaked simply because African Americans wanted to work, get an education, live in decent communities, raise their families, and vote.**[12]

Twenty-eight-year law enforcement veteran Matthew Horace, whose experience spans nearly every state in the country, and his co-author Ron Harris, a journalist and instructor at Howard University, offer a compelling and unforgettable account of implicit and explicit racism in American policing in *The Black and the Blue*.[13] They note that the Black Lives Matter movement has decisively helped call attention to the questionable number of shootings of black men, a problem they argue should concern us all. The problem is not limited to race, they point out, but affects other "out-groups" as well: "Here's a scary number that should give us pause," they write. "While black people are three times more

likely than other Americans to be killed by police, the mentally ill
are 16 times more likely to be killed by police."[14] This, too, is a civil
rights issue.

In *To Protect and Serve*, Norm Stamper said: "Pick a big city,
or a small one. Odds are, its police department has shot and killed
at least one mentally ill person."[15] As I recall, we had regular
encounters with people we knew to be mentally ill, and if a new
officer were to encounter them without knowing who they were,
someone would routinely explain it to them on the radio. We had
a middle-aged man we called Herbie who would often experience
seizures, and when we would send him to a hospital by ambulance,
he would sometimes become so violent that he would kick the
windows out of the vehicle. Sober, in jail as a trustee, he carried a
whisk broom, he wore little make-believe badges and dusted off our
uniforms when we had business there. He was kind, likeable, and
exceptionally polite—except when alcohol withdrawal caused him
to convulse.

We had a middle-aged woman frequently arrested for disorderly conduct in downtown Dallas. Whenever she was taken
into custody, she would always hike up her dress, squat down
and pee on the sidewalk—and the bigger the audience, the more
enthusiastic she was about doing it. We had homeless people in
the 1960s—some of whom were obviously mentally ill—but not to
the extent that exists today. We had lots of alcoholics, whom we
arrested frequently for drunk and disorderly conduct, and who,
during wintry weather, sought us out so they could go to jail and
stay warm. Some of these people were such sad cases that I recall
letting them finish their bottles before taking them in. Some would
say something like, "Officer, can you come by and get me in about
an hour?" Most of the officers I worked with would oblige, as would
I, if we weren't too busy, knowing full well that some of these people

smelled so bad that you could barely ride in the same car with them and that the stench would linger long after they were gone, leaving your relief angry for having to begin their shift riding with the windows down.

(A heads-up lesson here: Peace officers should take it upon themselves to learn how to deal with the mentally ill; if your department is too small to provide the training, find it yourself.)

Such opportunities to identify where we could do better explain why Horace and Harris insist, "Despite claims to the contrary, Black Lives Matter is not anti-cop, just as the women's movement is not anti-men, and the civil rights movement was not anti-white."[16]

In his book, *On the Other Side of Freedom*, civil rights activist and community organizer Deray Mckesson describes police officers as "ushers, shepherding men and women, and increasingly children, into subjection."[17] He bears witness to police officers creating conflict to resolve conflict.[18] He perceives police as bullies acting out an ideology of white supremacy, showing through their actions their belief that white lives matter more than black lives. As he sees it, "Defunding public education, gerrymandering, and scaling back the Voting Rights Act are all manifestations of this ideology."[19] If you believe he is wrong—and let us hope he is—you should help prove it, not by your arguments, but by your actions. Police officers and citizens share a common enemy, criminals and racists, and this, given the right approach, is a powerful association.[20]

Blue Culture: The Brotherhood

The belief that police officers will look after their own is so much a part of our folklore and print and cinema culture that, if it changed, it would be decades before people believed anything was different. As I mentioned earlier, it takes a resolute commitment to "protect and serve" to keep an ethos of "us versus them" from setting into an unmovable bias that alienates us from those whom we serve. As a police officer, you are going to expect that everyone you ask for information should be duty-bound to tell you what they know; and yet, if the so-called "blue wall" prevents you from being honest and forthright, then why should you consider yourself an exception? Think about it like this: If you adopt a gang-like ethos of loyalty at the expense of justice, then you are simply a gang member in uniform.

In *Us and Them*, science writer David Berreby reminds us that it is in our nature to favor those of our own kind, something he calls "kind sight."[21] It's like a shortcut to stereotyping or a delineation of us versus them. Wrap your mind around *kind sight* and *racial profiling* and see if you can come up with a difference. If you are a bigoted cop, you will have no trouble rationalizing racial profiling, because you will be able to give all kinds of reasons for profiling that have nothing at all to do with your hidden assumptions for doing so. As an ex-cop, I know this is true from countless observations and personal experience. As often as not, stop-and-frisk legitimizes hidden bias and the free-flowing rationalizations that follow.[22]

Listen to me very carefully now: Loyalty to one's fellow officers is expected, and a significant degree of allegiance is demanded, but when we let that sense of dedication denigrate our resolve to protect and serve the public, we undermine everything we are supposed to stand for, and we threaten the very ideal of justice.

Think about all the television and movie examples of police officers resorting to criminal acts to, as they say, "protect one of their own." For heaven's sake, it's considered an essential entertainment twist in attracting an audience. Loyalty is to be expected. We can't really function without it. But if we don't maintain the kind of integrity that gives rise to genuine public service as peace officers, then we can become a worse menace than the felons we arrest. The first step in managing your behavior in this arena is to be upfront with your fellow officers. This is not an easy task, but it is necessary, because failing to manage your behavior in this regard makes it impossible to live up to your oath *to protect and serve*.

In 1983, American television journalist Lawrence O'Donnell published *Deadly Force: A Police Shooting and My Family's Search for the Truth*. The book is about a police shooting in Boston in 1975, a case of mistaken identity where officers on a stakeout, while watching a car they thought had been used in an armed robbery, shot and killed James Bowden, Jr., as he left his mother's house after a visit. Bowden's widow hired O'Donnell's father, an attorney who was also a former Boston police officer, to find out what happened to her husband, because she knew—as did everyone who knew James—that he was not a criminal. It was a bad shooting, and the department attempted to cover it up. The rest of this book has a Kafka-esque feel to it, as O'Donnell meticulously and eloquently details the cover-up. O'Donnell says *Deadly Force* marked a new beginning in the scrutiny of police behavior. In the Preface to the 2018 new release of the book, O'Donnell said, "Police training is still not adequate, but it has improved. Police are no longer completely confident that they can cover up a bad shooting now that the news media is alert and ready to cover possible bad shootings by police."[23] Incidents like this are multifaceted tragedies: A loss of life; a miscarriage of justice; a crime committed to cover an accident; and thousands of dollars of wasted man-hours lost to committing crime rather than protecting the public.

It is a fact of human behavior, especially organizational behavior, that subordinates and supervisors are predisposed to close ranks and protect their own, but it is especially egregious when those of us being paid to enforce the law instead break it. This case resulted in a financial settlement based less on a court decree than upon a political promise.

O'Donnell says that, in those days, "cracking the blue wall of silence was virtually impossible," and that this book was "the single biggest breakthrough in the then-slim journalistic history of police use of deadly force."[24] But what hits me, like a left hook to the jaw, is not the case itself—which represents behavior I recognize from historical experience. What I have real difficulty understanding and accepting is the fact that when *he* was a police officer on the streets of Boston, O'Donnell's father also participated in a cover-up; he caught two burglars and let one of them go because he turned out to be a Boston police sergeant from another district.[25]

In response to a history of police corruption, the New Orleans Police Department in 2017 implemented EPIC—Ethical Policing is Courageous, a training program to inspire "active bystandership and peer intervention."[26] Former New Orleans superintendent Michael S. Harrington believes that it is an effective method of defeating the "blue wall of silence." Other deputy chiefs in New Orleans claim that ethical policing is contagious. Let's hope it is a successful program and that it catches on nationwide.

Body Camera Oversight

You will find studies that make contradictory claims for every practical and political point of view possible regarding the use of body cameras.[27] But in my view, body cameras are imperative in achieving effective policing.[28]

Police officers have long operated with an extraordinary degree of autonomy. It's hard to overstate the case of how this autonomy, from the very beginning of America's policing history, has led to a dynamic in which the word of peace officers has almost always come with the benefit of the doubt. Over time, this assumption led to the unwritten but acknowledged reality that most police officers felt they could pretty much do as they pleased and be cleared from wrongdoing, thanks to traditional public allegiance toward law enforcement.

In his book *Fire Shut Up in My Bones*, *New York Times* columnist Charles M. Blow wrote about an incident when he was stopped, along with some friends, by a police officer for an alleged traffic violation. The officer mistook a comb for a switchblade and drew his weapon. But it was what he said as he left that Blow has long remembered, and which makes my point about police autonomy. The officer said if he wanted to, he could make Charles and his friends lie down in the road, shoot them in the head and get away with it.[29] Some sense of accountability is necessary to keep attitudes like this in check.

Precisely because police work changes our biology, and because it is so easy to become jaded and bitter, more accountability is critical. Moreover, when it is commonly understood that all police officers are equipped with body cameras, the psychological effects for many people will cause them to behave better than they might have were these not in use. By the same token, as a peace officer, a camera on your person seeing what you see and hearing what you hear is a constant reminder that your sworn duty is to protect and serve and that your behavior will be a matter of record. In today's times, I would be very uncomfortable being on duty *without* a body camera.

In all incidents involving citizen complaints, video records of the incidents must be reviewed by management and, where possible, routine calls should be examined occasionally, too; because, as we have explored, prolonged periods of being exposed to elevated levels of stress exact a cost. How else will supervisors know when this is happening before it is too late? Airline pilots being responsible for the lives of so many people are routinely subject to supervised preflight checks. Police officers need the same level of scrutiny. If you cannot understand or accept that your mental health is a public concern and that periodic reviews are necessary for your own well-being and are in the public interest, then you should be reassigned or made to seek employment elsewhere.

Body cameras are not foolproof. They miss a lot of peripheral action and emotional content that affects all participants. But they are far, far better than relying on the memories of everyone involved. Police officers who have a habit of their body cameras "not working" when video evidence is required should be terminated. In February 2019, Memphis lawmakers proposed a law making it a felony for police officers to intentionally turn off their body cameras.[30] The calls for such penalties are likely to increase until policy violations become exceptionally rare and attributable only to technological glitches. The body cameras worn by police officers can provide straightforward evidence of an increasing inability to handle stress, and therefore—for the sake of accountability and possibly even to prevent such incidents before they occur—they must be reviewed.

Unfortunately, some small police departments are starting to opt out of using body cameras, citing budget limitations. Hopefully they can be persuaded otherwise. After all, if they are policing responsibly, the cameras should prove to be legally cost-effective.

Cleaning Up Dirty Harry

The image of the rogue cop who disregards the rules—who roughs up suspects and takes no prisoners, so to speak—is so much a part of American cinema that it can't be stamped out of our psyche. In far too many cases, we see this imitated by peace officers who aren't on the big screen but are instead on the streets where we

live. No one is more intransigent in law enforcement culture than
the officer who believes that he or she knows what's going on, what
needs to be done, and doesn't need or want training or advice. If
these officers think training is an unnecessary inconvenience and
they can't be convinced otherwise, they are bound to fail. You are
going to work with officers who, when reminded that their duty to
protect and serve the public is sacrosanct, are going to go off spit-
ting and sputtering about "goddamned liberals," or something
to that effect; I'm telling you now that these people are neither
sufficiently educated nor temperamentally suited to be police
officers. These people have been conditioned. As psychologist
Robert Burton explains it, "the feelings of knowing, correctness, conviction, and certainty aren't deliberate conclusions and
conscious choices. They are mental sensations that happen to
us."[31] Moreover, those of you who will rise to management must
understand (and act on the knowledge) that when you continue
to employ known racist peace officers, you lose community credibility.[32] We can see evidence of this in award-winning journalist
and editor Jill Leovy's remarkable book, *Ghettoside: A True Story
of Murder in America*, where she notes that the hardcore police
officers working in the toughest districts were "often seen as damaged goods by the LAPD."[33]

Every major police department in America, by nature of size
alone, is bound to have at least some officers in uniform who are
not suited for police work in situations where they must deal with
the public. They should be assigned duties accordingly—or again,
be required to seek employment elsewhere. Of course, officers may
accumulate citizen complaints for simply doing their jobs, and
everyone experienced in policing knows this, but statistics showing that complaints are not taken seriously by management are
problematic. The telltale heads-up that police officers are unsuited

for their job is when officers become so hardened in attitude that they will listen to no one about how to go about their work. This is not peculiar to police work: Every major career field is rife with know-it-alls who resist all methods of training and in too many cases become grandfathered into jobs they should be forbidden to perform. Of course, some of the physical changes that officers experience are involuntary, and holding them entirely account-able for actions under which they do not maintain control without mental health supervision is irresponsible; management should anticipate the potential for such issues and be held accountable when they do not.[34]

In the FBI, the agents assigned to finding serial killers are reassigned after a certain period, because the burden of so much horrific information is too much to bear without periods of relief. The same should apply to all men and women who address daily conflict and who are overexposed to humanity's worst behaviors. A person can only witness so much deviant behavior before cyni-cism takes over. Peace officers are expected to cope with stress with an almost superhuman ability and to be held to account for being unable to do things none of us are biologically designed to do.

Police work carried out in complete compliance with the ethos to serve, protect, and keep all safe, in my view, is far harder and much more complex than most of us have grown up appreciating. Our whole educational system is based on relegating the study of human behavior to specialists, and yet we are decades behind in providing the knowledge of what we have learned to the men and women who need it most.[35]

Policing, as I've noted, is not rocket science; it's a hell of a lot harder than rocket science, precisely because of the imprecision at work in that there are no completely right answers, and the matters at hand can be settled only in measures of degree.

In Fear for Your Life

Most of the laws in this country support the fact that you will be justified in shooting someone when you are in fear for your life and you have reason to believe that the person you are confronting poses an immediate mortal threat to you.[36] In the past, most juries have been reluctant to disregard this, so they usually find in favor of officers who have taken a life under these circumstances. But the evidence is overwhelming that this policy has been stretched too far, and in some cases, it is used simply as a means of covering up a careless disregard for human life. Times are changing, due in large part to the ubiquity of smartphone cameras.

Take out your smartphones and do a web search for the police video of the Mesa, Arizona shooting of Daniel Shaver, in January 2016. (The video release date was December 8, 2017.) This, ladies and gentlemen, is a blatant example of murder on video, plain and simple, and yet, the officer involved was cleared of second-degree homicide in the shooting. This young man was not a threat to the officer involved, but he was indeed in fear for his own life—for damned good reasons. He was sobbing while being subjected to a series of arbitrary commands, by a cop in search of an excuse to shoot. Keep watching it, and if you cannot determine that you are witnessing a wanton homicide, then I question your suitability for law enforcement. This officer was seeking a reason to execute this young man, not because he was in fear of his own life, but because he was simply not fit for police work, period. You tell me the reason he shot Daniel Shaver—when and if you *can* figure it out, because I can't. This kind of deplorable incident makes achieving the public trust impossible. The so-called experts who testified that this shooting was justified should be fired for cause.

On April 4, 2015, patrolman Michael Slager, a white North Charleston, South Carolina police officer, shot and killed Walter Scott, an unarmed black man, after a routine traffic stop. Scott was shot in the back running away, and the shooting was captured by a bystander's video. Slager pled guilty when his "in fear for my life" excuse was not believed, and on December 7, 2017, he was sentenced to 20 years in prison. Check out the video online and consider the absurdity of the defense of being "in fear for your life" as an excuse for shooting Walter Scott.[37]

In August 2018, a Dallas jury convicted former Balch Springs police officer Roy Oliver of murder for shooting a fifteen-year-old boy in a vehicle that Oliver had claimed was trying to run him and his partner over.[38] But cameras showed the car moving away from, not toward, the officers—and Oliver's partner admitted that he was at no time in fear for his life. Unfortunately, this kind of incident is going to occur increasingly in the future, until such time that the long-held assumption that police officers don't need to worry about being held to account is history. When—and only when— peace officers understand they will not automatically be given the benefit of the doubt in investigations over the use of deadly force, an awareness calculation about accountability will kick in, in your mind and the minds of all peace officers, that has not existed in the past.[39] Reality is, after all, what reality is, and in time the importance of being lucidly and judiciously aware will become a part of an unconscious assumption that it is important to not be careless regarding the value of a human life—whether the life is yours or that of a stranger, badge or no badge.

In October of 2019, a Dallas jury found Amber Guyger, a white female and a former Dallas police officer, guilty of murder, for shooting 28-year-old Botham Jean to death in his own apartment that she mistook for her own residence. When Guyger opened the door to the wrong apartment and found a black man who was reportedly eating ice cream, she said she was "scared to death." Guyger was subsequently found to have made racially-disparaging text messages in earlier phone conversations and a fellow officer at the trial testified about Guyger's bravery in having run toward the action when five Dallas officers were gunned down in July of 2016. A decade ago, my guess is that she would have been found innocent and described as having made a horrific mistake, or she might have been found guilty of manslaughter instead of murder. Time will tell whether the verdict of murder in this case was simply due to the unique circumstances, or whether it is a sign of things to come.[40]

First, as I often argue, police officers who experience fear too often should find another occupation. I have been involved in many police incidents that included physical assaults, but the only times I recall being in fear for my life involved traffic incidents and car chases. (In one chase, I had the good sense to break it off for safety's sake, long before it would become policy to do so.) As sworn peace officers in every major city with years of experience come to know, there are people in uniform who shouldn't be—and some of these individuals are looking for someone to shoot so they can bask in the limelight of a Dirty Harry celebrity status.

One night, on the Dallas North Central Expressway, there were a half dozen squads involved in a chase. I was monitoring it on the radio, and I was close by, so I headed in their direction, and I discovered that the car had been stopped, with several officers struggling with the suspect. I arrived at the same time as a lieutenant. Noticing that this lieutenant was wearing a white hat, the suspect assumed correctly that he was a supervisor and shouted, "Police brutality!" saying that he was being beaten up. To this, the lieutenant—caught up in the excitement of the moment—cracked the suspect's head with a metal flashlight. "Do you mean like that?" he said.

When I was in uniform, the notion that police officers in general are fearful would have been thought absurd, and I don't think things are that different in this regard today. Police officers are generally ready and eager to go where they are needed, when they are needed. This is in no small way what gives the work its special appeal. Accountants may dream of figuring out a financial strategy that saves their company; architects aim for a prize-winning design; physicians yearn to save lives. And police officers are perpetually seeking a bank robbery in progress.

In *Breaking Rank*, Norm Stamper says that white police officers are afraid of black men, and that *he* used to be afraid of *everyone* at first, but got over it—except he continued to be afraid of black men.[41] In the same book, when he tells how he was asked to go on a call where a suspect was threatening to kill his wife and kid, he comments that cops *live* for such assignments.[42] My take is that his language has slid in the direction of what I characterize as "safe police defensive rhetoric," where this subject is so often discussed (when you're talking about a police shooting, which always revolves around the "get out of jail free" card: "I was in fear for my life"). I don't think Stamper is purposely being disingenuous. I think he is just extending the semantics in keeping with the way the conversation is routinely dealt with by law enforcement organizations who are on the defensive by nature of legalese.

That white men see black men as being more of a threat than white men in our culture is a slam-dunk assumption; our entertainment media are infamous for making them seem that way. But that most white cops would be routinely *afraid* of anyone does not fit with my experience. Of course, any situation can escalate until one's fear is simply a reflection of the actual danger you are facing. But as a peace officer, you are after all wearing a side arm, and with your radio you can have a squad car cavalry arriving in minutes.

Moreover, it's likely that your biological reward system has learned to yearn for being where the action is.

In his book *To Protect and Serve*, Stamper has a chapter titled "A Scared Cop is a Dangerous Cop."[43] He says, "scared cops are a danger to themselves, and to the people they've been hired to protect and serve."[44] Neuroscientists Jaak Panksepp and Lucy Biven tell us that our fear system "can become hypersensitized when we have been frightened badly enough or for long enough. From birth, this capacity for free-floating fear is built into our brains; initially it can be activated by only a few unconditional stimuli, but experience can create fearful memories that henceforth can be triggered by previously neutral events of the world."[45] They note that, like all animals, we learn to fear from experience. So, in my view, any police officers who are truly fearful in the presence of all black men represent a danger to all black men and to themselves—and are thus unsuited for law enforcement. And so, not to be misunderstood, I'm not suggesting that officers should not always be cautious and wary when circumstances warrant vigilance, regardless of whom they are facing. But if a bad experience with anyone results in an unnatural fear of everyone, everyone's safety is at risk.

While I fully support laws that protect police officers when in fear for their lives, it is also my view that we need to actively identify officers unsuited for duty and remove them from serving before the (currently inevitable) incidents of unnecessary and abusive force take place. With more and more shooting incidents occurring in which video evidence contradicts officer testimony and more rests on the assumption they were in fear for their lives, a once-presumed trust is not a given.

There are far too many shootings where a fear for one's life was grounds for a plea of innocence, but where the videos show this plea defies all human logic, common sense, and any viable sense of human morality. These kinds of incidents threaten the integrity of the concept of law and order. In his book *The Gift of Fear*, security specialist Gavin De Becker writes about the kind of intuition that warns us—though we can't explain why—with that little nagging voice that says, "something is not right here."[46] It's often the case that when we do not listen to such a warning, we are sorry. And indeed, when you focus as a police officer on your work for an extended period, you can't help but configure your subconscious with circumstances in which your silent partner will whisper to you that something is wrong with this picture. If it's too warm for people to be wearing jackets, and you see someone at a distance wearing a heavy coat walk into a 7/11, you won't need to think about it: Your silent partner will let you know immediately that something is wrong with this scene.

This brings me to the notion of bias as a vital feature of context. Where are you more apt to expect that you might have to shoot someone: In the neighborhood where you live or the one where you work? In a poor neighborhood or in a rich one? In the day or at night? At a woman or a man? At a person who is black or one who is white?

Not all the warnings our silent partner whispers to us are valid: Some are just lightning-fast assumptions based on scant observations and mistaken subconscious assumptions. However, I believe that if you regularly take into consideration the algorithmic context of your situation—like where you are and how the location influences your assumptions—you will be more inclined to make accurate judgments. With practice and mental preparation, when you encounter dangerous situations, you won't just see what you expect to see based on biased assumptions, but you will see what is before you as it really is.

The December 20, 2018 online edition of *Scientific American* includes a column titled, "Is the Psychology of Deadly Force Ready for the Courts?"[47] This piece by Zachary Siegel features the testimony of psychologist Laurence Miller in the trial of Jason Van Dyke, who—in 2014 in Chicago—shot Laquan McDonald in the back 16 times as the teen suspect was walking away from officers. Miller essentially assembled the same information on the biology of human behavior that we have been reviewing here and presented it in Van Dyke's defense as a slideshow titled, "The Neuropsychology of Deadly Force Encounters." In other words, Van Dyke's stress from his police work was put forth to explain why he should *not* be held accountable for his actions. Watch the YouTube video of this shooting and tell me in this circumstance, as the officer, if you would have been in fear of your life—which was Van Dyke's claim. If your answer is yes, you are in my view excused from further consideration as a viable candidate as a peace officer.[48]

Using the routine stress of police work—and its accumulating effects on the parasympathetic nervous system of law enforcement officers—as a defense in such cases will backfire in the long run, I suspect. What a shameful betrayal of the public trust, indeed, if police departments were to embrace this kind of defense instead of using the same knowledge to prevent such incidents in the first place.

Unfortunately, the tactic may continue to be used. In October 2018, in a Chicago court, Jason Van Dyke was convicted of second-degree murder; he *had* been charged with *first*-degree murder and 16 counts of aggravated battery with a firearm.[49] If this conviction on a lesser offense is credited as a success of the "damaged psyche defense," others may want to use similar defenses. This will lead to further politicization of law enforcement—and damage the profession's reputation even further, because letting officers continue to work until obviously overstressed is clearly supervisory negligence.[50] This subject must become a police management obsession until an effective strategy is fully understood and implemented.

POLITICS AND POLICE

Incidents involving police misconduct bring us front and center to politics, because this is the public pressure point where police management and politicians so often clash over tactics and results, or a lack of results. But police departments that become overtly political in their response exact a social and political cost, because they can't help but alienate significant segments of their citizenry in doing so. I suggest an alternative that you may find surprising: A strategy of nonviolence.

As you may recall, Mahatma Gandhi used his strategy of nonviolence effectively to sway public opinion in favor of Indian independence. It may seem counterintuitive, but the same approach is applicable to police department public relations. When police department spokespeople push back against public criticism, the reputational damage incurred almost always outweighs the benefit gained. No matter what is said about defending the reputation and tactics of law enforcement, there are simply too many shootings in the news, too many incidents involving unarmed individuals, too many videos of police striking people who are not resisting. The only way to uphold the reputation of police departments is to emulate Gandhi, which in *our* case means doubling down on the objective and oath to protect and serve. When the public feels that police abuse is occurring, efforts to fight public opinion simply exacerbate the problem. The act of defending indefensible violence is self-defeating.[1]

In academia, the term *ideological amplification* describes the process by which ideological or goal-driven groups move farther in the direction they are leaning because they bond over their stated ideals as they go. Recall the Western movies where a lynch mob gathers and ratchets up its fervor, ultimately resulting in a hanging. Similarly, it's far too easy for military units and police departments to become overtly ideologically driven, while remaining oblivious to how oppressive their actions are, simply because they are not subject to their own tactics. Again, all you must do to appreciate the reality of such oppression is to identify with being a citizen of the community where you work and not a peace officer. I've personally been reflecting on this reality for more than 50 years.

You may already be aware that geographically our neighborhoods are forming more and more along the lines of political ideology.[2] Some have noted that there are biological differences driving our politics, with studies showing that, when they engage in political thought, liberals and conservatives rely on different brain regions.[3] Conservatives are apt to have larger amygdalas than liberals.[4] Moreover, you are likely to be treated differently by liberals and conservatives, because they each have different expectations about the duties of peace officers. Conservatives tend to view crime as stemming from a lack of self-discipline and an inability to delay gratification, with poverty being an unacceptable excuse for violating the law. Liberals are more likely to acknowledge that poverty and crime are systemically linked. Conservatives are more likely to demand harsh punishment for crime, while liberals are more likely to stress rehabilitation.

My experience and studies suggest that conservatives are strong advocates of law and order, and liberals are more likely to be concerned with police misconduct than conservatives. You mustn't let this get in the way of your objective, however, which is simply to enforce the law and to protect and serve.

Instead of being distracted by politics, look at the facts. Statistics that show lethal force is used more often on minorities—especially young black men—than on whites serve as proof that, instead of a war on cops, we have a documented tradition of not holding law enforcement accountable.[5] This has gone on for so long, even mere suggestions that police need to be held accountable are followed by cries of anti-cop bias. Retired LAPD police sergeant Cheryl Dorsey says, "Police abuse and excessive, unnecessary force, deadly force is not an aberration. Police abuse is a too frequent occurrence in communities of color and where poor whites reside. Be clear, everyone is in danger."[6]

In August of 2019, Attorney General William Barr spoke to the Fraternal Order of Police, saying that there must be zero tolerance for resisting arrest, declaring that it will save lives.[7] And he is right, it's damned good advice and it will save lives. Complying and complaining later if one feels wronged is the smart and safe thing to do. But then Barr went after social justice reformers, as if there is nothing in need of reform, at a time when hate crimes are increasing at an alarming rate and when the disparities of the criminal justice system are so often front-page news. This kind of tough on crime talk is taken by some as a traditional dog-whistle signal to crack down on minorities, and even if it is made with the best of intentions, the perceptional harm is done. Barr missed an opportunity to make an important point and double down on the oath of public service and yet his tone of get-tough rhetoric reinforces a public distrust of the police. Worse, rank-and-file police officers who hear people with the authority of the Attorney General say things like this often take this kind of message as reassurance that their past behavior of crossing the line regarding physical abuse is thus grandfathered and deemed greenlit and appropriate.

There are two books that do more damage than good for peace officers: *Cop Under Fire*, by Sheriff David Clarke Jr., and *The War on Cops*, by Heather Mac Donald.[8] On the cover of Mac Donald's book is a blurb by Thomas Sowell saying, "This book will save lives." In my view, it will cause the reverse. Both works amount to despicable political polemics that have no place on the shelf for peace officers who take the edict or their oath seriously. You don't just serve the members of the political party you belong to.

Speaking as a former police officer, I find irony in the absurd claims about a war on cops; instead, the evidence clearly suggests we need to declare a war on unconscious bias and acknowledge that the way these young men have been depicted in media, literature, and entertainment has worsened their treatment. It's that simple, and it's that hard. Arguing that to examine or repair this reality equates to a war on cops is a sign of a disgraceful inability and unwillingness to understand the nature of the problem.

Mac Donald claims that gains in urban safety that have begun with a proactive policing strategy will be lost if the demonization of law enforcement doesn't end.[9] But the claim that there is a war on cops, or that they are being "demonized" because serious public attention is being applied to police behavior is ridiculous. Of course, the public is going to speak out when YouTube videos clearly conflict with what the police departments are telling them.

If you are a police officer anywhere in America, and you feel you are engaged in a war against the media or the public because of the expectation of being held to account for your actions, then you need to turn in your badge, pack your amygdala in ice, and find a new occupation. Peace be with you, but I don't want you policing my neighborhood. I do not doubt that Clarke and Mac Donald are well-intentioned and that they sincerely believe their positions are justified, and yet it is brazenly clear to anyone who has seriously studied the history of racism and police behavior in this country that their books are irresponsibly superficial.

Mac Donald says that the *New York Times'* claims in November of 2014 that "the killing of young black men by police is a common feature of African-American life and a source of dread for black parents coast to coast," is "pure hysteria."[10] One cannot study this subject to any degree of depth without understanding and appreciating the concern the parents of people of color have for their children's safety when they come into contact with the police.

Clarke declares police brutality to be a myth, that it is no longer systemic, and he imagines he can hear liberals gasping when he says it.[11] Referencing other popular conservative positions in an attempt to win approval from his audience, he says brutality may be best described as foreign terrorists, or as "Planned Parenthood harvesting baby parts to sell to the highest bidder, but not American policing."[12] He argues that "what liberals want us to forget—is that there's a qualitative difference between violence and self-defense."[13] An officer of the law in any capacity who uses the word liberal as pejorative, as Clarke does repeatedly, instantaneously alienates half of the people he or she is sworn to protect.

Mac Donald and Clarke set out not to service the public interests of all citizens, but to make a political polemic appealing only to like-minded constituents. You might legitimately accuse me of something similar, except: My case is based on the premise that if you can see the problem of racial bias in policing as the biological and cultural problem that it is—rather than as a one-dimensional problem, as painted by the ilk of Mac Donald and Clarke—you can hopefully appreciate that it really is multidimensional and not a partisan issue at all. My aim is not war, but peace, and the assurance that everyone deserving of respect receives it—including members of the public and police officers.

In *The Coddling of the American Mind*, attorney Greg Lukianoff and psychology professor Jonathan Haidt recount how students at Claremont McKenna College prevented their classmates from attending a speech by Heather Mac Donald while referring to her as being a white supremacist.[14] This, in my view, is not the way to address this kind of issue, but it may very well portend a generational change in the way law enforcement is perceived in America—and police departments should take note and engage students in dialogue whenever possible.[15]

Law enforcement officials who take sides politically alienate those of the other party, period. Everything they say and do becomes politically suspect, whether it contains political bias or not. Police officers who make public proclamations to the effect that the President of the United States hates the police do not possess the kind of discernment necessary to wear the uniform.[16]

In *The Audacity of Hope*, Barack Obama wrote:

> **If we Americans are individualistic at heart, if we instinctively chafe against a past of tribal allegiances, traditions, customs, and castes, it would be a mistake to assume that this is all we are. Our individualism has always been bound by a set of communal values, the glue upon which every healthy society depends. We value the imperatives of family and the cross-generational obligations that family implies. We value**

community, the neighborliness that expresses itself
through raising the barn or coaching the soccer team.
We value patriotism and the obligations of citizenship,
a sense of duty and sacrifice on behalf of our nation.
We value faith in something bigger than ourselves,
whether that something expresses itself in formal
religion or ethical precepts. And we value the con-
stellation of behaviors that express our mutual regard
for one another: honesty, fairness, humility, kindness,
courtesy, and compassion.[17]

That Sheriff David Clarke Jr. would call President Obama "the
Cop-Hater-in-Chief" demonstrates everything that is wrong with
mixing partisan politics with the policing of the nation.[18] But to
have a United States president speak as Donald Trump did in July
2017, suggesting that the police not be too nice and not to worry
about roughing people up, is a disservice to the police and the
public.[19] The history in this country of abusive police behavior,
especially in the context of having been instigated because of a
political ideology, is horrific, with hundreds of thousands of documented reports.[20] Suggesting it is acceptable for police officers
to routinely rough people up to send a message does just that—
and the message is to ignore the history of racism, for political
reasons.[21]

And now, it seems, the argument even threatens to divide peace
officers along racial and political lines.

On September 4, 2018, Michael McHale, president of the
National Association of Police Organizations, Inc., wrote a letter
to Mark Parker, Chairman, President and CEO of Nike, condemn-
ing Nike's decision in supporting Colin Kaepernick in their "Just
Do It" Campaign—in part on the grounds that Nike's campaign

"perpetuates the falsehood that police are racist and aiming to use force against African Americans and persons of color."

On September 5, 2018, Sonia Y. W. Pruitt, National Chairperson for the National Black Police Association, wrote a letter to Mr. Parker expressing dismay about their inclusion in the letter; she declared that her organization in fact stands *with* Colin Kaepernick and fully supports his efforts.[22] This was an egregious missed opportunity by the National Association of Police Organizations, made all the more so because it was a letter by well-meaning public servants who simply do not understand the fundamental dynamics of bias and who do not have the humility and compassion to recognize that Colin Kaepernick taking a knee during the National Anthem is simply a desperate call for help for a problem that needs all of the attention it can get.

Imagine what the effect would be if, instead of taking offense, police officers nationwide had chosen to also take a knee, admitting there is a real problem and resolving to find a solution. This was, and still is, a strategic opportunity to come together and examine the complexity of bias and the simple reality of how the nature of bias is misunderstood. That something like this would occur in view of what has been learned about human behavior in recent decades is tragic, as politicizing the issue makes it impossible to address properly. An inability to receive critical scrutiny without a partisan pushback is childish, and it flies in the face of the public interest.

If police officers taking a knee in support of finding a solution seems out of the question, think about the problem in this context: We've already discussed Henry David Thoreau's argument that if we are the beneficiaries of an unjust system, we are responsible for putting it right. Thoreau's essay "Civil Disobedience" became the material that Mahatma Gandhi used to create a movement of nonviolence in India, followed by that started by Martin Luther King, Jr. in America.[23]

The humility and willingness of citizens to receive blows without fighting back resulted in a global groundswell of sympathy and empathy—and a paradigm shift in public opinion. Contrast this with the reality of myriad YouTube videos and television news clips of citizens who are not resisting but are being pummeled by police officers—and listen again to Thoreau: "There will never be a really free and enlightened State until the State comes to recognize the individual as a higher and independent power, from which all its own power and authority are derived, and treats him accordingly."[24] So imagine the global public reaction if we were to modify Thoreau's notion of civil disobedience and reformulate it as a true-blue positive police bias: Civil Dedication, Civil Devotion, Civil Commitment. And realize that all you are doing here is reinforcing your oath: You are giving no ground in the legitimate and necessary use of force; you are not being asked to submit to physical abuse; you would simply be guilty of refusing to defend indefensible actions. And even if you are right, and your actions were not over the line, just make your case without being disrespectful and reiterate your resolve to protect and serve. You only need to reflect on this strategy for a brief time to appreciate its potential for revolutionary change in the public's attitude toward police.

One last heads-up about politics: Political movements have a way of affecting public behavior and becoming police business. Donna Zuckerberg is a Silicon Valley-based classics scholar who received her doctoral training at Princeton University. In her book *Not All Dead White Men*, she describes a growing online movement called the Red Pill Movement, or "the manosphere," which misuses the classics of ancient Greece and Rome to justify misogynistic treatment of women.[25] Hopefully, this undertaking will dissipate and self-destruct, but if not, you may be hearing more about it in your community.

But a far greater threat is that of the rise of hate groups; the FBI has warned that extremist hate-group members make it a point to join and infiltrate police departments for both the training and the opportunities it offers to oppress members of minority groups.[26] Such individuals must be prevented from becoming officers of the law or, when found among police ranks, outed and removed without hesitation.[27]

Keeping the System Civically Responsible

As peace officers you have extraordinary power over the lives of ordinary citizens. This control is eclipsed and exceeded in orders of magnitude by prosecutors, who have a hold over those accused of crimes that is so formidable as to invite abuse without intending to do so.[28] Abuse occurs when the threat of prosecution bearing extreme penalties results in innocent people accepting a plea to a lesser charge, rather than taking a chance on spending many years in prison. The criminal justice system in America is desperately in need of reinvention.

We are taught that power is corrosive, and that absolute power is egregiously corrupt. Every agency of government that wields great power must be aware of the tendencies toward corruption or corruption will inevitably occur. As a peace officer, your best approach to avoid abusing your power is to always take care that your actions do not exceed those you would not want breached if you were simply a citizen and not an officer of the law. You will have hundreds of rules, regulations, and laws to follow, and yet the work itself allows for a great deal of autonomy and trust. Given the power you will have as a police officer and given the biological predispositions we've been discussing, police accountability must be a management obsession—or avoidable abuses will inevitably ensue. When they do occur but aren't addressed, things get out of control.

One more critical point about how we think about crime and punishment: I'm all in with utilizing the best thought-out methods for progressive rehabilitation in prison reform, based on the latest research in behavioral science. That too many convicts become repeat offenders requires our constant attention.[29] But crime and the ethos of punishment tend to addle our thinking in that the public and those of us in law enforcement begin to view crime and punishment as a tradeoff, an exchange in which a crime is committed and is then paid for by the punishment, and thus the process is judged sufficiently adjudicated. But no such exchange of value exists. Nothing a prisoner does erases the damage they created when they committed their crime.[30] And addressing this inequity is the most pressing issue in prison reform, because the impetus to punish and the assumption that a fair exchange has taken place and that the crime debt has been paid obscures the severity of the damage done: That's when we stop trying to rehabilitate and prevent crime and instead assume we've made things right—and we haven't even come close. Assuming we are applying a *quid pro quo* is absurd, and it muddles our thinking. Making up for horrific crime by "doing time" is analogous to the writing of a check that can't be cashed because of insufficient funds, and thus, we undervalue the pain and suffering of the victims—and even the remorse of the offenders who snapped, some of whom spend a lifetime regretting their rash actions. In *Until We Reckon*, Danielle Sered writes, "Retribution becomes more complicated when we recognize that those we are punishing are almost invariably also people we have failed to protect. Nearly everyone who commits violence has survived it, and while that in no way excuses their actions, it reminds us that state-conducted retribution for violence is carried out almost entirely against survivors of violence."[31]

This egregious disparity in valuation lets us off the hook too easily with the assumption that punishment for crimes committed is a just price paid—tragically, we go no further in our efforts to rehabilitate repeat offenders and to prevent crime in the first place by creating livable communities minus the kinds of stress we associate with living in war zones. Simply put, we accept the illusion. The fact that 97 percent of criminal indictments are plea-bargained suggests we have settled for a sense of exchange as evidence of our dedication in creating a just society, but our efforts always fall short of the solutions required, *because they lack the passion that justice demands.*[32]

In her book, *The New Jim Crow*, Ohio State University law professor Michelle Alexander shows precisely how we keep this dysfunctional system going:

> Today a criminal freed from prison has scarcely more rights and arguably less respect, than a freed slave or a black person living "free" in Mississippi at the height of Jim Crow. Those released from prison on parole can be stopped and searched by the police for any reason—or no reason at all—and returned to prison for the most minor of infractions, such as failing to attend a meeting with a parole officer. Even when released from the system's formal control, the stigma of criminality lingers. Police supervision, monitoring, and harassment are facts of life not only for all those labeled criminals, but for all those who "look like" criminals. Lynch mobs may be long gone, but the threat of police violence is ever present.[33]

Sleep on this.

When I was in uniform, for reasons I no longer recall, I questioned an ex-convict just released from the Texas State Penitentiary. What I do remember is what he told me about doing hard time. He said savvy inmates knew that it was a good strategy when you first got to prison to punch and pummel the first inmate within reach and to keep it up for days, then gradually over time calm down, become friendly and treat the guards with respect. It would accomplish two objectives. First, the other inmates would not be eager to mess with you, and second, you would likely get an early release, because the prison staff would take credit for having rehabilitated you.

Or perhaps it will help to see our system from an outsider's perspective. In 2008, Dmitry Orlov, a Russian engineer who immigrated to the United States in the mid-1970s, first published *Reinventing Collapse: The Soviet Experience and American Prospects*, a comparison of superpower similarities; in this book, he noted that, although the Gulag program had given the Soviets a decisive lead in the incarceration of its citizens, America had finally pulled ahead. He wrote:

> **In the end the jails race has been won by the Americans, who are currently holding the world record for the percentage of population in jail. Here, the judiciary meat grinder relies less on secrecy than on obscurity, gorging itself on the poor and defenseless, while being careful around the moneyed and the privileged. To mask its naked aggression against its citizens, the United States has traditionally used the fig leaves of constitutional rights and due process. But ill winds now blowing across the country have wilted this decorative flora, and not a week seems to go by without some new reports of abuses and atrocities.[34]**

Whether or not you agree with this biting assessment is less important than that you are part of a system in which millions of citizens do believe that Orlov is correct, and that a significant number of the citizens you serve are going to view your actions as if you live and breathe in a shadow of injustice.

Policing Aspirations

There are more examples of police chiefs like Norm Stamper who have devoted their working lives to police reform. While I have spent five decades thinking about improving policing, retired police chief David Couper has spent fifty-plus years doing something about it. Couper served as a chief of police in Burnsville, Minnesota and in Madison, Wisconsin for over 25 years. He is the author of *Arrested Development* and *Telling It Like It Is*, two works that offer advice based upon his tried and tested experience in improving policing, through a process of "professionalizing the ranks" as he puts it, with the aspirational goal that, "Only those who represent society's highest values serve as police."[35]

Couper argues that there are four major obstacles to serious and lasting police reform: Anti-intellectualism, violence, corruption, and discourtesy.[36] He advocates decentralizing police services, developing a sensitivity for understanding human behavior, and mastering conflict management and crisis intervention. Couper says higher education changed his life and his views about law enforcement, a sentiment that I can certainly attest to.[37] Couper says that when police officers begin to value people over property, and view their jobs as being problem solvers, rather than enforcers, they begin to work more effectively. I would add that their job satisfaction will improve as well.[38] Long ago, Couper envisioned police becoming experts in human behavior, persuasion, and experts in the appropriate use of force. He writes:

> **Changing police isn't just about changing a few things, but everything: hiring, training, leadership. Solving problems, community-orientation, and evaluation. It is about changing the very nature of the police function itself and the multiple ways that will have to be put in place to raise the intellectual capacity of police, curtail their use of excessive force, drive out the vestiges of corruption and racism, and implement a new culture of courtesy, customer focus, and restraint in using physical force.[39]**

I wholeheartedly agree. Long ago, Couper became an advocate for eliminating military bootcamp-like training for peace officers, even making officers' uniforms more like civilian clothes to enable officers to relate to citizens on more equal, and less intimidating terms.[40]

David Couper has an active online blog, *Improving Police*, where he offers his law enforcement experience and expertise in solving policing problems and where he interacts with anyone interested in police reform.[41]

ROLL CALL

Those of you just starting out are going to experience a learning curve that can at times be steep. You will have a training officer who will give you advice and instructions that don't make much sense at first. Your training officer may turn on your squad car's red lights to stop a vehicle in front of you, and you will not know why, because you didn't see what they saw. If you are not used to the radio chatter, what is going on won't make sense for a while. Walking down a street in uniform, you are likely to feel that you are sticking out like a sore thumb, as people will stop you and ask you questions that you haven't the slightest clue how to answer.

For a time, rookie police officers seem locked in an embarrassment zone as a rite of passage. I was with my training officer the first day after we'd had seatbelts installed in our squad cars. Taking the passenger seat, I buckled mine—even though my training officer didn't. Our first call was a light airplane crash in the Oak Cliff section of Dallas in an open field. When we pulled up next to the downed aircraft, my partner jumped out, and I couldn't figure out how to unbuckle my seat belt. A crowd had gathered, so I pretended to be talking on the radio and was about to use my pocketknife to cut the strap when I figured it out. Stories like this for rookie police officers are legendary in law enforcement. One night working out of the Southwest substation, being a rookie, I was sent to the Northwest substation because they were short-handed. While driving north of Hampton Road in my Mustang convertible (but in uniform), I saw a man in a gas station with his hands in the air with two men standing in front of him with their backs to me. I swerved into the driveway like Steve McQueen on a movie set, hit the brakes, jumped out of the car with my revolver, resting it on the open door of my car, and yelled at the men in the station—only to find out that the attendant was only explaining to his customers how he had been robbed at gunpoint the night before.

But one day, for some of you, everything is going to click. You'll suddenly realize what you are looking for are violations of the law—and there they will be, popping up right in front of you, in bold italics. If by this time you are working alone, you are likely to go through a period when it just seems you are always in the right place at the right time. In my day we called this the "black glove" stage. This is a period when you are beginning to set the temperament and tone of your career as a peace officer.[1] This is the point at which you most need to apply critical thinking to your work, because, as educator Stephen D. Brookfield put it: "Critical thinking happens first when we try to discover the assumptions that influence the way we think and act. Pretty much every action we take *is* based on assumptions that we have accepted, sometimes unthinkingly as accurate. Critical thinking involves deliberately trying to find out what these assumptions are."[2] Think about all of those television cop shows and movies you have watched. That was fiction. This is real. You are going to have many occasions when the unexpected causes you to rethink what you have always assumed to be true. Utilize these moments as a gateway to probable cause for further exploration. Finally, as serious as the career you have chosen clearly is, you are also for a time going to be aware that police work can also be fun. The trick is to make this feeling last.

Attitude is Everything

To keep your attitude in tune with your objective to protect and serve is going to take an effort analogous to daily mental housekeeping. Your duty is to serve the public by enforcing the law and treating the citizens you encounter with the respect they deserve. Your duty to your family is to come home safe. Your duty to your fellow officers is to look out for their safety as you do your own.

Every day brings a new context into play where you patrol. For example, a day may stack up something like this: You didn't sleep well; you had an argument with your spouse the night before over something silly; your son is being bullied at school; you have heartburn from last night's dinner; the dry cleaners didn't have your uniform ready; the deputy chief pissed you off because of what she said in the detail room before you started this shift; your ankle still hurts from chasing a suspect yesterday; you are working in a beat today known as "the snake pit"; you and your temporary partner—whom you detest—have just arrived at a disturbance call where the dispatcher reported shots fired; you get out of the car and meet a huge black man with both hands in his pockets.

Okay, now before we go any farther, my point is to have you realize that every day you are going to bring a semicolon-separated algorithmic context with you to the job, and—recalling all of the biological functions of your limbic system—I hope by now you can begin to appreciate the extreme importance of your attitude, because it sets the stage for your career as a peace officer and the very safety of the public you serve. I haven't said that much about our individual political orientations up to this point, and I want to emphasize that politically there is no "right" way to be, so to speak. But jobs in law enforcement often attract people with rigid opinions about how people should act and behave in the world, and thus these individuals are by nature less open to new experiences; and yet, as it turns out, law enforcement is a proving ground for being open to new experiences, because ready or not, they are your future. Be prepared. Recall and be prepared to respond to the rage circuit triggers that are set to go off if you are unable to establish *Order*, if you or the person you confront on the beat perceives *Insult*, or if either of you feel *Stopped*.

Your Beat: Community or Cortisol Canyon

Okay, pay close attention. What I'm about to say is extremely important, and it's as critical for your understanding as anything I've said up to now. The first thing to comprehend about your beat is that it's not really yours. Not surprisingly, police officers held to account for the crime statistics in the areas where they work intuitively develop a sense of ownership of the behavior of the citizens who live and work there. But you don't own this territory or these people. You work *for* them. Your job is to protect them and keep them safe. That police departments so often miss the whole point of their existence in this regard is a travesty.

The late Jane Jacobs, an American-Canadian journalist who transformed urban planning, had some strident comments about city policing, including this one:

> **Police can seldom be depended on to police them-selves. Their most common forms of crime are bribe**

taking, brutality, and bearing false witness. When police crimes are unmasked, it is usually done by investigative journalists, sometimes helped by brave informants from the inside and increasingly helped by scientists such as forensic biologists and demographers. The standard reform attempted is a new layer of oversight: a civilian review board to receive and deal with accusations by the public. Short public memory—every scandal is only a nine-day wonder—and sincere but sentimentalized public appreciation of the risks police run tend to undermine civilian review boards as long-term remedies.[3]

This was in 2004, before the ubiquity of cell phone and body cameras.

In his book *I and Thou*, Austrian-born Israeli philosopher Martin Buber noted that we relate to relationships with equals as "I and Thou," and with those to whom we relate only as a means to an end as "I and It."[4] Similarly, if you become embittered and calloused to the point of viewing the citizens in the communities where you work as dirtbags, scum, or worse, then you will likely act out accordingly. Not that you won't encounter people who work hard to earn these pejorative descriptions, but when you begin to apply this judgment to citizens at large, you cease to be a peace officer.[5]

If I were to have my way, every police officer would live for at least a year in the toughest neighborhood they patrol. It may be the only way to drive the point home about what it's like to live in a community that, in a disturbing number of ways, resembles occupied territory in a war zone. We have places like this in major cities all over this country, and too many of these communities are over-policed. I trust that none of you have grown up in similar conditions. Anyone? No hands in the air? Didn't think there would be; it's not surprising that people who grow up in these communities don't view law enforcement as a viable career option. But hopefully you can help change that by proving yourself an example of behavior worthy of emulation.

Pick a city: Dallas, Chicago, Atlanta, or Ferguson, Missouri. Imagine two young black men are walking on a sidewalk in a low-income residential area, a police cruiser drives by slowly, and one of the young men says to the other, "Nothing for us to worry about with those guys in the neighborhood." Sounds hysterically absurd when you consider the reality of such a scenario. It's more likely that these young men feel like quarry, prey, targets. And this, in my view, is *prima facie* evidence of law enforcement missing the point of their very existence.

In his book, *A Colony in a Nation,* MSNBC television journalist Chris Hayes puts our racist past and present in perspective. As the title suggests, we experience a two-tier and unequal system of justice when it comes to everyday community living.[6] And here you thought we are all equal under the law.[7] There is always a clamor for bringing expertise to poor communities, and this too often misses the point. As New York University economics professor William Easterly writes in *The Tyranny of Experts*: "The technocratic illusion is that poverty results from a shortage of expertise, whereas poverty is really about a shortage of rights. The emphasis on the problem of expertise makes the problems of rights worse."[8] First and foremost in my view is that the residents in any community, rich or poor, need to feel safe from criminal elements and from oppression by authority; otherwise, the very notion of community is suspect.

In *The Age of Insanity,* psychologist John F. Schumaker writes: "The mental health profession needs to examine its moral obligations as it searches for ways to contribute in a broader way to human welfare."[9] He wrote this in 2001, and look at where we are today with community and police public relations. Schumaker continues:

> The social welfare of the population is a sorely neglected goal of contemporary psychology. In the future, this devalued system must give way to one wherein mental health workers involve themselves actively in research and practice related to such issues as power inequality, distributive justice, democratic participation, social policy and the dynamics of oppression.

I know from my own studies that there are many health professionals who work tirelessly to improve living conditions for all citizens. It serves no one—and is simply unacceptable—to make partisan political arguments out of public safety issues that are critical to public health and national security.

When I was in the Dallas Police Academy in 1966, the Inspector-in-charge spent a lot of time talking about English law, because it has had an enormous influence on our law.[10] If you go all the way back to the 19th century and read the works of John Stuart Mill, you will see that the English had a good grip on the notion of community centuries ago. About individual freedom in civilized communities, Mill wrote that:

> The sole end for which mankind are warranted, individually or collectively, in interfering with the liberty of action of any of their number, is self-protection. ... the only purpose for which power can be rightfully exercised over any member of a civilized community,

against his will, is to prevent harm to others. His
own good, either physical or moral, is not a sufficient
warrant.[11]

Mill goes on to explain:

The only freedom which deserves the name, is that of
pursuing our own good in our own way, so long as we
do not attempt to deprive others of theirs, or impede
their efforts to obtain it. Each is the proper guardian
of his own health, whether bodily, or mental and spir-
itual. Mankind are greater gainers by suffering each
other to live as seems good to themselves, than by
compelling each to live as seems good to the rest.[12]

Mill noted that this assumption was not even new in his day.

Today, many law enforcement organizations seem to lack
a regard for the vital part of personal freedom that establishes
community. Just consider stop-and-frisk policies—based not on
probable cause that someone is about to harm another, but upon
a hunch.

Consider that Abraham Maslow's hierarchy of needs depends
upon having one's physiological and safety needs met before one
moves up the ladder.[13] You don't get to love and belonging if you
don't feel safe, in which case you can also simply forget about
self-esteem and self-actualization. If public safety is not a reality,
then there is no basis for a community to begin with. People who
break the law in all neighborhoods need to expect to be arrested,
and people who aren't breaking the law need to feel completely
safe from harassment and arrest—or the very basis for a community simply doesn't exist. What does exist instead is a community

drenched in stress—a cortisol canyon, I call it, because its streets are filled with people whose stress hormones runneth over.

In *The Goodness Paradox*, Harvard anthropology professor Richard Wrangham writes, "Every society has to find its own protection. To avert episodes of violence we should constantly remind ourselves of how easily a complex social organization can decay, and how hard it is to construct."[14] Consider the communities I have characterized as cortisol canyons: They have high poverty rates, high unemployment, high crime rates, and they are low on respect, and short on a sense of honor. Wrangham explains that human social tolerance comes from our having a low tendency for reactive aggression and that we depend upon proactive aggression for group safety. Police protection fits this bill, and yet, in cortisol canyon, reactive aggression is likely to be high, higher than average.

Now, add a long waiting time on 911 calls for help because the local police are shorthanded or are engaged in petty misdemeanor arrests for the sake of raising government revenue, and we've upped the community angst yet another level. If honor is missing, reactive aggression is just a hair-trigger away. Let me say again: If you want to gauge the effectiveness of policing in a given community, don't rely on numbers, just ask the people who live there if they feel safe. When they do feel safe and secure you may be able to see evidence that they respect your service, but until then, don't take it for granted.

So, try to imagine having grown up in a city where squad cars always seemed to be stalking citizens and where your experience didn't warrant that these officers likely were more interested in keeping you safe than in messing with you; in fact, their actions felt more like those of predators looking for a quick meal. Nonsense, you say; these are police officers whose sworn duty is to serve and protect—and you are right. But I've seen enough and experienced

enough to know that it doesn't feel that way to most of the residents
in low-income communities that are considered high-crime areas
by law enforcement, especially if you are a young black man.

How many times would you have to be stopped and frisked
when you were simply walking down the street to begin to resent
the intrusion? I suspect not many. Speaking for myself, after
about the third time of being stopped and searched in my own
neighborhood, I would be ready to reclaim some Southern honor.
Given my learning, life experience, and temperament, had I been
born black, I have little doubt that I would either be in prison or
long since dead, especially had I been born in the distant past,
a time that social critic Cornel West characterizes as a struggle
against nihilistic periods of oppression absent of meaning and
hope.[15]

In 2009, when the incident occurred in which Professor Henry
Louis Gates, Jr. was arrested by a police sergeant in Cambridge,
Massachusetts, I wrote a blog post about the arrest that included
this statement:

> **For a teachable moment to have occurred out of the
> incident with a Cambridge police sergeant and a dis-
> tinguished university professor it would be necessary
> to reenact the incident, to do a play-by-play enactment
> of everything said, of every gesture made, and of the
> voice inflection and tone of everyone involved, and
> then to read the laws covering this situation very care-
> fully. It would be an extraordinary learning experience
> for everyone who participated. From what I learned of
> the incident, and based on my own experience, I don't
> believe Professor Gates broke the law. What occurred,
> in my view, was that a learned scholar embarrassed a**

police sergeant in front of his subordinates, and the sergeant overplayed his hand and authority in the same manner that occurs all over the United States, day in and day out. The default position in this case is aggravated by the sergeant's need to maintain the respect of his subordinates. Moreover, the reason I am quite certain the Professor broke no law is that the police department dropped the case immediately. There was no case, and you can rest assured they wouldn't have dropped it if there had been one.[16]

The *LA Progressive* published the piece, and now I have several years of essays on their website.

So, ladies and gentlemen, go to any white, affluent neighborhood, stop and frisk people randomly, and I guarantee you will find lots of illegal drugs—especially opioids—these days.[17] You will also likely find yourself in court for harassment. Of course, you have no choice but to enforce the law, but you should also be aware that attitudes toward drug use are changing, and it's likely that broader legalization is on the horizon.[18] All you need to do is go to any affluent white neighborhood and start stopping and frisking people at random to see this exercise for the systematic oppression that it is. Could you claim that your probable cause was that you were in a high-opioid area? Do you think that a percentage of frisks in these white neighborhoods would produce arrests statistically in line with those in poor, black neighborhoods? Do you get my point? I see some frowns.

Okay, folks, let's look at our own Constitution, the 14th Amendment: "No State shall make or enforce any law which shall abridge the privileges or immunities of citizens of the United States; nor shall any State deprive any person of life, liberty, or property, without due process of law; nor deny to any person within its jurisdiction the equal protection of the laws." Now, the 15th Amendment: "The right of citizens of the United States to vote shall not be denied or abridged by the United States or by any State on account of race, color, or previous condition of servitude."[19] Sleep on it.

The reputation of all policing agencies is always a work in progress, and their mistakes, missteps, and examples of mistreatment will always be remembered longer than their honorable deeds. Those of us who champion law enforcement and decry the fact that there is so little cooperation from the community must learn to appreciate the reality that it's only when citizens feel safe and protected that anything akin to loyalty is due law enforcement. *Quid pro quo* is based on trust—and because of the history of past police-community relations, the price for earning trust is inexorably high.

Simply put: When the citizens in the communities where you patrol see you in uniform, if they are not committing a crime and they are not a wanted fugitive, your presence should make them feel safe. If it doesn't, there is something seriously amiss. In his painfully honest and insightful book, *Chokehold*, former prosecutor and MSNBC consultant Paul Butler writes:

> **Much of the conventional wisdom about racial justice is wrong. The civil rights movement did not do nearly as much good for African Americans as many people think. Having more black police officers does not mean that cops treat African Americans better. When the federal government takes over a police department, it does not necessarily improve the situation it seeks to address. About half the time, police violence**

actually increases after an intervention by the U.S. Department of Justice.[20]

In his book *Coming Apart,* libertarian political scientist Charles Murray attempts to explain why so many of our communities appear to be disintegrating economically.[21] Murray claims white males are simply less industrious than they were in the past and so he goes through a litany of selective communities that all share the same failing, in that the fault always lies with the people and never with the systemic circumstances they find themselves in. It's like criticizing goldfish for not being avid explorers and for spending their time swimming in circles, without noticing that the confining shape of the bowl matters more than the motivation of the fish. People growing up without adequate resources are analogous to vegetable gardens in depleted soil. There will always be people who shirk their responsibilities and try for a free ride on the taxpayer's dime, but to focus exclusively on the behavior of individuals instead of the conditions they find themselves in is at the least absurd, if not disingenuous.

For a neighborhood to be socially viable, physical and mental safety must exist as a sacred trust—making its members part of a genuine community, where shelter is ensured without reservation—because without emotional security, residents are not only psychologically homeless, they are existentially stressed and do not have the luxury of feeling safe. There are many economically-disadvantaged communities in America where the enforcement of petty offenses and misdemeanors is considered a reliable revenue source; this is the very antithesis of aspirational justice, equal treatment, and the spirit of our nation's founding documents.

In her book, *Punishment Without Crime,* law professor Alexandra Natapoff reminds us that a police officer's word is not enough for a criminal conviction for the wealthy, "But for poor, undereducated, black, brown, and other vulnerable people, that's often all it takes."[22]

When police departments focus on numbers, the result is over-policing, and this leads to underserving communities, as the busyness comes at the expense of being available for service when the public calls the police and no squads are available. And thus, over-policing leads to under-policing.[23]

When I first went to work in South Dallas, my partner was driving us back to the station toward the end of a very busy evening shift when we started passing people who were waving and yelling at us to stop and help them for reasons unknown to us. He did not stop, and I was exasperated. But my senior partner, who had worked there for years, explained that it was like this all over this part of town, and if we stopped our relief would be stuck at the station, and there would still be people all over the place needing help but not getting it. In time, it became obvious that he was right, but when working by myself I still couldn't ignore calls for help without stopping.

This puts a special emphasis on not over-focusing on petty offenses for the sake of numbers, in areas where at any moment the calls for help may be greater than could possibly be answered. A seemingly quiet night can become chaotic in an instant, and if half the available squads are out of service in pursuit of petty offenses for the sake of raising revenue, the cost is public safety, and the oath to protect and serve is rendered disingenuous. Moreover, as the 2015 DOJ Report on the Ferguson Police Department made clear, when a community sets out to derive its major source of revenue for governance from petty misdemeanor offenses, but those charged can't afford to pay the fines, the whole enterprise becomes a progression of criminal manufacture, as misdemeanors morph into felonies by way of oppressive policing.[24] At this point, an impression of rampant crime is reported in media (or shared on social media), leading to calls for more aggressive policing, and the whole process ratchets up a notch. Moreover, if the problems concerning community policing were not complicated enough, Kathleen Hall Jamieson, in her book *Cyber War,* shows how the Russians have been using trolls and bots in social media to inspire and incite distrust between the police and citizens in black communities.[25]

Socrates and Broken Windows Policing

No doubt I'm in political territory here, because this is where politicians win reelection, by appearing to be tough on crime.[26] But I ask you to review once again that the goal here is public safety, which includes your safety, and that of your fellow officers. Arrest statistics from poor neighborhoods always support the notion that extra attention is warranted there, and yet the act of paying closer attention increases the likelihood of more arrests, and an emphasis on petty offense for the sake of raising revenue obscures the possibility for being objective. Shamefully, in many low-income communities in America, the municipal and county administrations depend increasingly on revenue from traffic fines and misdemeanor violations. Retired police captain Howard Rahtz acknowledges this practice when he writes that, "Traffic stops for the purpose of revenue enhancement are at best ethically questionable." U.S. citizens are constitutionally guaranteed freedom from unwarranted government intrusion, and traffic stops without a public safety purpose erode that freedom.[27] That these measures contribute to an increase in cortisol—for officers and for the public—is painfully obvious.[28] In *A Colony in a Nation*, Chris Hayes writes about this practice in Ferguson, Missouri: "The model of cops as armed tax collectors didn't stop with simple traffic stops for speeding: The entire

municipal court system was designed to function like a payday
lending operation. Relatively small infractions quickly turned into
massive debts."[29] Any way you try to characterize this kind of civic
administration, it amounts to overt oppression because of an egregious lack of consideration for the public.

If justice is the goal, politicians left, right, and middle must stop
using peace officers as a governmental revenue source. Depending
on arrests and citations for misdemeanor offenses as a means of
achieving public safety is destructive and egregiously disingenuous.
If traffic safety can be improved by traffic fines, utilize digital photographic technology for apprehending offenders; you can mitigate the
public pushback by giving adequate warnings before exacting a fine,
and do not make failure to pay fines a jailable offense. Find another
means of requiring payment before receiving government resources.
Police officers who are preoccupied with racking up tickets, citations
and petty arrests for the sake of appearing to have the numbers to
make politicians look effective, and the revenue to run the government, are not available to do what they are needed for most, which
is to make our communities and neighborhoods safe places to live.

Digital traffic technology is the means to truly change the
behavior of people who drive, because a breach of traffic laws will
exact a penalty every time, while waiting on the chance of being
ticketed by an observant peace officer is so infrequent that it has
very little effect on behavior. People get caught so infrequently that
being in a hurry always seems to be worth the risk. Communities
that ban digital traffic cameras because of public outrage reveal the
political hypocrisy of claiming safety is the objective of their system
because digital camera technology works much better in changing
behavior than the chance of being observed and ticketed by a police
officer. Most of the people ticketed for speeding by digital cameras
do not commit a second offense.[30]

I'm sure you are also very much aware of the broken-windows theory of policing, which says that if you tend to the small problems, you will prevent larger ones.[31] Now, there are lots of compelling arguments against this policy, but I'm inclined to believe there is at least a grain of truth in the concept, at least when it comes to the aesthetics of the physical and structural environment. For example, if many windows are broken and graffiti is ubiquitous, then adding to it certainly has less impact than did the first example. But I will also point out that many economically-disadvantaged neighborhoods are places of low respect, where the police don't respect the citizens and the citizens don't respect the police. Do you suppose statistics will tell us that we will find more violence in such places? Think about it. The New York Police Department equates the broken window policy with increasing the quality of life, but I will argue the reverse.[32] The rationale is that a lawless environment invites criminal activity, and that petty crimes portend major crimes, and indeed there is a grain of truth in these assumptions as well. But the aggressive policing that some justify with the broken windows objective dramatically increases the stress level in these communities, and their obsession with metrics leads to misclassifying offenses, which further leads to fudging the numbers for the sake of management cosmetics. A simple and direct method of determining the quality of life by polling the residents who live there is overlooked.[33] As it turns out, the reduction of criminal activity due to broken windows policing is modest at best, but I will argue that the emotional angst of the oppression that results is deep and lasting.[34]

So, let me be clear about community quality of life: It occurs when people feel safe because they *are* safe, and *not* when they are the subject of incessant harassment over offenses that do not receive such attention when committed by neighbors who are deemed nonthreatening. Numbers are meaningless when you are being accosted on the street or your house is being broken into—and a call to 911 doesn't help, because the squads on duty are busy writing tickets to add to municipal revenue (while not affecting the number of traffic accidents).

What we have today in most communities is broken policing. Sue Rahr, the former sheriff of King County, Washington, and Stephen K. Rice, associate professor of criminal justice at Seattle University, have written an empowering paper titled "From Warriors to Guardians: Recommitting American Police Culture to Democratic Ideals."[35] They use an example from Plato's *Republic* about society's need for guardians who bear the sacred trust of keeping the community safe. Plato was none too fond of democracies, but he knew what they aspired to be. He described three types of government: Tyrannies, democracies, and aristocracies.[36] Socrates and Glaucon discussed the issue of where the guardians of society might be found and that their selection would be no easy matter, that they would need to be "dangerous to their enemies, and gentle to their friends; if not they will destroy themselves without waiting for their enemies to destroy them." Imagine if Socrates had had the benefit of YouTube. Socrates further argued that these guardians must be philosophers and must by nature be lovers of wisdom and knowledge.[37]

That the edict for justly protecting and serving a community was known centuries ago but seems lost in the 21st century seems existentially heartbreaking, but worse—much worse—it's really a moral indictment of our intent. You can come up with elaborate rationalizations, some of which sound quite plausible, but none measure up to the fundamental idea of justice. Democracy demands that our citizens are safe from criminality and oppression and that exceptions of any stripe move us toward tyranny. To value the safety of citizens less than their usefulness as a misdemeanor revenue source is a blasphemous slap in the face of human decency. Socrates would have none of it, and neither should we.

About the selection of our guardians, Plato wrote:

> **Let us note among the guardians those who in their whole life show the greatest eagerness to do what is for the good of their country and the greatest repugnance to do what is against her interests ... And they will have to be watched at every age, in order that we may see whether they preserve their resolution, and never, under the influence either of force or enchantment, forget or cast off their sense of duty to the State.**[38]

So we aren't exactly reinventing the wheel when it comes to community policing. Philosophy professor Edwin J. Delattre reminds us of Alexander Hamilton's warning: Too little authority leads to anarchy, and too much authority leads to tyranny.[39] One moral message of *Blue Bias* I hope you take to the streets with you is that you must be careful that you do not become a guardian in affluent communities and a warrior in impoverished ones.

Time for Some Quick Review

Nearly a century ago, Walter Lippmann pointed out that "the subtlest and most pervasive of all influences are those which create and maintain the repertory of stereotypes."[40] It's as if these socially agreed-upon pictures in our heads represent a social defense mechanism that obscures reality in favor of assumptions that are accepted by tradition to keep us safe. Thus, it is socially accepted that we will see what we expected to see.

When occasions arise that trigger this vast repository of learned assumptions that is stored in our subconscious, we experience the associated biased emotions as reality. And as we justify them, we are subject to confirmation bias.[41] Stereotypes are just shortcuts—snapshots or notations—some double-stamped with stigma. Now, pause for a moment and think about the signals, cues, and clues you look for when trying to find criminal actions. Shortcuts, snapshots, and pictures in your head will all speak to you as probable cause. I'm not saying you shouldn't pay attention to these things. I'm just pointing out how important it is for you to realize precisely what you are doing and why it works the way it does.

You should also fully understand by this point that asking people if they are racially prejudiced is a senseless thing to do, since our conscious selves don't have direct access to our subconscious. As my own experience has borne out, one may be a racist without admitting it and sometimes without being aware of it, but statistics prove without a shadow of a doubt that racism is still very much alive. That African Americans are arrested disproportionately causes some police officers (and members of the public) to conclude that this fact alone amounts to probable cause that they must deserve it—while being oblivious to the unfairness and blatant bias at work in such thinking.[42] That peace officers can be this narrow-minded and egregiously uneducated today is, to my thinking, completely unacceptable. That there are events that can be metaphorically described as D.W.B. (Driving While Black) is a declaration itself of probable cause.[43]

By any objective standards, the American criminal justice system's disproportionately harsh treatment of minorities is a national disgrace. In Until We Reckon, Danielle Sered writes, "We have built a culture of incarceration in a way that has developed communities of color so disproportionately as to make the lineage from slavery through Jim Crow to our current jails and prisons undeniable."[44] It makes a mockery of our country's founding principles about being born with equal rights. If you have the slightest doubt about the veracity of this statement, Michelle Alexander argues persuasively in *The New Jim Crow: Mass Incarceration in the Age of Colorblindness* that the war on drugs has created a new Jim Crow era, meaning that the racial caste system in America has not been eliminated so much as simply redesigned. I implore you to read her book and *Chasing the Scream: The First and Last Days of the War on Drugs*, by Johann Hari, which offers a history of the so-called war on drugs—with a perspective every peace officer needs to be aware of.[45]

Overcoming racial bias is an incredibly demanding thing to do because, as you know by now, the emotional coding that establishes racial bias takes place beneath our conscious awareness. And for law enforcement officers, the prescription to overcome it includes mindfulness, introspection, counseling, resolute supervision—and continuous effort.

It's critical to understand that when you work in neighborhoods with large ethnic minority populations, negative interactions with residents will either reinforce whatever prejudices you have already learned or will set the stage for implanting prejudice in the future. Thus, the seeds for racial profiling are sown in a rich mixture of emotional experiences that in time will set up like concrete, unless you are resolute about maintaining a sense of objectivity and resolved to participate regularly in reflection and introspection to keep the nature of bias in perspective.

Again, this is not rocket science: It's a hell of a lot harder than rocket science, and we're not benefitting as we should from knowledge gained through unrelenting research in neuroscience, human psychology, primatology, and anthropology. Using the analogy of rocket science, think of the *Voyager* space probe, which is now many astronomical units beyond our solar system; by comparison, our progress in race relations hasn't made it to the moon yet. We are still sputtering in a low-earth orbit.

Because we like to consider ourselves to be far above behaving with animalistic inclinations, we prefer to ignore any reminders that we have them, and we pay a heavy price for not facing the truth. And yet, we are territorial and tribalistic creatures. In the words of anthropologist Robert Ardrey, "The territorial imperative is as blind as a cave fish, as consuming as a furnace, and it commands beyond logic, opposes all reason, suborns all moralities, strives for no goal more sublime than survival."[46] As we take such things as home, country, personal space, and group identity seriously, our inherent physiology enables us to adapt to and rise to any occasion.

To remain connected with one another, and with our humanity, we have learned that peace officers need to be well-versed in the humanities. As naturalist E. O. Wilson makes clear in *The Origins of Creativity*: "We are ruled by emotions inscribed in our DNA by prehistoric events little known and only partly understood. Meanwhile, infinitely puzzled, we have been catapulted into a techno-scientific age that may in time serve instructions to robots well but not the ancient values and feelings that keep us indelibly human."[47]

Many of you will spend years patrolling low-income neighborhoods where most people know nothing of anthropology, psychology, neuroscience, and the literature that binds humanity as one species, one people. So these citizens don't need human "doings" as police officers as much as they need human beings. If you really want to make a difference in the lives of your fellow man, here is your chance. Poverty is psychologically debilitating; if you don't understand it as such, you will have a very hard time understanding why some of the citizens where you patrol don't see the world as you do. If you expect them to, you are setting yourself up to foster resentment for circumstances you do not understand. Respect is a commodity that is often hard to find in poor communities; one of the reasons gangs form is that inspiring fear is a shortcut to gaining respect. If you are unable to show a modicum of respect for the people you serve, it will become obvious over time, and it can accompany you like a contemptuous halo for everyone to see but you. It takes a lot of patience and dedication to try to relate to people who have little hope for the future and whose basic distrust of the police, in so many cases, is justified. It's hard to understand without effort what it is like for people who crave dignity but see little hope in acquiring it—people for whom it feels their status is a curse and whose way of coping is to suffer a smoldering rage of resentment and sadness, and who harbor an internal need for a redress for what they perceive as perpetual shame and humiliation.

I'm not asking that you see yourself as a social worker whose job it is to educate people who have not had the benefit of a liberal arts education, something that I call an existential education.[48] I'm just pointing out that if you don't truly understand the existential angst that you are going to witness daily, you will likely suffer a deep-seated sense of anxiety and frustration. In doing so, you are likely to become so judgmental about the citizens you encounter daily, your own resentment will be met with theirs—and the stress may shorten your life. Your experience and accrued sense of contempt will cause you to disregard the need to treat the people you encounter with the respect they are due.

When our primate cousins encounter social hierarchy, their hormones adjust accordingly. So do ours. For example, when a low-ranking male ape suddenly finds himself in an alpha male role, his levels of testosterone will shoot up accordingly. Put a uniform, a badge, and a gun on a man or a woman, and precisely the same thing happens. I know this is true from personal experience and extensive study and soon you will also feel these effects.[49]

When police officers and citizens come together, a brain chemical reaction occurs in all present. Those who view the officer as someone to trust are likely to experience increased levels of oxytocin—sometimes called the moral molecule.[50] Those who see the officer as a threat will experience an increase in adrenaline and a spike of testosterone.

As primates, we are wired for the potential of conflict escalation. Because of repeated exposure to extreme social situations, police officers are apt to suffer the consequences of their wiring working all too well. In my view, it is not an exaggeration to say that law enforcement officers are chemically conditioned to turn on their internal aggression switch and get an instant response. But the very fact that our hormones can induce behavior ranging from subservience to alpha dominance according to circumstance, suggests we can also be flexible and therefore, we are trainable.

As police officers, you are required to be assertive, and in doing so repeatedly you will become accustomed to surging levels of adrenaline and higher-than-normal levels of testosterone. When incidents occur that call for you to rise to the occasion, thus causing elevated hormone levels, you may experience an automatic stance of privilege. Metaphorically, you become a full-feathered peacock. This sense of status-entitlement can too easily become corrosive; people filling alpha roles come to feel that dominance is their prerogative. It's a kind of situational arrogance that comes after multiple incidents in which one is expected to be the dominant individual—because the act of appearing dominant is chemically self-reinforcing.[51] This is where we sometimes see the rage circuit for "Insult, Order, and Stop" set at hair-trigger status.[52]

Fortunately, there is another side to the brain chemical rewards associated with police work: Namely, the ability to derive pleasure from empathy and altruism. The opportunities to experience both are ever-present in law enforcement. These rewards reinforce the stated goals and oaths of most law enforcement agencies. This is the reason that some people are drawn to becoming peace officers and why they can't imagine ever doing anything else. The tending instinct, as you will see, is a prime example.

Self-assurance and self-confidence are other best-case examples of the results of the appropriate use of authority in the performance of a peace officer's duties. For some officers, though, positional power begins to manifest as volatile resentment, triggered when their orders are not followed immediately or when the actions of others are experienced as acts of disrespect. Especially when an officer's unconscious bias machine has imperceptibly identified the person encountered as someone assumed to be of a lower class and unworthy of respect, an explosion of hormones will be stimulated simply to regain one's sense of official superiority.

At the same time, because of the sensitive nature of your duties, we must hold you accountable, even, or especially, when you cross the line from being of service to citizens to abusing them, subverting the very reason for your existence. In my view, police officers who manage to control themselves in dire situations and perform their duties as expected are exemplary human beings, and when you behave this way you should be appreciated as such.

Police work, as noted earlier, ranges from boredom to excitement on steroids and, having experienced feelings toward the latter end of that scale many times, I would describe them as a dopamine rush that one not only gets used to, but also in some cases learns to crave, seeking them at every opportunity. Nearly a half century has passed since I served as a police officer, yet I still miss the adrena-line-rush "jackpots."

In large metropolitan areas, emergency calls are a routine part of police work. It seems fair to ask that law enforcement officers and their management be aware that being conditioned to seek excitement can bring about an unconscious effort among officers to up the ante for the benefit of what amounts to an addictive experience.

In every occupation, we find people who do not belong and whose behavior damages the reputations of their organizations. Unfortunately, although the qualifications for peace officers are very high, we are not yet experts at weeding out people who don't have the temperament for police work. And although all hierarchal organizations tend to close ranks when threatened, law enforce-ment organizations, by nature of their dangerous and difficult role in society, are especially bound emotionally to bond in loyalty to one another; it would be unnatural, even disappointing, if they weren't. The dark side of this loyalty, however, is where the most dangerous and malfunctioning inclinations of our animalistic behaviors come into play. It begins when officers who have become accustomed to using excessive force experience approval or indif-ference from management.

In 2014's *Rise of the Warrior Cop*, Radley Balko, a blogger and investigative journalist who has dug deeply into topics such as police misconduct, drug policy and civil liberties (and whose resume includes both the likes of the *Washington Post* and *Fox News*), writes: "Cops who rat out other cops tend not to remain cops for very long. Lying and exaggerating in police reports and on the witness stand isn't just common, it's routine and expected. It's a part of the job."[53] Under these conditions, the cure can be worse than the disease.

Balko explains that his book isn't anti-cop; it's anti-politician, because the latter make the rules that turn the former into bad cops.[54] I feel the same way, and you only need to read the DOJ Report on the Ferguson Police Department to appreciate what kind of behavior a system results in when the demand for revenue is a higher priority than public safety.

Balko says there are two forms of police militarization: Direct and indirect. The first references the use of the military for domestic policing. Indirect militarization happens when the police simply become more and more like the military.[55] His book shows how the increasing politically-inspired use of military equipment supplied by the government is escalating the process and Balko's advice serves as a warning that we need to mitigate the further militarization of the police, before we wind up in a police state. It is indeed often the case that police officers need overwhelming force to stop criminal acts of violence, but when SWAT team police units with military vehicles and tank-like armaments enter a neighborhood and conduct their business, even when they are successful, they take something away from the residents' existential sense of safety and community that can't be easily restored.[56] Using military force for domestic disturbances can be so overwhelming as to escalate violence.

But we know without question that people behave differently when they're aware someone is watching. Even a happy face on the wall in a break room is likely to increase donations in a voluntary coffee fund.[57] In some ways, the growing paranoia in America about living in a surveillance society is justified. But when it comes to law enforcement, we have unfortunately proved the point that justice can't be both blind and just if we human beings clearly have a biological predisposition that threatens our impartiality when we are under stress. This is where the technology of bodycams can come into play. In some cases where police officers have begun to wear cameras, complaints of abuse have dropped. I believe this happens because officers are not as apt to lose control of their emotions when their actions are being recorded. Likewise, the people you encounter or place under arrest are less inclined to resist, act out, or become belligerent when they are aware that their actions will be documented. To achieve objectivity, law enforcement needs oversight. We have the technology to protect both police officers and citizens, and the expense of doing so pales in comparison to the cost of the social anguish we might so avoid.

From my own experience, I know there are times when you must act angry even when you're not, simply to quell a disturbance. Repeated frequently enough, however, this kind of experience can easily lead to increased adrenaline and testosterone conditioning for instantaneous aggression, just as working out with weights increases muscle strength. Just as actors and actresses learn to bring forth on cue and express the full range of human emotions while being in complete control every step of the way, surely, with extensive training, you can expect to play your part in society and act as you need to act without losing complete control of your emotions.[58]

Regardless of race, creed, or color, every citizen in this country is due the respect afforded every other citizen. Police organizations have a duty and a moral obligation to protect and serve, and the best way for management to meet that obligation is to serve the public interest as intended. To do this requires recognition of our basic human tendencies and acceptance of visual and audio scrutiny of police actions to better protect both officers and the public.

Malcolm Gladwell begins and ends his book *Talking to Strangers* with a discussion about Sandra Bland, a young African American woman from Chicago, who was driving through a small town near Houston, Texas, when she was stopped by a state trooper for failing to signal a lane change. Three days later Sandra Bland was dead, the state trooper was eventually fired, and the incident cost the state nearly two million dollars.[59]

Gladwell's book is fundamentally about how we misread and misinterpret one another. The transcript Gladwell provides of the interaction between Sandra Bland and the trooper is an excellent training exercise in what can go wrong between a law enforcement officer and a citizen. If traffic stops are going to occur in your future, then the lessons of what went wrong here may be crucial to your success. Compare the YouTube videos of the incident with Gladwell's transcript and narrative, and then decide for yourself what you would do differently given similar circumstances.

Now here is the thing that calls for your undivided attention. All through *Blue Bias* I have been telling you about topics like body language, facial expressions, and alpha behavioral signs so you can effectively read the people you come into contact with, and yet, Gladwell's book is filled with examples of how easy it is to misread these cues. So, it's hard to overestimate how important it is for you to come to grips with the reality of just how complicated human behavior is and how easy it is to come to simplistic and biased assumptions that are the exact opposite of what you think is happening or that you are witnessing. Now, I'm not trying to confuse you; I'm just hoping to drive the point home that being truly objective in police work requires an agile mind, wary and skeptical of the rigidity of black and white assumptions. In a nutshell, it's all too easy to become totally convinced that you are right, when you couldn't be more wrong.[60]

TENDING TO COMMUNITY

I n *Breaking Rank*, Norm Stamper writes:

> Although two-thirds of all police departments claim
> they are engaged in "community policing," most of
> them practice nothing more than an arid, cynical
> form of public relations. Real community policing is
> predicated on the potentially frightening notion that
> people in a democracy have the right and the author-
> ity to act on their own to make their communities
> safe. And to hold their police accountable for *helping*
> them do so. Community policing is the community
> *policing itself.*[1]

Real freedom, as Harvard Law School professor Cass R. Sunstein
notes, is the ability to navigate one's way through life while successfully managing the obstacles in one's way.[2] The ability to do this
effectively is what makes any community a viable and good place
to live.

In his book, *This View of Life*, evolutionary biologist David
Sloan Wilson identifies core design principles necessary for a viable
community: A strong sense of group identity; collective efforts;
everyone pulling their weight; inclusive decision-making; monitored behavior; sanctions for violations; quick conflict resolution;

local autonomy; and polycentric governance, which simply means having more than one center that can respond authoritatively.[3] For residents of any neighborhood to experience genuine freedom via community policing, the core design principles above are necessary—and it appears that Norm Stamper came to a similar conclusion long ago.[4]

Until theory hits the streets and enters the daily protocol of community law enforcement, nothing changes. *The Retrieval of Liberalism in Policing,* a book by former FBI agent and current professor of criminal justice at Radford University, Luke William Hunt, has an admirable goal—and yet, this book by an academician for academicians is unlikely to immediately benefit police and the public. I have only the highest regard for university scholarship, but it is time for academics to consciously broaden their reach.[5] Now, I get a feeling of exhilaration just walking on a college campus. Our institutions of higher learning represent our nation's intellectual capital. And yet, what they pay us back is far too little for the public investment we make in their existence.

Physicist Jeff Schmidt, author of *Disciplined Minds,* gets to the heart of my argument when he writes: "Professional training ... lessens people's sensitivity to elitism, weakens their commitment to fundamental change, and decreases the militancy with which they pursue their ideals."[6] Schmidt decries the "political and intellectual timidity" of those in a position to know better.[7] That the great strides made by behavioral scientists are not adequately shared with, and used by, the agencies charged with enforcing our laws and keeping the peace leaves us as a society hobbled and held back, not to mention disillusioned and bitter.[8] It's as though the schooling socialization process in which the best students learn the rules and abide by them is creating people who have learned not to rock the boat.[9]

Luke William Hunt is a brilliant scholar, and his goal to improve policing is desperately needed. But in his book, he discusses such academic concepts as Kantian dignity, aristocratic dignity, comportment dignity, and meritorious dignity.[10] And then, he does what so many academics do: He argues that some say this, and some say that, and he offers no clear guidelines for police officers in uniform. It may as well be a private conversation among members of an elite club.[11]

Equal justice under the law requires no veil of ignorance; it requires instead that each citizen, regardless of race, creed, color, gender, sexual orientation, religion or political persuasion, be treated with the respect and individual sovereignty that the United States Constitution provides, regardless of the community where they encounter officers of the law. And if the blindfold is keeping our Lady of Justice from seeing this (because of the biases that are built into our laws and algorithms), maybe she *does* need to remove it. What we need for community policing is a paradigm-level attitudinal shift in the approach of law enforcement officers, so officers hit the streets from day one having a much richer knowledge of how our minds work. This brings us back to the Roll Call notion that *attitude is everything*, because attitude is crucial in making community justice a reality.

Jeff Schmidt remarked a couple of decades ago on what he called "attitude crimes." He noted that if you talked back to the cops and you were black or Latino, you were likely to spend a night in jail.[12] The "punishment for attitude crimes is rampant,"[13] Schmidt said then—and it remains true today.[14] Now think of the impact of all those years spent reinforcing this mutual disrespect with numerous examples of implicit and explicit bias. Of course, minority citizens living in economically-poor communities don't need to theorize or philosophize about justice; they are painfully aware that they rarely experience the same treatment by the police as citizens in affluent neighborhoods.

To truly turn the corner on equal treatment under the law, we need new ways of thinking about old biases. My earlier comment that attitude is everything understates the case; for policing to change in America requires an *epic* change in attitude on the part of police officers. If this were to occur, the attitude of the public would eventually follow.

Psychologist Shelley E. Taylor published *The Tending Instinct* a few years ago, which offered an alternative to the fight-or-flight instinct, arguing persuasively that the female instinct for tending to and befriending is just as pronounced, just as necessary, and very often the better alternative. This line of thinking is worth extensive research and exploration by law enforcement agencies.[15] The differences in the use of deadly force by men versus women officers is enough probable cause to investigate and learn what it suggests.

Remember the sympathetic nervous system and the engagement aspect that takes place in the realm of our eyes, ears, and face, and the notion that a high-pitched voice is considered nonthreatening? It turns out that women are better at interpreting nonthreatening facial expressions.[16] Remember the late Fred Rogers of *Mister Rogers' Neighborhood,* and his almost lyrical rhythmic and prosodic intonation when addressing children, which millions of toddlers found mesmerizing and enthralling? They found Mister Rogers' voice appealing, precisely because his tone was more feminine than masculine. Or consider the stress level of listening to Johnny Mathis singing *Chances Are,* versus Clint Eastwood gritting out the words, "freeze" or "make my day." Numerous studies suggest that women peace officers may be more inclined and able to calm things down—and tend to be better in deflecting personal insults.[17]

There is a great lesson here that's been pretty much lost when it comes to police work. Shelley E. Taylor calls our attention to our gender differences in how we respond to others, especially in matters involving conflict. In 2002, she wrote:

> **Eight percent of the nation's police officers are women, and as their numbers have risen, so has our recognition of the value their tending skills bring to the job.**[18] **In most respects, men and women in the police force look much the same, but in potentially volatile situations, women's abilities to manage situations that might escalate or turn violent have proven especially useful. Women handle domestic violence, neighbor disputes, and rape cases especially well. They are also far less likely than male officers to have complaints filed against them by members of the communities they serve.**[19]

About gender biological differences, Taylor writes:

> **Oxytocin's effects are enhanced by estrogen, which means that, in a woman, its effects on stress responses and social behavior will be magnified by the simultaneous presence of estrogen.**[20] **But the impact of men's hormones on oxytocin may be exactly the opposite. Androgens appear to antagonize oxytocin's effects, which means that whatever effects oxytocin may have on men may be reduced in the presence of male hormones. Since male hormones like testosterone often increase in response to stress, the impact of oxytocin on men's biology and behavior under stress may be quite minimal.**[21]

In *The Moral Molecule*, neuroeconomist Paul J. Zak states:

> The empathy deficit we see in men isn't just a tagalong to being more aggressive. Testosterone *specifically* interferes with the uptake of oxytocin, producing a dampening effect on being caring and feeling. At first this sounds like nothing but a negative. But by making young males—the hunters and warriors—not only faster and stronger but less nice, testosterone also makes them less squeamish about crushing skulls in order to feed and protect the family.[22]

While aggressive force is occasionally a necessary part of the duties of police officers, surely we are beyond skull-crushing.

Zak continues, "By having testosterone block oxytocin's actions, nature saw to it that roughly half the population would be moderately empathy-impaired, which meant ruthless, even unfeeling, when it came to punishment—no giving in to tears or excuses. Males became society's original enforcers for all matters large and small."[23] That regarding gender, we are wired differently biologically is a given. The assumption that nature "saw to it" seems less certain, however, than the fact that nature recorded it. Just as certain is that Stone Age behavior is what is making our communities unlivable. All too frequently, our news headlines involving the behavior of police officers make the case for more oxytocin and less testosterone.[24]

It's important to point out at every opportunity that male police officers encounter other men daily who are much stronger than they are and it's not unheard of that male officers are often overpowered during physical altercations. And yet, every time a similar incident occurs, and a female officer is involved, some form of gender bias makes the news.

In fact, firearms trump physicality: Even babies have strength greater than what is required to pull a trigger. If this were not the case, only the strongest among us could be peace officers, unless they were always to patrol in groups. Police dispatchers do not have the option of sending large or small officers to quell disturbances. If you are 5'7" and weigh 170 pounds, and the person you are arresting is 6'7" and weighs 300 pounds, and he says he is not going to jail—and you are alone—your situation has just become dire. A call for backup is appropriate in such a case, regardless of your gender.

In the 1960s in Dallas, the only female officers I recall were in the juvenile bureau. There may have been others, but I do clearly recall the mindset at the time was that having women on patrol was simply unthinkable. The women who broke ground by demonstrating that women could be as good as, or in many cases better than, men in quelling disturbances lived through decades of harassment.

In David Simon's book *Homicide*, published in 1991, there are references to women police officers as "secretaries with guns."[25] In my view, we need a lot more women in patrol. When it happens that we have parity in the number of women and men in uniform, the statistics concerning all aspects of overaggressive police will abate. Police departments with a reputation for brutality are reflecting irresponsible management and an oxytocin shortage. Neuroscientist R. Douglas Fields points out that men score higher on sensation-seeking than do females, and that lower salivary testosterone levels correlate to reports of boredom; this appears to support my personal observation that men are more likely to unconsciously escalate conflict for the sake of the dopamine rush it provides.[26]

According to neuroscientist Jaak Panksepp and psychotherapist Lucy Biven, "Abundant animal research suggests that in general, females are biologically less prone to anger than males. Differences in circulating sex hormones, even in humans, are at least part of the reason for gender differences. Testosterone clearly makes males more assertive and aggressive than females."[27]

In *To Protect and Serve*, Norm Stamper suggests that one way to humanize a police department would be to feminize it.[28] He presents a roundup of studies by the National Center for Women and Policing (NCWP) showing that female officers are equally competent with males, less likely to use excessive force, more apt to implement community-oriented policing, more effective in improving their departments' response to violence against women, and able to help reduce problems of discrimination and harassment.[29] In *Breaking Rank*, Stamper said he agrees with Joseph Wambaugh's assertion (when he left the LAPD) that at least half of a police department's sworn personnel should be women.[30]

Racism and Redefining Reality

As sworn peace officers, you are going to frequently meet people whose very presence endangers you and those whom you are charged to protect and serve. You must become astute enough to recognize these persons as such without internalizing the assumption that everyone you meet intends to hurt you. The fact that you don't routinely assume such a threat in your personal life should be instructive and insightful to you, especially when you encounter people of a race other than your own. Most of the people you encounter are not dangerous criminals.

In his book, *Character and Cops*, Edwin J. Delattre takes issue with those teaching sensitivity training, because they seem to be saying that all white people are racists.[31] This would indeed be an oversimplification. But all it really takes for white people to see black people as different or to feel that black men are more dangerous than white men is to have grown up in a culture where such assumptions are accepted as reality.[32]

San Francisco police sergeant Adam Plantinga discusses racial profiling in his book *Police Craft*, and the way he does so reveals his frustration and exasperation at knowing that bigotry and racism are at play in police work, while not being able to resolve the issue.[33]

Again, and it's impossible to overstate the case, in police work all that's necessary to result in more unarmed black men being shot by officers is the existence of an implicit assumption that black men are more dangerous than white men. That's all. You don't have to *hate* people with a different skin pigmentation; if you simply perceive them as being slightly different—just enough to expect them to act and behave differently toward you—then your reactions to their presence can cause you to treat them much differently than you would someone you trust.

In their book *In Context*, Nick Selby, Ben Singleton, and Ed Flosi, all veteran law enforcement officers, examine 153 cases of unarmed civilians having been shot by police officers. They state that they sought to be objective, and I think they were; they were willing to admit human error where it applied. They also admitted that they were unable to answer the question about whether or not in individual cases black men were treated differently than white men.[34]

Psychologist Stephen Pinker is an amazing scholar who keeps reminding us that things are better than they seem and that the future is brighter than we are led to believe. In his terrific book *Enlightenment Now: The Case for Reason, Science, Humanism, and Progress*, Pinker says:

> **By now you should be skeptical about reading history from the headlines, and that applies to the recent assaults on equal rights. The data suggest that**

the number of police shootings has *decreased*, not increased, in recent decades (even as the ones that do occur are captured on video), and three independent analyses have found that a black suspect is no more likely than a white suspect to be killed by police. (American police shoot too many people, but it's not primarily a racial issue.)[35]

In my opinion, based on personal experience and years of study: Pinker is wrong on this point, not about the number of instances being less, but the likelihood of race being a factor, and I suspect his bias for opting for the better angels of our nature is causing him to do what he has warned us against doing: Assuming too much from the headlines. Writing about criminal offenders, Pinker alludes to a "swaggering mindset, amplified in a culture of honor."[36] But this culture of honor swagger also applies to many peace officers, and I know this from personal experience, past and present, and I also know from the numerous examples already mentioned that Pinker's examples are inadequate.

In fact, the same year Pinker's book was released, a story in the *Washington Post* on August 29, 2018, by Logan Strother, Charles Menifield, and Geiguen Shin (all scholars in relevant fields) told how they collected online data from web-based repositories that had only recently become available about police shootings. In 2014 and 2015 most of the individuals were indeed white, but because white citizens make up 62 percent of the population, the fact that only 51 percent of those killed were white demonstrates they were underrepresented in the shootings. By comparison, African Americans (who made up 17.9 percent of the U.S. population) were disproportionately more likely to be killed by police (they made up 28.1 percent of the results) as were Latinos.[37] Their conclusion was that the disproportionate killing of black suspects and Latinos was a downstream effect of institutionalized racism—fitting in with our discussion here of implicit bias.[38]

Given our cultural heritage, our literature, daily news, our television and big-screen histories, there is enough reason for our brains to believe that black men are more dangerous than white men. The most elementary reason for this is that the color difference, in our culture, *is a noticeable difference.* Our silent partner would be derelict in its duty had it not picked up on this blatant fact, because attention to such differences is its job. However, the perception of black men being a greater danger is egregiously more apparent than real: It's just not true. Negative stereotypes of black men stand out in our entertainment genres exactly as intended for the effects expected in drawing larger audiences. The same could be said at various times for other groups, such as, for example, Muslims.

Undeniably, too many unarmed black men have been shot because of this ubiquitous cultural stereotype, while others have been beaten, given longer prison sentences, or stopped and frisked repeatedly. The damage is done, and for those who are now deceased, it doesn't matter if we call it racism or simply a mistaken assumption, because they are still dead.

Former prosecutor Paul Butler reminds us that, "The police kill, wound, pepper spray, beat up, detain, frisk, handcuff, and use dogs against blacks in ways they do not do the same to white people."[39] Do you not think this observation warrants further exploration?

Let's go back to the notion of probable cause. Considering what has been said so far, ask yourself if there is reason for you to believe that our culture presents black men as representing more of a threat than white men because reinforcing stereotypes makes for better newscasts and entertainment, attracts a larger viewing audience, and sells more movie tickets? Hatred is not required for biases that result in a cost to human lives; all it takes is a different opinion about the actions of other people based on skin pigmentation or any identifiable distinction that makes them stand out.

So, how do we solve this problem? No hands in the air?

Ladies and gentlemen, this is your problem to solve. I don't have a surefire way to overwrite the existence of implicit biases. But pretending to be colorblind is no answer. What we do know for sure is that we can't deal effectively with biases if we don't know they exist. As I have pointed out, my IAT test shows a preference for Europeans over African Americans, and I am an adamant supporter for ending all aspects of racial bias, implicit or explicit, that in any way result in bigotry. So, perhaps I have solved my own problem without being able to tell what made the difference, but I'm satisfied based on my history of policing that somehow my silent partner got the right message.

My advice is to get to work and take the online Implicit Association Test (IAT) series of exams and apply reflection and introspection to gain the perspective you need to perform your duty. This is your job and your problem. When you take what has been said up to this point about black men and minorities in general and then apply it to Muslim Americans, your perspective should sharpen into clear focus. As soon as you hit the street on patrol, you will fail or prevail by your own savvy and initiative. Therefore, it is critically important that you become truly interested in the psychology of human behavior, especially your own.

You don't have to be a racist or a misogynist to make errors in judgment about women and minorities. All it takes is being human. All you must do instead is let your silent partner off the hook for making literal assumptions about matters that require careful and thoughtful analysis. As peace officers you can and will make a difference if you give it your best effort.

In summary, when we arm men and women with a badge and gun and send them into conflicting situations, we change their brain chemistry by turning them into alpha males and alpha females; for some, this will literally change the physical anatomy in their brain. We set you up to drive whatever biases you have already assimilated deeper. And we know enough about human behavior to recognize that unless you can become hyperaware of how bias works, you will be subject to continuously making the same mistakes in judgment. It is not at all uncommon for civil rights activists, even, to discover they have internalized a white preference, or for feminists to find they have issues about the roles of women. The only thing this really means is that their subconscious reflects what it knows. It is a mistake to assume that showing a white preference or a straight preference on a sexual orientation test is a sign of overt hostility. But it is also a mistake to assume that such biases left unaddressed will not result in hurtful discrimination.

We know that the physical and mental effects for some officers will be such that they will become primed for rage, posing a threat to themselves and others. We know that some officers will become so hooked on the adrenaline rushes that come with the job that they will subconsciously do things to ratchet up the excitement level, which will pose a danger to all concerned. We know that no matter how well you understand your role in society and the divergent behavior of your fellow human beings, there is always more to learn, and that if you adopt the right attitude in the beginning and stick to it, you may have a career that offers rewards you are likely to find nowhere else. Finally, remember: We may be primates, but we become people when we remember to remember that we are primates.

Communities as Metaphoric Rage Centers

As we've discussed, as a nation, we are miles from the mark of the ideal that our blindfolded Lady Justice is supposed to represent. Historian Jon Meacham's book *The Soul of America* is a cogent history of American strife in search of our better nature. From America's beginning we have lived—and continue to live—in the shadow of racial hatred that ebbs and flows like an erratic ocean tide. From the days of slavery, through the Civil War, Reconstruction, Women's Suffrage, the Great Depression, World Wars I and II, the Red Scare, and the Civil Rights era, to the present, issues of race are never far from surfacing as acts of violence.

Just like other animals, we human beings don't function well when oppressed: When animals are caged, to relieve their stress, they pace back and forth. Inmates in jail develop similar habits. When we live in oppressive conditions, we act out and become violent. All over this country, we can find peace officers so ill-informed as to declare that racism is a thing of the past, and yet, given our history, that anyone today can be so uneducated is staggering.

In communities such as those I have referenced as "cortisol canyons," neuroscientist R. Douglas Field's rage triggers metaphorically permeate the air like socially-planted land mines, or like booby traps set to go off at the slightest sign of trouble.[40] More often than not, in these communities, race appears to play a role in providing that added impetus that prompts the pulling of a trigger. Here, every letter in LIFEMORTS is a trap, and they bear repeating here: Thoughts of Life and Limb in these communities are always matters of concern, because physical harm is always a distinct possibility; in these neighborhoods Insults are as ubiquitous as song birds; worries about the safety of Family members are constant; the Environment echoes the distress of neglect and insufficient tax revenue; Mate (or spousal) issues are exacerbated by all the other threats, as is the reality of low-paying jobs and chronic unemployment; Order is trumped by perpetual chaos; Resources are always lacking; feelings of Tribalism are always in play; and a sense of being Stopped or Oppressed is ever present.

As philosopher Raoul Martinez reminds us:

> **All privilege is built on accident and injustice. Unravelling the intricate dynamics of power, privilege and prejudice takes commitment and humility. It is a lifelong journey. No one gets it right all the time, and understanding one form of oppression is no guarantee of understanding another. It takes persistent effort to dispel the alluring myth that one's advantages are somehow deserved. It is a myth that returns again and again in countless ways to justify the unjustifiable.**[41]

Our collective history is an eternal tribalistic struggle that shapes us and our communities and laws. Officers of the law have been the ones enforcing, in many cases, unjust laws. Many of the communities where you are going to work are subject to extraordinary stress as matters of degree; they all have a heartbreaking history of race relations. And they all deserve justice.

Nothing Less than Passion

Before he passed away in 2007, Robert C. Solomon—a professor of business and philosophy at the University of Texas at Austin—left us with a passionate aspirational argument for achieving societal justice. In his book, aptly titled *A Passion for Justice*, Solomon's theme is that "justice is not a utopian plan for the perfect society, but a personal sense of individual and collective fellow-feeling and responsibility."[42] This is ideological ground zero for peace officers, because it gets to the heart of the reasons for your sworn oath to protect and serve. But to understand the emotional appeal for justice, one must be familiar with the history of injustice, because it's not possible to review the horrific unjust past without experiencing overwhelming feelings that redress is imperative.

Solomon argued that nothing less than a passion for justice can and will achieve justice, and unless and until we cultivate our emotions, our efforts for arriving at a just world will be meaningless.[43] Solomon was adamant that we should not argue the case for justice via borrowed opinion, but that the task requires our own convictions, and again, this is precisely the ethos needed to guide law enforcement officers. If you are not 100 percent sold on the idea of fairness, then we might be better served by tilting at windmills than policing with the expectation of achieving justice.

Solomon points out that, "Justice, according to Plato, is first of all a personal virtue."[44] He also says this virtue must exist in the souls of those who seek to achieve justice.[45] "The problem with the idea that justice is a kind of convention or a contract adopted by people for their mutual protection is that it fails us when we need it most—that is, when there really is some monster of injustice against which we want to defend ourselves."[46] Solomon calls our attention to the fact that, "Plato's inclusion of women as guardians of the republic was a remarkably novel and precocious idea in a society that still considered women chattel."[47] That it has taken us a couple of thousand years to catch back up to this observation (confirmed by our research regarding gender and conflict resolution) should inspire reflection.

Guardians and Warriors Revisited

Norm Stamper points out that the guardians in Plato's *Republic* responsible for ruling the cities belonged to a class of "philosopher Kings," and that former King County sheriff Sue Rahr likely had a more literal idea of guardians when she and Stephen K. Rice submitted their paper advocating adopting the ideal of guardianship.[48] Stamper argues that, when defending against enemies—which in our case would be criminals—warriors are indeed needed. Warriors, in Stamper's view, include people like Nelson Mandela, Martin Luther King, Jr., Mahatma Gandhi, Harriet Tubman, Rosa Parks, Sojourner Truth, Viktor Frankl, and others of similar reputation.[49] (Cultural warriors, yes; but physical guardians or protectors of the public? I don't think so, except in a moral sense.)

It would be prudent to keep this question open for continuous reflection. A friend of mine who retired recently as a police chief in Texas suggested that we should turn our oath around, making it "*To Serve and Protect*," saying the change of emphasis is significant because the anticipation of the need for force is thus diminished. No doubt you will at times take on the persona of a warrior as a peace officer, or a guardian, and how you see yourself as a police officer is likely to evolve, but your continued mindfulness in this regard is critical to your sense of purpose and accomplishment.

The role you will take on the street is, ultimately, something only you can decide and shape. Perhaps if you can stay abreast of the notion that reasonable people can disagree semantically about the fundamental approach to the work, then you might be wise to simply treat it as unfinished but damned important business, because the ideal of justice is at stake. Plato's guardians were indeed philosophers, and it's true that an auxiliary or warrior class would keep the peace on the streets. But if we have learned anything in the past two millennia, it's that we don't know nearly enough about how our minds work to keep our emotions in check under duress.

In his leadership class, Norm Stamper says, "To develop fear-lessness you have to *lean into your fears*. You have to become a *warrior*."[50] My take is that if our primary goal is justice and you want to internalize a genuine blue bias *to protect and serve* or *to serve and protect*, then you must *lean in to learning*. If you don't have a sophisticated understanding of how our brains function with beliefs, bias, and our biological predilections under stress, you aren't sufficiently armed to protect yourself and those you serve. A true-blue bias is about paying an extraordinary amount of attention to many things that have routinely gone unnoticed. In my view, justice demands it.

Solomon observes that:

> Justice is, first of all, a matter of individual virtues and feelings, but both justice and the individual are defined within community, and justice ultimately has to be the concern of the community. But this Platonic image of harmony between the individual and the community has all but been destroyed in contemporary thinking, and our views about justice tend to get split between the two ungainly metaphors of the isolated, naturally selfish or at any rate self-interested individual and the impersonal, abstract, impartial institution—the state, the law. What gets lost in the middle is the essential sense of ourselves as being members of concrete communities, living and working together with other people.[51]

The alienation that results amounts to peace officers and citizens identifying as parties in a contest between us and them.

Solomon alleges that there is no such thing as freedom independent of community, and I will argue that this observation
highlights the oppressive nature of over-policed communities.[52]
Solomon further advises us to be careful in distancing ourselves
from the world of animals as if we are somehow exempt from such
comparisons, because we humans may come up short in the assessment, and that we might want to observe our simian cousins, as
they sometimes are better at practicing community than we are.[53]
For this, he references Jane Goodall's research showing that effective alpha males rely on much more than brute force to maintain
their positions in the hierarchy.[54]

Solomon writes:

> **We are bound by our biology, our culture, our circum-
> stances, and our characters. It is no argument against
> freedom and autonomy to say, against so much recent
> philosophy and ideology, that freedom and autonomy
> have their limits. Nor is it an argument or excuse for
> excessive government to insist that society is prior to
> individual rights. The Greeks had it right: to live a
> good life, live in a good society. The idea that the good
> life is something prior to and opposed to society as
> such is a bit of insanity that only the anonymity and
> agoraphobia of modern urban society could inspire.[55]**

Solomon delves into the crux of the psychological angst that, if
not acknowledged or understood, bedevils the work of peace officers, although he does not mention the field of law enforcement in
this context. He tells us that, "Without care and compassion there
can be no justice."[56] He also notes that "justice is a complex set of
passions to be cultivated, not an abstract set of principles to be

formulated, mastered, and imposed upon society."[57] But imposing a set of laws upon society is precisely the edict of contemporary policing, and in most cases without much worry spent over methods, let alone the essential psychological predilections that govern human biology. Solomon further counsels:

> **Justice begins with compassion and caring, not principles or opinions, but it also involves, right from the start, such "negative" emotions as envy, jealousy, indignation, anger, and resentment, a keen sense of having been personally cheated or neglected, and the desire to get even. Our sense of justice is cultivated from these "negative" emotions. I would not say that a person who has not suffered some pain or injustice cannot feel compassion, but there is a fairly straightforward sense in which a person does not yet know what pain and injustice are.**[58]

And later he observes that, "One cannot care about fairness without getting furious and even vengeful at those who break the rules and corrupt the practice." Solomon warns us that, "To pretend that one can be compassionate and fair-minded without at the same time giving outrage and even hatred their due is to eviscerate the moral sentiments and with them our sense of justice."[59] This reminds me of the history of the South.

On the cover of *Just Mercy: A Story of Justice and Redemption,* by Bryan Stevenson, *The New York Review of Books* calls this nonfiction book every bit as moving as *To Kill A Mockingbird*; inside, novelist John Grisham compares Stevenson—a New York University law professor and executive director of the Equal Justice Initiative—to Harper Lee's fictional character Atticus Finch. I concur on both counts. *Just Mercy* is about Stevenson's work in the Deep South on behalf of death-row inmates and children sentenced to prison as adults. The book shows in great depth how a country that aspires to depend on the rule of law is so often subject to the rule of racial bias, a traditional bias so deep in the bedrock of Southern culture that it is accepted as common sense, oblivious to the immoral arrogance that it represents. Stevenson writes, "The opposite of poverty is not wealth; the opposite of poverty is justice."[60] By the way, fair warning: Another printing of this work has been adapted for young adults. So perhaps you should become familiar with it yourself.

If you are a sworn peace officer who does not truly understand justice in a historical sense along with a sincere appreciation of how our minds work, instead of cultivating your positive emotions, you will likely double down on your negative sentiments. Doing so will ensure that you wind up bitter and disillusioned. Don't let it happen to you.

LEARNING CODE 3

Regardless of the occupation, when it comes to the complexity of social relations, few of us learn everything we need to know, and it shows. Why do so many people reach a point at which they assume they know everything they need to know? Where does such arrogance come from? Why do so many people stop reading? In his book, *Call Sign Chaos*, former Secretary of Defense and retired Marine Corps general James Mattis repeatedly emphasizes the importance of extensive reading, noting that each promotion in the Marine Corps comes with a mandatory reading list. General Mattis writes:

> **We have been fighting on this planet for ten thousand years; it would be idiotic and unethical to not take advantage of such accumulated experience. If you haven't read hundreds of books, you are functionally illiterate, and you will be incompetent, because your personal experiences alone aren't broad enough to sustain you. Any commander who claims he is "too busy to read" is going to fill body bags with his troops as he learns the hard way.[1]**

So, as a police officer, make no mistake, your call sign, your very reason for being in uniform, is to mitigate social chaos; bringing peace and order to bear is the very reason people call 911. You are expected to be a spontaneous leader with instantaneous solutions for all sorts of situations that have gotten out of hand, and if you do not follow the general's advice you will make novice mistakes from a lack of both knowledge and the confidence that comes with a sincere effort to learn everything you can about your work. When you arrive on the scene of a call for police, you are expected to know more about establishing a peaceful order than anyone present, and you already know from learning about primate behavior that being an alpha authority requires much more than brute force. Moreover, in the field of human behavior, so much remains to be discovered in the behavioral sciences that it is in your best interests to stay attuned to the cutting edge of research, because your health, well-being, and that of the public you serve and the officers you work with depend on it.

Self-Education is Critical to Good Police Work

I trust that by now I have constructed a compelling argument that the knowledge required to do a better job of policing in America is an urgent matter. To achieve the status of a profession, police officers must act the part and doing so requires learning that's well beyond the norm. Far too often, and for far too many people, formal education and training can, when people accept their credentials as an educational limit, produce a self-restricting attitude toward subject matter boundaries in which one's level of academic achievement experience suggests it is futile or not worthwhile to venture on with further study. In other words, if the subject at hand seems too advanced, then further exploration is avoided. But, if one's education works as intended, every course or degree will end in a thirst for more knowledge, meaning it's not an end to learning, but a new beginning. Optimal learning requires that the subject matter is not so difficult that comprehension is not possible, but far too often, subject difficulty and the qualifying protocols of formal education represent a dead end or barrier, so that inquiry goes no further.

You have been introduced to the science of brain chemistry and it is admittedly a difficult subject because of its complexity, but this field is exceptionally relevant to law enforcement and to you personally. Research in this field has really taken off in the last two decades.[2] If you are committed enough to get this far, then all you need to comprehend what the study of brain science offers law enforcement is persistence and that you continue to be interested in new research.

Adult educator Stephen D. Brookfield says that he often explains to his students that he frequently reads and rereads text only to realize he has no idea what it means, but of course his point is that he persists and thus he is ultimately rewarded for doing so.[3] It has been my experience that many peace officers tend view their jobs in a very narrow frame of reference, believing that they already possess all of the knowledge they need to work effectively, and in my view, this is why we still have so many examples of aberrant police behavior on YouTube.

In his book, *The State of American Policing*, David J. Thomas writes:

> **After dedicating 20 years of my life on the front lines of policing—being a street officer, working for five different agencies, and training thousands of officers in every subject imaginable—I have always wondered why the profession has been so slow to change. Why**

has the profession circled its wagons and fought against change? I remember teaching my first class of veteran officers, and one sergeant asked: "Why can't things stay the same?"[4]

Now, don't get me wrong, there are literally thousands of men and women in uniform who are doing a great job as peace officers. But what keeps law enforcement from becoming a profession echoes in the sergeant's question: There are simply too many police officers who don't have an appreciation of the value and urgent need to become sensitized, motivated and chemically-rewarded for learning what they need to know but don't know, and aren't even curious about learning what they still need to master.

Earlier I mentioned that Norm Stamper said it's necessary to lean into one's fears to overcome them, but to lean into learning is simply to become truly interested in the human condition, because it's your job.[5] Moreover, the reward that so many officers leave undiscovered is this: More intensive learning can also be as exciting as a call warranting red lights and siren.

Cerebral Jackpots

We've already covered the fact that a genuine interest in police work can result in "flow," or periods when time loses its significance because of the intensity of your focus. But you can also get the benefit of a gambler's endorphin rush. When it comes to formal education, unless we are truly in the thrall of our subject matter, having our attention hijacked by repeatedly having to answer questions that we didn't ask tends to shut down lots of people's sense of curiosity. For example, upon leaving school, some people are so turned off by having had to spend so much time studying subjects they had no interest in that they stop reading, sometimes for the rest of their lives.

But when you are deeply interested in all aspects of your work, you can get what I call a slot-machine dopamine effect, simply from striving to better understand it. If you have ever played a slot machine, then you know that each time you spin, you anticipate a possible reward. Sometimes you win a little, and if you play long enough, you may hit a jackpot. Now, if you won every time you pulled the lever, it would become boring, but the anticipation of winning is highly stimulating—it's an evolutionary biological feed-back system that has given us the drive for curiosity levels necessary to meet the demands of survival. Intensive learning, born of a deep desire to know is thus chemically rewarding—when you pursue a subject you really care about, you are constantly pulling the lever, and if your spin turns up new information that adds significantly to what you already know, it's exhilarating when your knowledge reaches a critical mass of sophistication, because a new inquiry can result in a kaleidoscopic readjustment—a dramatic re-understand-ing and reorganization of your knowledge is possible which means you have hit a *cerebral jackpot*—your *dopamine rush* comes without the need of a code 3 emergency call. Follow me so far? This is pre-cisely why so many people pursue hobbies with such enthusiasm. When you oversee your own learning, you can set the pace and manage the complexity, so that you are always intellectually able and ready to take the next step. For peace officers, it begins with examining assumptions you've always taken for granted, but never seriously questioned, and thus, graduating from a police academy is when your learning begins in earnest and when your curiosity should shift to a higher gear.

Again, it's worth restating that the dynamics of the rewards of learning are a complicated process, but it's simple enough to understand that, for learning to become a self-reinforcing activity, your understanding must achieve a critical level of sophistication, so that adding new information causes a gray-matter commotion, resulting in a cerebral reorganization. You don't have to experience a car chase or a robbery in progress to reap the benefits that come with an endorphin rush: All you must do is to care deeply about what you are doing, enough to strive to learn all you can so that you remain interested enough to experience an overt sense of curiosity. Got it?

My observations about the pleasurable rewards of learning come from personal experience. I understand what it's like to have hated school, to the point of dropping out, only to develop an insatiable interest in myriad subjects later in life. Through many years of interacting with college professors whose enthusiasm for learning often shows itself as a passionate sense of curiosity, I'm enthralled by the power of self-directed inquiry and eager to spread the word about its value. Many years ago, despite not having a college degree, I was offered to be fast-tracked into the doctoral program for adult education at the University of Surrey, in the UK.[6] I was honored by the offer but declined because I felt it would be too restricting for my studies, and it would have been financially difficult at the time, but most of all I felt it would have detracted from my advocacy for self-education.

Once again, *think of an education not as something you get but as something you take.* Learning is a fundamental human need. Adult educator Peter Jarvis expressed surprise that Abraham Maslow didn't include the need for learning in his hierarchy of needs theory.[7] I have also wondered about this lack of acknowledgment, and I consider it an error.[8]

My own experience, from having hated schooling to becoming a student with an unquenchable thirst in myriad subjects, is that I can't help but wonder why early on in our formal education that we are not given the formula with great fanfare for becoming truly interested enough in *something* to achieve a critical mass of knowledge, so that adding to it becomes a chemically-satisfying experience. Surely, although the formula for each of us may be somewhat unique, the recipe for all is similarly concocted.

So deep is our need for learning that giving it free reign is the means and wherewithal in life that enables us to come up with a meaningful existence, with the ability to deal effectively with the existential angst of being mortal beings. After many years of studying and reflection, the only way I have genuine confidence that policing can be substantially improved is if you police officers on the street become truly interested in your work, making it a profession by becoming existentially inquisitive.

Vital History

If you will commit to learning in detail of the horrific atrocities that have occurred routinely in the history of policing in America, especially regarding race relations, you will begin to appreciate why this knowledge is absolutely necessary, just to allow you to understand how your presence in uniform is being perceived by citizens whose knowledge of the history may also be limited, but who have experienced a legacy of feelings passed down from one generation to the next from the residue of a brutal heritage. Until you have a genuine historical understanding of slavery in America, the Civil War, Reconstruction, the backlash against Reconstruction, the Jim Crow Laws, Plessy versus Ferguson, and a thoroughly intimate knowledge of the history of policing regarding the horrific treatment of black and brown people, you cannot maintain enough sociological equilibrium to walk the streets in uniform with the confidence that you know what you are doing in the context of tradition.[9] I trust if you learn to fully appreciate the history of policing in America, you will believe as I do, that such an endeavor on your part to understand the unabridged history of policing will lead to a personal commitment acknowledging that racial reparations are long overdue in police-public conduct. I will guarantee you this: Once you fully understand this existentially-anguishing period of our history right up to the present, in many instances, you will have no reservations about whether there was enough *probable cause* for the Black Lives Matter movement to have begun.[10]

So, now it's time to act. There are so many people engaged in so many lines of work in this country, whose knowledge and their level of interest in their field is just barely enough to get by. For myriad reasons, the pilot light of their curiosity was either never really lit, or it flamed out. But when this happens in law enforcement, the casualty is justice. Just going through the motions as a police officer results in sloppy work, which, with the power and authority you wield, can ruin lives simply because of a lack of thoughtfulness and mindful conscientiousness on your part.

The Power of Curiosity

Igniting or reigniting your sense of curiosity is easier than most people may think. It takes, as I said earlier, achieving a sophisticated level of knowledge, so that adding to it becomes chemically rewarding. I will go so far as to say that for some people you can begin without any enthusiasm at all, but if you continue to study of your own volition, you will eventually ignite the flame of your curiosity when your knowledge reaches a point in which the knowledge becomes a part of your identity. You can become the go-to person in any field, simply because so many jaded folks just don't make the effort. And being known for one's knowledge is rewarding.

Once your level of interest achieves what I call a big picture perspective, or metaphorically, the view from 30,000 feet, relevance will begin to appear like pop-up targets at a shooting range. Patterns will become clear and connections that were hidden before will become glaringly obvious. And at this point, you will likely wonder why you didn't see these influences before. We are after all, an overspecialized culture, and a big part of the reason that our problems are so difficult to solve is because our focus is often too narrow. Albert Einstein declared that the truest sign of intelligence is imagination, and yet, we are often far too restrictive when faced with complexity as each expert prefers to stay in the box of their respective discipline, and all the while other experts with relevant knowledge are nearby but are seldom asked or included in relevant discussions.

But when your desire to learn more becomes something akin to a burning desire, you will find significance everywhere. It's almost like having an internalized sonar system constantly pinging the horizon, set upon anticipating the discovery of any and everything that might be relevant. There are so many related subject matter disciplines that never seem to arrive under the same umbrella of purpose. Anthropology, biology, history, neuroscience, sociology, primatology, psychology: All these disciplines and many more apply to policing and yet the problems of policing are most often discussed absent of any mention of some of the most critically-important aspects of human behavior.

We are now at another threshold for making your career in law enforcement pay dividends that are rare in so many lines of work. In his book *The Second Mountain*, *New York Times* columnist David Brooks likens our life journey metaphorically as consisting of two mountainous objectives: The first "is about building up the ego and defining the self, the second is about shedding the ego and losing the self. If the first mountain is about acquisition, the second is about contribution."[11] This is simply becoming engaged in a kind of service to others that offers rewards that upon reflection when one is old will stand out as having been priceless experiences. It's about doing things that matter, really matter. Consider all the pushback and criticism aimed at law enforcement by people who believe you are mistaken and the satisfaction and sense of accomplishment you can obtain simply by serving as an example of the kind of behavior as a police officer that will cause them to reconsider and see things from your perspective. These experiences and your memories of them can become a legacy that will outlive you.

David Brooks writes about people who miss climbing the first mountain and wind up in a valley depressed and with shattered dreams.[12] My life experience suggests that police officers often wind up here because they have mistaken the first mountain for something that it isn't. It happened to me. So many officers have experiences like mine, in that they can't see that their egos keep them from the myriad opportunities they are missing: To police as if everyone's life matters and to remember that often the smallest acts of kindness and compassion become the most worthwhile remembrances.

CONTEMPLATION
AND SELF-REFLECTION

Serving fellow citizens in your community offers special rewards
that can often go unnoticed and thus be underappreciated
because of a lack of awareness. In his essay *Compensation*, Ralph
Waldo Emerson shared this advice:

> **Every man in his lifetime needs to thank his faults.
> As no man thoroughly understands a truth until he
> has contended against it, so no man has a thorough
> acquaintance with the hindrances or talents of men
> until he has suffered from the one, and seen the
> triumph of the other over his own want of the same.
> Has he a defect of temper that unfits him to live in
> society? Thereby he is driven to entertain himself
> alone, and acquire habits of self-help; and thus, like
> the wounded oyster, he mends his shell with pearl.[1]**

Emerson reminds us that our "strength grows out of our weak-
ness" and that "the wise man throws himself on the side of his

assailants. It is more his interest than it is theirs to find his weak point."[2]

As a police officer on the street you are in a unique position to help people, from solving small problems, all the way to matters of life and death. The compensation is there, to be found in their sense of gratitude, for your having done the right thing. But as peace officers, you are accountable to interests that often conflict: You are answerable to your supervisor, your fellow officers, and the public you serve. Buffeting the conflicting headwinds that come from these sources of influence requires a keen sense of duty and self-awareness, or else you will spend too much time feeling defensive and you may lack the ability to explain your behavior under difficult circumstances, unless you are exceptionally aware of being aware. By now I hope what I'm saying makes sense. If the way you treat people is inconsistent with the way you think you treat them, it means you have an attitude problem, and no one needs to know this more than you do.

Training Your Silent Partner

It's time for you to step up as a Training Officer. Your student, as you will know intuitively by now, is your silent partner. Your job as TO is to train your silent partner and to hold him or her responsible for their impulses, actions and biases. Given this responsibility and growing interest in your work, instead of dreading new training programs, as your desire to learn escalates and grows in intensity, you will seek them out, and your increasing level of expertise may at some point enable you to contribute to the classes you attend.

Jennifer L. Eberhardt is a professor of psychology at Stanford University. She is a law enforcement consultant, and she trains police officers about the genealogy and ubiquity of implicit bias.

She is the author of *Bias: Uncovering the Hidden Prejudice That Shapes What We See, Think and Do.* Her book is an exceptionally insightful and inspiring read. Eberhardt reminds us that, "Implicit bias is a kind of distorting lens that's a product of both the architecture of our brain and the disparities in our society."[3] That's what we must fix, because this distortion is a distortion only because our subconscious has assumed that what we have witnessed growing up was accurate. It's analogous to a map with mistaken coordinates. So, we have some remapping to do.

Eberhardt writes about how she grew up in nonwhite neighborhoods and had not been around white people until she was in middle school, which meant that she had not developed an ability for recognizing white faces, because as she notes, all of us become comfortable with what is familiar.[4] It's a common folklore observation that all races have difficulty telling other races of people apart. Eberhardt's childhood experience reflects her arguments that implicit bias forms as we experience life.

Eberhardt cites studies of police-stop data that clearly show evidence of implicit bias.[5] So here is a method of training your silent partner that I derive from Professor Eberhardt's work. These aren't her suggestions; they are just what I glean from reading it. To deal with our level of implicit bias, it is first necessary to identify it.

First off, take the IAT and test your silent partner. You can't know what's in his or her subconscious until you have a sense of what their assumptions are to date.[6]

Next, imagine the value of being able to review every public contact you have as a peace officer. For service calls, traffic stops, citizen encounters, felony arrests—every time you come into contact with another person on official business you record the date and time, the nature of the contact, the location, the gender, ages, and race or ethnicity of the individuals, the cordiality of the contact and that you give each one of these categories a 1 to 10 grade with 1 as great and 10 as exceptionally not. This may seem like a lot of trouble and that may have been true when I was in uniform, but not today. There are cell phone apps for about every kind of data collection idea you can come up with, so many that you should also be aware that there are apps for citizens to secretly record police stops.[7]

Now, if you are thinking at this point that you don't need this kind of information, my position is that the more adamant that you are in feeling this way, the more you need to review your interactions with the public. You have nothing to lose but your illusions and you have a lot to gain in the way of becoming much better at your job, because the better you are able to understand your own behavior, the less vulnerable you are to having others accuse you of doing things you are unaware of. If you are accustomed to treating some categories of people with less respect than others, and you don't consciously know it, or don't want to explore the matter, then you haven't appreciated the value of Emerson's advice.

Valuing Your Data

So, consider what you could do with this data. Your bodycam records, if available, combined with your own records, will, over time, reveal the degree of your biases. When you compare age, gender, race, neighborhood, nature of contact and cordiality with your grade perception, you will have what you need to begin remapping your subconscious. This remapping is not easy, but there is research to date that suggests there is hope for overcoming our internalized mismarked map of what we have mistaken for reality.

How do you score regarding gender, age, and racial differences? Are there noticeable and measurable differences in the way you interact with people? Do you act differently toward people according to the neighborhood you are in? Does the gender, age, or race of the person matter?

If you can review your bodycam recordings, is your tone different regarding the categories above? Does the neighborhood you are in influence your tone? How about the words you use in addressing individuals? Is there a difference in the respect you show individuals depending upon the whom and the where or their race in particular? The possibilities for this kind of attention to what heretofore has been lost are tremendous insights into fixing the things in law enforcement that we know that are broken and that successful efforts at reform are too slow in addressing.

Again, it's worth reiterating that, while collecting the data above may appear cumbersome and somewhat bureaucratic, with today's technology, collecting the above information from a single encounter can easily be accomplished in less than two minutes. Some police departments have police-stop data that collect all or part of this information, and in the future, you can expect continuous improvement in data collection and in formal reviews of the data by supervising authorities.

One of the reasons we are so slow in making significant progress in police-public relations is that the wherewithal and the motivation to change has to be both bottom-up and top-down. Unless those of you on patrol on the street really care about these issues as much as your supervisors do, solutions will be slow in coming or not at all. Thus, hopefully a big-picture perspective may help me make my case.

Earlier I asked you if you believed in free will. Now I'm not going to delve deeply into this matter because it could take a couple of more books just to capture the arguments for and against free will. Do a little research and you will be amazed at the number of

scientists who challenge the notion that we have free will.[8] I admit
to being wobbly on the subject at times. It is indeed complicated,
but it's worth periodic reflection, because keeping the idea in play
can help you recall how important it is to be mindfully aware of
your actions and of all the chemical hormone concoctions sloshing
around in our heads that spew forth when our limbic system picks
up on threats, before our frontal cortex is even aware of what is
going on. To gain some semblance of personal control in such circumstances takes an extraordinary sense of mindfulness. Suffice it
to say that knowing our gray matter starts in on perceptual actions
milliseconds before we are consciously aware of them should maintain our attention and reflection. Do we think people with epilepsy
have free will? What about schizophrenia or dementia? How about
PSTD, post-traumatic stress disorder? Our whole criminal justice
system is predicated on the assumption that we are more than the
sum of our biological predilections.[9] I'm not trying to convince you
one way or the other on this topic, and some kind of middle ground
is likely a more appropriate assumption anyway, but the reason the
notion of free will should be of future interest to you is that if you
are going to spend your life as a career peace officer, understanding
your own motivations and being able to make sense of them, and
explain them beyond simple appearances is critically important.
You can't do it effectively if you don't fully appreciate the complexity at play in doing so. If, as a peace officer, you experience a high
level of conflict and dangerous action on a routine basis over a long
period of time, it will affect your biological makeup. Your mindful awareness is critical to your wellbeing, and that of those you
serve and work with; therefore, you have your probable cause to
remain interested. It's also critical that you understand that citizens
in overpoliced communities also experience biological changes
from frequent stress, and young men who are routinely stopped

and frisked for no apparent reason, other than their age and race, can be just as stressed out as you are, and it can lead to conflict that could have easily been avoided with a little forethought. Stress begets stress, adversity feeds on itself. We are contextual creatures. Free will and probable cause are worthy of your continuous attention; reflection and genuine mindfulness are as much about caring as they are about training.

Another way to think about the viability of free will is to consider how much of our biological system functions without our awareness. We don't need to concentrate on our blood flow, breathing, digestion, or to alert our immune system to fight foreign viruses; sleep and dreaming are experiences that occur which we just seem to let happen. So, where did the assumption come from that our consciousness is the supreme authority over our motivations? Jonathan Haidt's notion of our conscious self as the rider on the back of an elephant may understate the case.

HONOR REVISITED:
A TRUE-BLUE BIAS

So, time for some GPS reorientation. Perspective, as I hope you have inferred by now, can significantly dissipate the pain of existential angst, but only if you apply yourself. We now revisit honor.

Recall how I keep reminding you that we humans are tribalistic, that we are primates, and that to understand our actions in the present we must go way back in time (as Robert M. Sapolsky asserts)?[1] I'm going to put on my amateur anthropology hat now and suggest that primitive men did not lack for a sense of meaning and belonging. Their mythical and magical beliefs about the world made even the humblest among them cosmic creators.[2] Imagine having truly believed that you had the ritual power to cause the sun to rise in the morning!

Now, of course, these ancestors of ours were seriously deluded (as our descendants will also likely conclude about us someday), and like all humans they suffered the psychological problems that come part and parcel with being born self-aware mortal creatures. But it's likely they were better at tribalism than we are. We still have

271

the biologically-based, chemically-driven tribalistic inclinations big-time, but the beliefs that comprise our worldview are not only somewhat loosely held, they are also under constant attack by those who see the world differently.[3]

British scientist Robert Winston describes our predicament: "As a species, we are not physically designed for large and anonymous cities, low-level stress, fast food, addictive drugs and the fracturing of communal life." He adds that, "We are forced as a species to walk through life laden down with the genetic baggage of five million years of savannah psychology and the inherited traits that preceded the hominids."[4]

So, we moderns suffer a brand of alienation previously unfamiliar to our species. While our communications technology is retribalizing the world with exponential speed, the psychological shelter that culture traditionally provided in prehistory is becoming more and more elusive. Today, all tribes are subject to relentless criticism by others with opposing views, and this is new and unprecedented, historically or prehistorically. For all of us, living is about mattering, and if you don't matter, the obvious question is what the hell is the acceptable point of that?

Take Abraham Maslow's hierarchy of needs, presented here in ascending order: Physiological needs, safety, love/belonging, esteem, and self-actualization.[5] For our ancient ancestors, tribal life rendered these needs more easily satisfied: Tribal life would have once provided both actual and existential shelter, the likes of which we are still searching and grasping for. Nearly a century ago, Austrian psychoanalyst Otto Rank observed the clash between the natural world and the one created by modern man.[6] In fact, we unconsciously absorb and respond to our respective cultures each day, just as we do to fresh air and sunshine (or their lack), which is why we do so many things without knowing why. Achieving, gaining or reclaiming honor in an unjust society presents those who physiologically *need* this honor with an unacceptable lack—as well as standards of judgement that are themselves oppressive.

As Francis Fukuyama reminds us in his book *Identity: The Demand for Dignity and the Politics of Resentment*, "The desire for the state to recognize one's basic dignity has been at the core of democratic movements since the French Revolution."[7] Likewise, the incident that sparked Arab Spring was the result of a street vendor's humiliation.[8] The lesson should be obvious that the antidote to the modern politics of resentment is respect.

Our Behavioral Roots

In *Coming Home to the Pleistocene,* written by Paul Shepard shortly before his death in 1996, the philosopher observed that, despite seemingly immense variety in the structures of human societies, all of them are really just variations "on the species theme—whose human traits are Paleolithic." In other words, we still possess Stone Age predispositions. He further asserted that, "The greater the degree to which a person or society conforms to our Paleolithic progenitors and their environmental context the healthier she, he, they, and it will be."[9]

Primatologist Frans de Waal suggests one possible path: "We are stuck with a human psychology shaped by millions of years of life in small communities so that we somehow need to structure the world around us in a way recognizable to this psychology."[10]

Now, I'm not implying that our ancient ancestors' lives were to be envied. No doubt, for millions of years, their lives were likely "nasty, brutish, and short," but my best guess suggests that it's highly unlikely they experienced the kind of alienation we have created in the name of civilization, and they had much more time for leisure and socialization than modernity affords us—and this alone would have likely eased their stress in a manner that is simply not possible for most working people today.[11]

We are a highly-adaptive species, and our historical efforts at forging civilization are rife with catastrophe—evidenced by a written history dominated by tyrants, tyranny, slavery, genocide, torture, and every kind of oppression imaginable. This record of social strife documents the price we are paying for a paradigm shift away from our Paleolithic past and its simpler way of life.

In *The Only World We've Got*, Paul Shepard notes how "The virtual collapse of hunting and gathering, the central activity of the ancient culture, would surely have affected the very heart of human existence."[12] I suspect we are still in search of tribal feelings lost. Shepard continues, "All major human characteristics—size, metabolism, sexual and reproductive behavior, intuition, intelligence—had come into existence and were oriented to the hunting life."[13]

Against a backdrop where I'd argue our politics and economics also make us ill-equipped to negotiate our differences among diverse groups of people, we have created communities where the shelter of tribal life has been replaced with fear, resentment, and a contempt so great that it has devolved into disgust. Thus, residents live day-to-day on the verge of hair-trigger rage, only to encounter peace officers of similar temperament. These are places where public safety is never experienced by residents as a sure thing; in our profession, we call them "high-crime areas."

In *Civilized to Death*, Christopher Ryan writes, "The more we understand what human life was like before agriculture, the more civilization looks like a pyramid scheme. Disparities of wealth and power were among the first things to emerge when people settled into villages and towns."[14] Wealth and power disparities lead to constant struggle and stress for those who are lacking in both. This has been a significant factor for many people throughout human history, particularly since the invention of agriculture.

Now, compound this existential human dilemma by comparing life in the high-crime areas that I have characterized as *cortisol canyons*, and hopefully you may feel some empathy and concern for those who live in zip codes that conjure racial stigmas, class stereotypes, and the stress thus imposed. Imagine living in a neighborhood where you never feel safe, not just from bad actors, but also from being detained and questioned by police officers, just for being present. What we call high-crime areas, residents call home. And from me to you, this is just probable cause for perspective.[15]

Again, I return to the notion that we might be better served if Lady Justice removed her blindfold and that some of our social problems in resolving criminal justice can only be addressed politically. Blind justice is not working as intended. Injustice must be seen and acknowledged before it can be addressed. In *Locked In*, Fordham University law professor John F. Pfaff says, "The term 'criminal justice' is a misnomer; criminal justice is, at best, a set of systems, and at worst a swirling mess of somewhat antagonistic agencies."[16] America's criminal justice system is a vengeance industry, and those within it dramatically underestimate the pain and suffering that occurs because of its failure to prevent preventable crimes, including by those within the system.

Criminal Justice Reform

Considering all that has been brought to your attention to this point, do you see probable cause to believe that our system of justice in America is hopelessly in need of reform?[17] Our courts are backlogged, and it's not a stretch to suggest that a considerable number of the citizens who serve on juries couldn't pass a citizenship test, let alone comprehend the dynamics of bias to the degree necessary to understand and contain their own biases. Moreover, the fact that attorneys routinely employ psychologists to take advantage of biases jurors don't even know they have adds a whole new level of disingenuousness to the pursuit of justice.[18]

Most punishments rely on the accused's own admissions of guilt, which are historically unreliable.[19] Prosecutors routinely cross ethical and legal lines because they deem winning more important than justice. Sentencing statistics on the way white citizens are treated versus minorities shout "double standard." Unfortunately, it's clear that many judges do not themselves understand how our minds work in relation to bias and that an overwhelming number of studies show that they are themselves subject to manipulation in rendering decisions based on the context in which they are made.[20] Jury trials are often more about stagecraft and skillful emotional manipulation than a means of arriving at just verdicts.

I'm telling you these things not because you can change or fix the circumstances, but only to point out how important it is that you be competent and conscientious. If you are having a dreadful day and your work reflects it, you can and will introduce citizens who don't deserve it to this criminal justice system. Your work can save lives, and it can also ruin and take lives. The quality of policework and that of the whole justice system depends upon your attitude— and the attitudes of all those whom we have chosen as guardians. As Socrates argued, we are dependent on their temperament, just as our community is going to be dependent on your disposition.[21]

Honor

In reexamining and rethinking this subject, I hope I have succeeded in providing you with enough probable cause to inspire

you to pursue a philosophical perspective on honor, to the ends of self-preservation as a peace officer and to attain the goal of policing as you would prefer to be policed as a citizen.

University of Houston philosophy professor Tamler Sommers argues in his book *Why Honor Matters* that honor does indeed matter more than is commonly accepted today in academia. Although I don't agree with him on some issues, I think he is onto something big—and that, as they say, somewhere in this haystack, we will find a pony. Sommers does remind us that honor, while difficult to define, is of vital importance to us; on that matter, I agree. As he outlines:

> **Honor, at its best, promotes individual virtues like courage, self-reliance, hospitality, and personal integrity. Honor contributes to a sense of community, solidarity, and collective responsibility. In other words, honor gives us back our tribal significance. When properly harnessed and directed, honor can advance social progress; it can unify oppressed groups and provide effective frameworks for resistance and freedom. Well-functioning honor cultures exhibit great wisdom in handling conflicts in a wide range of contexts from rural neighborhood bars to inner-city schools and even the criminal justice system.**[22]

If you think back to the beginning of this class, I reminded you that you have chosen a noble profession. But it can't be noble without this something we call honor. Your honor as an individual officer of the law umbilically ties you to your fellow officers. In turn, your department is bound to honor the citizens served—for whom honor is due—or you are in violation of your most important objective. In fact, I believe, as Sommers says, that reclaiming honor can put us on track to solving some of our most pressing problems. For, although I've already pointed out some of the costs of honor when it is dark, thoughtless and unrestrained, I've made little note of its positive social utility.

In his book *Don't Shoot*, criminologist David M. Kennedy, who has dedicated his life's work to understanding inner-city crime, observes three aspects of community: *Law enforcement, vital citizenry*, and *the streets*.[23] He reminds us that we "can't do community development if people are afraid to go outside."[24] But the notion of honor is still applicable in the streets. In the HBO series *The Wire*, for example, Omar Little (played by Michael Williams) says, "A man's gotta have a code." Though fictional, this has a truth that has stayed with me ever since I first heard it uttered. It also rings true with an assertion made by University of California anthropology professor Alan Page Fiske and Northwestern University moral psychologist Tage Shakti Rai, in their book *Virtuous Violence*, that most violence is morally motivated.[25] Along similar lines, in *The Honor Code*, British-born Ghanaian-American philosopher Kwame Anthony Appiah writes, "Honor isn't morality; but the psychology it mobilizes can unquestionably be put in the service of human achievement."[26]

Police Drama

David Simon's series *The Wire* is one of my all-time favorite television series. I credit Simon for achieving a valuable public service in bringing to light a blistering array of appallingly neglected social issues. Omar Little was also one of my favorite characters, heroic in a tragic sense. At the same time, it is not entirely lost on me that Omar Little, Stringer Bell, Avon Barksdale, Marlo Stanfield, and Brother Mouzone also stand out as creative reinforcements of the assumption that black men are exceptionally dangerous. This social reality is steeped in the bedrock of our entertainment industry so deeply that most often we don't even see it so much as we just take it for granted, even though the truth of the inference is more apparent than real. Yet our whole approach to policing in so many communities is predicated on mistaking appearances for reality.

David M. Kennedy literally places both blame and responsibility for repair at the feet of law enforcement:

> **We have taken America's most vulnerable, most historically damaged, most economically deprived, most poorly educated, most stressed, most neglected, and most alienated neighborhoods and imposed on them an epidemic of imprisonment. We have given America's poor black communities an iatrogenic condition. They cannot stand against it. It has become an independent source of terrible damage, like racism or terrible schools or official neglect or vanishing jobs. It is one thing that will prevent anything else from working, make meaningless all of our aspirations for better schools and economic development and community uplift. Nothing else will work until we fix it.**[27]

Cultural anthropologist Ernest Becker likens society itself to a codified hero system, lamenting that it would be a devastating release of truth if we were to admit our need for heroism. He says:

> **Only those societies we today call "primitive" provided this feeling for their members. The minority groups in present day industrial society who shout for freedom**

and human dignity are really clumsily asking that they be given a sense of primary heroism of which they have been cheated historically. This is why their insistent claims are so troublesome and upsetting: How do we do such an "unreasonable" thing within the ways in which society is now set up? "They are asking for the impossible" is the way we usually put our bafflement.[28]

You and I will have to let the politicians answer Becker's question, but by now I hope you can see that the quest for heroism is just a desperate search for honor—in the simplest sense of counting as a human being. I hope you also see that you have it in your power to do your part by simply treating the public you serve, rich and poor alike, as if their lives really matter. This is the best foundation of a blue bias for Plato's guardians, because without the wherewithal to live lives that matter, honor is absent, allowing contempt and resentment to become the order of the day.

Dealing with What's to Come

We are faced with deep-seated political issues in this country that must be addressed to have any hope of having a desired effect on the rate of crime. Moreover, the constant chatter about providing jobs for those in the inner cities of America is way out of sync with reality. And for those of you who are young, with a lengthy career in law enforcement ahead of you, you need to be ready for a realistic future.

In *Homo Deus*, Yuval Noah Harari observes that, "In the twenty-first century we might witness the creation of a massive new unworking class: people devoid of any economic, political or even artistic value, who contribute nothing to the prosperity, power and glory of society. This 'useless class' will not merely be unemployed—it will be unemployable."[29] But Harari's concern goes far beyond lamenting economic statistics. As he says: "The crucial problem isn't creating new jobs. The crucial problem is creating new jobs that humans can perform better than algorithms."[30] Harari writes about what he calls "the great decoupling," when he hypothesizes human beings will lose our economic usefulness as our value is overtaken by code and automation.[31] Just imagine what is going to take place in employment as delivery and taxi drivers, perhaps even pilots, are increasingly replaced by autonomous vehicles.[32]

But, let's face it: We have already witnessed the creation of groups of unemployable citizens, not because they are "useless," but because they have been systematically oppressed, geographically ostracized, and overtly discriminated against in every manner possible.[33] In his book *Tribe*, Sebastian Junger said, "Modern society has perfected the art of making people not feel necessary. It's time for that to end."[34] Junger acknowledges something is missing today that we only notice in the event of disasters. He says, "What catastrophes seem to do—sometimes in the span of a few minutes—is turn back the clock on ten thousand years of evolution. Self-interest gets subsumed into group interest because there is no survival outside group survival, and it creates a social bond that many people sorely miss."[35]

Criminologist David M. Kennedy reflects back to a bleak reality:

What has been going on in America, what has been going on for a long, long time, *is obscene*. All of it. All sides of it. The 2.2 million people in prison, the dead cold in their graves, the children and husbands and wives and lovers and parents left broken behind, the lawless cops on the street, the hero

cops blowing through doors to almost no purpose at all, the dying kids who'd rather protect their killers than talk to the law, the community silence about the kids killing kids, the communities who see cops as the enemy and the cops who see the communities as the enemy, the front yards and parks and bodegas occupied by drug crews, on and on: all of it, obscene.[36]

A profound lesson of Robert M. Sapolsky's book *Behave* (and his *Book TV* video lecture about the book) is that, despite our experience and biological predilections, we have the capacity to change. Contrast police officers, high on their tribal cocktail of testosterone and low oxytocin, with the chaos they create working in districts where they assume an us-and-them relationship with the citizens they are supposed to serve, communicating their disgust through body language, verbal abuse and the frequent use of excessive force. Stew on this image in your mind for a few minutes, because it is happening right now all over this country, as are examples of police officers doing the right things for the right reasons.

Respect

Imagine for a moment that honor is sunshine; if this were the case, the communities I mentioned earlier (that I characterized as cortisol canyons) are always cloud-covered and often beset with a dismal fog—resentment, so palpable that bitterness seems to echo off the dilapidated, neglected buildings that serve as reminders that these neighborhoods don't count. There are lots of hardworking citizens who live in these localities, and they are always very much aware that it's cloudy all the time. Most of these folks would trade their heroic aspirations for a little respect, or for any evidence that their lives are considered important by the public at large, that their opinions count, that what they say is worthy of an audience, and that their community is worthy of economic investment.

Now clearly, most of the systemic problems mentioned above are out of the realm of your individual authority to address. These matters are indeed political, and police and our military, as noted, must by design be apolitical. But for those of you who work in these communities and are coming face to face, day to day, with the symptoms, you need a deep understanding of the pall of existential angst that hangs over these areas.

It should come as no surprise that when honor is reduced to words on paper, words and not honor will determine not what honor is, but what honor was. In other words, honor exists in the presence of your actions, and if honor is missing, its absence can't be compensated for with rhetoric. Thus, when you denigrate the citizens in these neighborhoods when they question the sincerity of your behavior, you cannot help but cross the line. Your conduct as a peace officer and the ideological philosophy of your department matters. True-blue law enforcement in a democratic republic cannot exist without reciprocal honor.

Of course, you can get by in law enforcement without this kind of a 30,000-foot perspective, and you may well have the empathetic temperament to perform your duties well without developing a deep psychological understanding of the whats and whys of the behavior you are witnessing and participating in each day. But deliberate reflection will enable you to dissipate your own unavoidable frustrations. You are going to be in constant need of this added perspective to dissolve your angst, keep your frustration in check, and to relate to the citizens you serve with a sense of empathy and respect that makes room for honor. Police work is all about attitude, and to keep your spirits up—considering the behaviors you are going to witness—requires perspective with a routine that is akin to housekeeping.

In *Consilience: The Unity of Knowledge*, Edward O. Wilson reminds us that nothing in life "makes sense without theory."[37] You need not be a scientist to develop your own theories about life, and don't fool yourself for a minute into believing that cops aren't big-time theorists. In an informal and unconventional sense, your assumptions will shape your perspective as a peace officer, and if you continue to explore your interests in the humanities, it can help to keep you interested in your work. This effort will provide you with a stalwart defense against cynicism.

If you make a lifetime career of law enforcement, you are going to experience the best and worst of human behavior up close and personal, and the worst is very likely to stretch your faith in the worthiness of your fellow man to the limits. Coping and maintaining your existential equilibrium while constantly confronting the kind of behavior that makes a mockery of human decency is going to require an ongoing resolve. This includes keeping your spirits up, so that you do not project sarcasm, because your attitude and demeanor will be contagious to your fellow officers and the public. Lots of peace officers can manage a career without showing the psychological wear and tear of dealing with human beings at their worst, and yet, that they are at least somewhat jaded is a reliable certainty.

Stephanie M. Conn says that being a cop-turned-psychologist gives her "a unique vantage point to understand both the policing and the counseling professions," and as proof she has written a terrific book to help peace officers and emergency responders remain resilient in work that notoriously saps emotional energy.[38] In *Increasing Resilience in Police and Emergency Personnel*, she writes about how common cynicism is in policing and that she has "met very few police officers who didn't speak sarcasm as a first language."[39]

Being an ex-cop-turned-philosopher, it is my belated experience that resilience is bound to perspective: One depends upon and reinforces the other. Perspective is the big-picture purpose that keeps your personal problems from skewing your objective. Perspective summons motivation. If I had been able to view police work in the context that I was to assume only a few years after quitting earlier, I would have stayed in uniform. I would have been able to put the cynicism that comes with the territory in perspective. This is why an attitude toward continuous learning is so important: It can make the difference in looking forward to your next shift or dreading it.

You have the capacity to bring change in the metaphoric form of sunshine to the communities where you work. The ball is in your court, and the Blindfolded Lady has her fingers crossed hoping that you will become the type of guardians for your respective communities that Plato had Socrates imagine. Plato's ideal of the most efficient and effective government would be presided over by philosopher kings who are both intelligent and wise. If he were here today, I'm betting he would observe that we could sure use some philosopher cops.

EPILOGUE

Every time I refer to myself as an ex-Marine in social media, invariably some former Marine speaks up with a reminder that, when it comes to the Marine Corps, one is never an ex. I suspect that there is something similar at work in law enforcement. Despite a half century of absence, when the five Dallas officers were killed running toward a shooter in July of 2016, the incident felt personal. I suspect it's because you can't help but summon forth the faces of officers you have worked with as a means of emotionally processing this kind of news.

Looking back on my police experience, what bothers me most today is the extent of the indifference and arrogance so many of us exhibited, myself included, about how our actions of aggressive policing for the benefit of racking up arrest numbers, for personal advancement and ultimately to oblige the political purposes of elected officials, disparaged and degraded the lives of many citizens we were supposed to be serving. Today, in spite of what has been learned in the time since, this reckless disregard in so many communities continues and in some cities, the evidence suggests that not only have things not improved, they have gotten worse because the driving force of their municipal economies rests on collecting fines for misdemeanors from citizens already mired in poverty.

I find it deeply ironic and disappointing that, while doing research for this book, I would stumble on a study commissioned by the Johnson Administration in 1967, when I was in uniform, that, had the recommendations made been implemented, we would likely have long ago come much closer to creating the kind of community policing that treats all citizens as being worthy of equal treatment and respect in the manner that I have advocated in this book.[1] *The Challenge of Crime in a Free Society* places great value on the thoughtfulness of why we have high crime rates to begin with. The report is imperfect, as are all studies that undertake subjects of such complexity, but had this intensive study not been politicized, ignored, or in many cases treated as hostile, American policing would without question be in much better shape today. The study includes this statement:

> **The most effective way to prevent crime is to assure all citizens full opportunity to participate in the benefits of society. Especially in inner cities, achievement of this goal will require extensive overhauling and strengthening of all social institutions influential in making young people strong members of the community—schools, employment, the family, religious institutions, housing, welfare and others. Careful planning and evaluation and enormous increases in money and personnel are needed to expand existing programs of promise and to develop additional approaches.[2]**

They made over 200 recommendations.

The report focused on poverty, unemployment, the lack of affordable housing, redlining, overt and systemic racism, and the much-needed acknowledgement that education for police officers and those who administer the criminal justice system needs to teach them to be capable of constantly being cognizant of the restraint and thoughtfulness needed to treat citizens with respect, when the duress of stressful circumstances makes it difficult to do so. The authors advocated that police recruits and all personnel engaged in the criminal justice system be deeply interested and vested in public service with knowledge and interests in sociological studies and liberal arts. That this analysis called for sweeping changes in the criminal justice system that were not implemented given the political ideology, then and now, does not surprise me, but that we knew, even in my day, much of what really needs to be accomplished does.[3] It's not too late. Now it is up to you.

Oscar Wilde is credited with saying something to the effect that "nothing worth knowing can be taught."[4] Having spent a great deal of time and effort putting together insightful information in hopes of passing it on, I'm still sympathetic with Wilde's assertion, because unless one thirsts for knowledge, real knowing is unlikely, and unless we temper the anticipation of knowing with a commanding strain of both curiosity and skepticism, we default to our unconscious biases, without appreciating that the easiest lesson to learn in life is that things are often not as they appear, and yet, of all of life's lessons, it's the hardest lesson to remember, when it really counts to do so.

Actor Peter Falk, as Lieutenant Columbo in the long-running television series of the same name a few years ago, provided an example of a point I've tried to make in myriad ways. Lt. Columbo always had one more question to ask; to catch a guilty party off-guard, he never settled for appearances at face value. Of course, this was fiction, but insatiable inquisitiveness is an incredibly valuable attribute for peace officers, and it's a promising formidable weapon against unconscious bias.

I lost count of the working subtitles of this book. It's gone from featuring primatology to focusing on a rethinking of policing and deadly force, but it always comes back to the certainty that our subconscious records appearances of reality, with a powerful gravitational force that pressures us just beneath our conscious awareness to lean toward what we have accepted as being real, whether we agree with it or not. And what is so disheartening is that when you explain this in detail, for some people it's an easy sell; they will agree instantly that it makes sense and that it's very likely true, and yet, the very next day they will default to their earlier position, as if nothing in their view has changed; while other people simply cannot conceive that they are subject to subconscious influence that they are consciously unaware of. They remain absolutely convinced and adamant that if they do not harbor a conscious racial bias, then they can't possibly have one. This is precisely the modus operandi of unconscious bias. Simply put, our subconscious directs our daily lives without our conscious awareness, and yet, our organic cerebral apparatus has grown clever enough to explain away our behavior, even though very often we don't have a real clue that can objectively explain our actions. But this is where you come in as investigators, because we have evidence of what has happened: We have mountains of research data and the cases that you make can embody the very ideal of justice. Delve into this subject with the determination that once and for all you are going to get people to see bias as it really is, and you will begin to understand why the subject of racism has plagued us for centuries. And perhaps, it helps explain my frequent doubts about publishing *Blue Bias* because of the reoccurring feeling that it will be ignored or reviled by so many of the very people who could benefit most from reading it. On a morning talk show discussion about racism I heard Professor Eddie S. Glaude, Jr. argue that we need to create a world where "racism can't breathe;" achieving this would most assuredly require a society where racism can't hide behind a badge.[5]

I have never stopped reflecting about my police experience. Having spent decades reviewing the literature of those who speak on behalf of the police and those whose views are critical of the law enforcement, I've given these matters an extraordinary amount of attention and reflection. These reflections were tempered with a flood of memories of the explicit racism in my community when I was growing up, and by the fact that the overt explicit racism was in those years so pervasive that had these sentiments been illustrated with clouds, it would have always looked stormy.

While researching and discussing this work with others, there have been many times when just mentioning bias and racism in present-day context resulted in silence or a glazed-over look, followed by an expressed desire to move on, as if this was no longer a relevant subject. But the clouds are still with us; they have thinned in many regions of the country, but there are still lots of places where storm clouds are always on the horizon. Racism today exists in the bone marrow of our culture, and in many parts of America, the *Make America Great Again* mantra is simply a thinly-disguised appeal for white supremacy.[6]

While extensively reviewing the literature about the history of slavery and Post-Reconstruction in America and thinking back on my experience in the 1960s, I recently came to an existentially-horrifying conclusion that in the past, hatred in many parts of the country was so vile, and so deeply ensconced in tradition, that I believe in many cases, when a black suspect was arrested and charged with a crime, his guilt or innocence was secondary to the realization that the contempt for his race was so psychologically satisfying to racists, that to have one black man in custody who would be punished severely was enough of a reward, in and of itself, to make his guilt or innocence beside the point. And reviewing the evidence of what is happening today, I don't doubt that this level of hatred still exists in some parts of America.

How does knowing things like this help one begin to focus on positive news and viable solutions for dealing with both implicit and explicit racism? The literature dealing with issues of racial prejudice is so profoundly focused on negative experience that I believe we may miss many opportunities to find meaningful remedies. I do not for a minute doubt the research showing how as very young children, we prefer faces of our own respective race, but in reviewing so much data that shows how we are predisposed to internalize prejudice at a very early age, it occurs to me that we might be able to turn this tendency around in some instances and mitigate our penchant for discriminatory categorization.

For example, in *Stony the Road*, Henry Louis Gates, Jr. mentions Uncle Remus, depicted in the 1946 Walt Disney movie *Song of the South*, and portrayed by James Baskett. Uncle Remus is one of my first, and most vivid and lasting memories of early childhood. Born in 1943, I must have been three or four when I saw the movie, but Uncle Remus singing "Zip-a-Dee-Doo-Dah" with a bluebird on his shoulder was to me the kindest, nicest and most appealing human being on planet Earth. The Disney studio removed the movie from distribution because of charges of racism and I don't doubt it was racist in its adult context, but it clearly wasn't taken that way by this toddler, and it makes me wonder if our predilection for similarity as children may be much more nuanced than we are led to believe, and that there may be opportunities at a very young age to neutralize, deter, or even reverse the internalization of racial prejudice.

Reading *Stony the Road* and watching the PBS presentation on the period of Reconstruction and the backlash that followed after the Civil War, it becomes crystal clear that it's possible to appreciate that the existence today of a sentiment of white supremacy is simply a residue of the Southern angst, expressed as a revulsion for Northern Aggression, the disingenuous reasoning Southerners attributed as the cause of the Civil War.

In the 1940s and '50s, when I was growing up, the open and loudly shared conceit that most of the adults I encountered left no doubt of the superiority of the white race, and stereotypical clichéd assumptions served as conversation starters. In the 1960s, when I was in uniform on the streets of Dallas, I had no idea about how extensive and egregiously harsh the history of overt and explicit racism in policing was in the past, and had I known, I can't help but at least hope that the knowledge would have positively influenced my behavior. The clues of overt racism, however, were everywhere in the Jim Crow South.[7] But we didn't learn about the brutal history in school: Texas is infamous for expurgated textbooks. At the Dallas Police Academy in those days, if they mentioned the racial history of policing at all, they must have glossed over it. And in the communities that I grew up in, the sentiment of white being right came with a sense of righteous arrogance and indignation that is currently regaining social traction in America as I write these words.

I have frequently used the term GPS in a metaphorical sense to get our philosophical bearings in this work. Having read of the life experiences of so many African American and Latino American citizens and so many peace officers, both black and white, it is my firm conclusion that to attempt to work as a police officer without a thoroughly-grounded understanding of the history of policing, especially in the treatment of minorities, is to be not just existentially lost, but doomed to repeat past mistakes, because you will, in effect, be culturally illiterate in the context of being able to relate to citizens as if you are living in the same existential time period.[8]

You can't fully understand the communal ground you walk on today in a law enforcement context if you don't understand the bedrock genealogy of the culture where you work. And thus, mindfulness, grounded in a deep understanding of the historical knowledge applicable to the life experience and cultural heritage of the members of the community you serve, is the most effective method of staying in tune and in touch with your parasympathetic nervous system, your frontal cortex, and the people you are charged to protect and serve.

In August of 2019, CBS News contacted more than 150 big city police departments to inquire about training regarding racial bias. Nearly 69 percent confirmed that they have implicit bias training and yet 59 percent reported that they do not yet have a way to measure the results of their training, while reporting that some officers resent the training, believing that it interferes with their ability to do their jobs.[9]

In January of 2017, a Pew Research Center survey of nearly 8000 police officers working in departments with 100 or more officers found that 92 percent of the white officers believed that all of the changes required to give black citizens equal rights with whites had already been made, while just 29 percent of black officers agreed.[10] If you have read this book up to this point, I trust you will find this revelation disturbing. That an idealistic and out-of-touch awareness of racial issues is so pervasive among peace officers dramatically limits the number of officers willing consider the hidden effects of implicit bias; it instead suggests that they already know everything they need to know on the subject. So, as statistics demonstrate, acts of hidden prejudice continue and the rationalizations offered as justification just get more sophisticated but remain ultimately disingenuous. If we fail to apply what we have learned from science in policing, we will continue to experience Stone Age behavior and the disparity will continue to be glaringly obvious in criminal justice statistical data.

Having spent years contemplating how to better explain how implicit bias works and how to mitigate its effects, the current resurgence of explicit bias and outright hatred being instigated by partisan politics in America is one of the most disappointing cultural experiences of my lifetime. But as law professor Justin Hansford points out, "racial justice movements in this country have always been met with a backlash."[11]

Philosopher Richard Rorty predicted in 1998 that at some point in the future America would become politically disillusioned with the status quo and elect a *strongman president*, who would promise revolutionary change, resulting not only in economic disaster but wiping out the advances won by women and minorities during the past half century.[12] The presidential election in 2016 confirmed Rorty's prescience, as rising hate crimes have demonstrated. Turning the tide of politically-orchestrated contempt is a difficult task for law enforcement because of the emotional contagion acts of hatred incite, and the shame of it all is that these crimes are totally preventable.

On a recent episode of *Meet the Press*, Senator Kamala Harris pointed out that since Russia is involved in trying to exploit the issue of racism in America as a means of fostering political division, it makes racism an issue of *national security*.[13] This is a profound observation, and if law enforcement could take the lead in explaining the true nature of both implicit and explicit bias and lead by example by showing how we can eliminate them, it would represent a long-overdue moral milestone and a stellar achievement in police community relations, while simultaneously upholding our national security. We need to meet this issue head-on. For law enforcement agencies, there is no such territory as neutral ground: Either peace officers are upfront in dealing with the existence of racism or it continues as it has for centuries.

"Denying Racism Supports It"—this headline in a *New York Times* column by Charles M. Blow nails this vital point, and where law enforcement is concerned this incisive reflection cannot be overstated.[14] To continue to employ peace officers who are known to be overtly racist is to undermine the very foundational premise of a just society.[15]

There are millions of positive interactions with police officers and the public that occur daily in America; often many of these incidents are the result of police heroics with lives and property saved that go unnoticed and do not garner the media attention they deserve. And while the percentage of incidents that may be characterized as misconduct may be small in comparison, it is clearly demonstrable that too many of these acts are egregious examples of a lack of training, a misunderstanding of how unconscious bias affects our behavior, a lack of self-control, a lack of the temperament necessary to perform their duties as required, or all of the above combined.

The complexity of human biology makes it clear that we still have many more questions than answers, and it's important to call attention to the fact that so much research relevant to the subjects in this book is recent, with the expectation that much more will be conducted in the near future. But the question that begs an answer, in my view, is why conventional education and training causes so many people in so many occupations to conclude that they already know everything that they need to know to perform jobs in which a lack of necessary expertise is glaring.

Being open to new information and striving to better understand one's own behavior and human behavior in general is an essential key to making progress. Simply put, the fact that caring really matters can't be overemphasized, because an elevated ethos of concern results in the heightened sense of awareness necessary to get things right from the beginning.

When one begins to understand the history of race relations, divisive politics, the complexity of human biology, human psychology, and the way our minds work with relation to bias, then I can only conclude that a position of impartiality is unavailable to peace officers. Not to tender an opinion and a posture about the verifiable existence of racism is unacceptable, because as a peace officer you must be an antiracist simply to keep from being complicit, as Ibram X. Kendi advocates; thus, as he argues, "a radical reorientation of consciousness" may be necessary, or you can't help but continue to support systemic racism.[16] Not surprisingly, white supremacists assert that antiracism is a code word for anti-white. But what else would we expect them to say?[17]

Professor Kendi is unequivocally right about the effort needed to eliminate racism in all of its subtle and overt manifestations: All of us who have grown up with our subconscious observing systemic racism require an active awareness of antiracist acknowledgement as a stalwart defense against seemingly intuitive, but implicit racist assumptions, born from simply observing the world, not as we want it to be, but as our life experience subtly chronicled it, while we weren't paying close attention. Simply put, ending racism depends upon wide-awake vigilance; it's the only hope of exposing hidden bias. Racial prejudice, implicit or explicit, is oppressive, it's subconsciously pushy, and it requires exertion to neutralize it, and in a society such as ours, where racial bias is embedded in the bedrock of our culture, there are no exceptions. If we are to defeat racial prejudice, then doing nothing is not an option: Everyone must participate, especially peace officers.

Critics of this book will no doubt point out that it is idealistic in the extreme, and that most officers hardened from experience will tend to dismiss it out of hand, and I think in view of the Pew survey mentioned earlier that in many cases they are right. I wish, however, that I had had this kind of advice when I wore the uniform. If this effort can inspire even a small percentage of police officers on the street today, I will consider the attempt to have been worthwhile.

Police chiefs, administrators, and supervisors may deem this book overly critical of their profession. I offer no apology for having presented it with respect to strict standards of accountability, and a high regard for literature rightly critical of law enforcement, because I firmly believe that social justice demands a full accounting for the behavior of peace officers, with full transparency, but even so, I can't imagine supervisors not wanting their officers to read it, especially those who want to be chiefs someday.

NOTES

INTRODUCTION

1. Mihaly Csikszentmihalyi, *Flow* (New York: Harper & Row, 1990), 3. We will be returning to what Csikszentmihalyi termed the "flow state" more, starting in the first chapter.

2. My Dallas Police Department (DPD) service spanned April 1966-July 1970, which were eventful years in American civil rights history. For reference, my time in DPD started just three years after the Dallas assassination of President John F. Kennedy.

3. Gordon W. Allport, *The Nature of Prejudice* (New York: Simon & Schuster, 1979), 9. This is still an excellent reference for understanding the nature of racial bias, and it is still referenced in thousands of research papers.

4. Our chemical predispositions will be addressed in detail in future chapters with respect to the hormone oxytocin.

5. Raoul Martinez, *Creating Freedom: The Lottery of Birth, The Illusion of Consent, and the Fight for Our Future* (New York, Vintage Books, 2016), 216.

6. Martin Luther King, Jr., "Letter From a Birmingham Jail," The Martin Luther King, Jr. Research and Education Institute, (April 16, 1963) 2019, https://kinginstitute.stanford.edu/king-papers/documents/letter-birmingham-jail.

7. Peter Wade, "75 Percent of Republicans Say White Americans Are Discriminated Against," *Rolling Stone*, March 9, 2019, https://www.rollingstone.com/politics/politics-news/poll-white-discrimination-806242/. Wade reported that 75 percent of registered Republicans believe that white people face racial discrimination while 62 percent of Democrats disagree, but the majority of Democrats, Republicans, and Independents agree that African Americans and Hispanics face discrimination.

8. Steven Pinker, *The Better Angels of Our Nature: Why Violence Has Declined* (New York: Viking, 2011), 668.

9. Edwin J. Delattre, *Character and Cops: Ethics in Policing*, 6th ed, (Washington, DC: AEI Press, 2011), 468, "Every police officer in America affirms or takes an oath to uphold and defend the U.S. Constitution and therefore its Bill of Rights." The motto "To Protect and Serve" was the result of a contest in February 1955 by the Los Angeles Police Department's *Beat* magazine and the winning entry was submitted by Officer Joseph S.

Dorobek. Today there is almost a universal acceptance of the expression as the essence of the police oath.

10. Michelle Alexander, *The New Jim Crow: Mass Incarceration in the Age of Colorblindness* (New York: The New Press, 2010). If you have any doubts about the unfairness in today's criminal justice system, this book will help you erase them.

11. Jeff Greenberg, Sandel L. Koole, and Tom Pyszczynski, eds., *Handbook of Experimental Existential Psychology* (New York: The Guilford Press, 2004), 74.

12. Richard Conniff, *The Ape in the Corner Office: Understanding the Workplace Beast in All of Us* (New York: Crown Business, 2005), 85. Conniff writes, "We seem to have evolved to deny the existence of social dominance even as we pursue it with all our hearts." Also see Leonard Mlodinow, *Subliminal: How Your Subconscious Rules Your Behavior* (New York: Pantheon Books, 2012), 110, 116, 119-23, 130-1, 134.

13. Mihaly Csikszentmihalyi, *The Evolving Self: A Psychology for the Third Millennium* (New York: HarperCollins, 1993), 48-51. Also see: Lawrence J. Friedman, *The Lives of Erich Fromm: Love's Prophet* (New York: Columbia University Press, 2013), 100; Erich Fromm, *The Sane Society* (New York: Henry Holt, 1955), 25-29; and Erich Fromm, *The Anatomy of Human Destructiveness* (Greenwich, CT: Fawcett Publications, 1973), 129-147. Nature is the key in this case: Man is truly an adaptive animal, and yet we do not perform well when we are, even metaphorically, caged.

14. Paul Butler, *Chokehold [Policing Black Men]: A Renegade Prosecutor's Radical Thoughts on How to Disrupt the System* (New York: The New Press, 2017), 26.

15. Jennifer L. Eberhardt, *Biased: Uncovering the Hidden Prejudice That Shapes What We See, Think, and Do* (New York: Viking, 2019), 140, 143-152. Eberhardt says that while researching iconic imagery she couldn't shake the loathsome examples that relied on ape imagery. Henry Louis Gates, Jr., *Stony the Road: Reconstruction, White Supremacy, and the Rise of Jim Crow* (New York: Penguin Press, 2019), 109, includes on that page a despicable Plate XIV, "The Evolution of Man by Ernest Haeckel." In the image is the progression: "Chimpanzee, Gorilla, Orang, Negro."

16. The science offered throughout this text is presented not as a final word on the issues being discussed, but as a work in progress.

17. Pinker, *The Better Angels*, 370.

18. Ernest Becker, *The Denial of Death* (New York: The Free Press, 1973), 209.

19. Paul Goodman, *Growing Up Absurd: Problems of Youth in the Organized Society* (New York: Review Books Classics, September 11, 2012).

WELCOME TO MY POLICE ACADEMY

1. Csikszentmihalyi, *Flow*, 3.

2. Csikszentmihalyi, *Flow*, 3. This is the source of the citation at the top of the page.

3. Delattre, *Character and Cops*, xxi. I highly recommend this book as a corner post in your personal law library.

4. Michael J. Nila, *The Nobility of Policing: Guardians of Democracy* (Salt Lake City, UT: FranklinCovey, 2008), 9.

5. All the books by Stephen Pinker listed in this bibliography represent a treasure trove of information for anyone engaged in the business of human behavior.

6. Christopher Chabris, and Daniel Simons, *The Invisible Gorilla: And Other Ways Our Intuitions Deceive Us* (New York: Crown Publishers, 2010). *The Invisible Gorilla* is a slam-dunk case demonstrating the power of selective attention: We are so prone to seeing only what we expect to see that, when we try hard to focus, we can miss what is right in front of us. Even a person in a gorilla suit.

7. Csikszentmihalyi, *Flow*, 52. Csikszentmihalyi points out what he calls a "microflow" of activities that help us cope with boredom, and that complexity is a key to enjoyment and learning (when the challenge meets our abilities and is not overwhelming).

8. Chris Hedges, *War is a Force That Gives Us Meaning* (New York: Anchor Books, 2002), 3, 10, 37, 62-63, 158-159, 167, 176. Hedges shows clearly that war is drug-like in how it accentuates meaning in life.

9. The notion of thinking of an education not as something you get, but as something you take, has been a central thesis of my work from the beginning.

10. Charles Hayes, *September University: Summoning Passion for an Unfinished Life* (Wasilla, AK: Autodidactic Press, 2010b), 48.

11. Johann Hari, *Chasing the Scream: The First and Last Days of the War on Drugs* (New York: Bloomsbury, 2015), 172.

12. Hari, *Chasing the Scream*, 175.

13. Hari, *Chasing the Scream*, 176-184.

14. Robert M. Sapolsky, *Behave: The Biology of Humans at Our Best and Worst* (New York: Penguin Books, 2017), 154-173.

15. Delattre, *Character and Cops*, 43.

16. Mihaly Csikszentmihalyi, *Creativity: Flow and the Psychology of Discovery and Invention* (New York: Harper Collins, 1996), 87. Csikszentmihalyi points out that, without a burning curiosity, we are unlikely to stay interested long enough to make a significant contribution.

17. Ellen Kirschman, Mark Kamena, and Joel Fay, *Counseling Cops: What Clinicians Need to Know* (New York: The Guilford Press, 2015), 13.

18. Dean Crisp, *Leadership Lessons from the Thin Blue Line* (New York: Page Publishing, 2017). Check YouTube for some of Dean Crisp's lectures.

19. Becker, *The Denial of Death*, 4-5, 160-170.

20. Robert W. Fuller, *Somebodies and Nobodies: Overcoming the Abuse of Rank* (Gabriola Island, BC, Canada: New Society Publishers, 2004), 79. Fuller says, "We reach our full maturity and stature when we see ourselves in our heroes and find our heroes in ourselves."

21. Csikszentmihalyi, *Flow*, 52, "Enjoyment appears at the boundary between boredom and anxiety, when the challenges are just balanced with the person's capacity to act."
22. Csikszentmihalyi, *Flow*, 66-70.
23. Csikszentmihalyi, *Flow*, 72-77.

THE ROOTS OF BIAS: TRIBALISM & CULTURES OF HONOR

1. It has long been my opinion that publicly-funded research should be readily available for critique and public comment. There are academicians who strive to have their discoveries become public knowledge: Robert M. Sapolsky, Steven Pinker, Mihaly Csikszentmihalyi, E. O. Wilson and others mentioned in this book are good examples.
2. Becker, *The Denial of Death*, 209. Becker warns repeatedly about overspecialization and leaving to "experts" that which is vital to living.
3. Morris Massey, *The People Puzzle: Understanding Yourself and Others* (Reston, VA: Reston Publishing, 1979).
4. This tape or video can still be found for sale on the Internet.
5. William F. Allman, *The Stone Age Present: How Evolution Has Shaped Modern Life: From Sex, Violence and Language to Emotions, Morals, and Communities* (New York: Simon & Schuster, 1994), 247-249.
6. Paul Bloom, *Just Babies: The Origins of Good and Evil* (New York: Crown Publishing, 2013).
7. Bloom, *Just Babies*, 6.
8. Bloom, *Just Babies*, 14.
9. There are many good books on this subject listed in the bibliography: Allman, *The Stone Age Present*; David Berreby, *Us and Them: Understanding Your Tribal Mind* (New York: Little Brown and Company, 2005); Joshua Greene, *Moral Tribes: Emotion, Reason, and the Gap Between Us and Them* (New York: The Penguin Press, 2013); Jonathan Haidt, *The Righteous Mind: Why Good People are Divided by Politics and Religion* (New York: Vintage, 2013).
10. Antonio R. Damasio, *The Strange Order of Things: Life, Feeling, and the Making of Cultures* (New York: Pantheon Books, 2018), 20. Damasio shows just how deep this ethos resides in living organisms: Bacteria can detect defectors not pulling their weight and block them. He says we would be foolish to reduce our sophistication to the level of bacteria, but equally foolish not to recognize that bacteria have governed our lives from the beginning.
11. Nicholas A. Christakis, *Blueprint: The Evolutionary Origins of a Good Society* (New York: Little Brown Spark, 2019), 311, 315. Christakis notes that many people are readily willing to pay a personal cost in order to punish someone who has wronged them or their group.
12. Christakis, *Blueprint*, 266-268. In-group bias is formidable in that categorization, no matter how trivial, can foster the emergence of ethnocentrism and xenophobia.

13. Two very good books on this subject are *Us and Them: Understanding Your Tribal Mind* by David Berreby; and *Moral Tribes: Emotion, Reason, and The Gap Between Us and Them* by Joshua Greene.

14. Gerhard Falk, *Stigma: How We Treat Outsiders* (Amherst, NY: Prometheus Books, 2001). Gerhard Falk has written a compelling work meticulously describing the dynamics of stigma.

15. Jack Holland, *Misogyny: The World's Oldest Prejudice* (London: Constable & Robinson Ltd., 2006), 270-271.

16. Frans de Waal, *The Bonobo and the Atheist: In Search of Humanism Among the Primates* (New York: W.W. Norton and Company, 2013). For our simian cousins, the bonobos, however, females set the tempo for behavior.

17. Kathleen Taylor, *Brainwashing: The Science of Thought Control* (New York: Oxford University Press, 2004), 186. A January 17, 2017 post by the Pew Research Center reports that there is a significant difference in the attitudes of male versus female police officers and that the latter are less aggressive and less likely to have fired their weapon on duty—11 percent of women compared to 30 percent of men.

18. Rachel Louise Snyder, *No Visible Bruises: What We Don't Know About Domestic Violence Can Kill Us* (New York: Bloomsbury Publishing, 2019), 6.

19. Snyder, *No Visible Bruises*, 189.

20. Edward O. Wilson, *The Social Conquest of Earth* (New York: Liveright Publishing, 2012), 254. Wilson says, "Societies are mistaken to disapprove of homosexuality, because gays have different sexual preferences and reproduce less. Their presence should be valued instead for what they contribute constructively to human diversity. A society that condemns homosexuality harms itself."

21. Bloom, *Just Babies*, 143-144.

22. Kenji Yoshino, *Covering: The Hidden Assault on Our Civil Rights* (New York: Random House, 2006), 23.

23. Yoshino, *Covering*, 23. This book adds a perspective about universal equality that is more often than not missing from public discussions about discrimination.

24. R. Douglas Fields, *Why We Snap: Understanding the Rage Circuit in Your Brain* (New York: Dutton, 2015), 307.

25. Fuller, *Somebodies and Nobodies*, 127. Fuller also calls stereotypes, "The enemy of respect and recognition."

26. Berreby, *Us and Them*, 117-118; Sapolsky, *Behave*, 85-87.

27. Fields, *Why We Snap*, 329-330.

28. Raphael S. Ezekiel, *The Racist Mind: Portraits of American Neo-Nazis and Klansmen* (New York: Viking, 1995), xxi, "The militant white racist movement, in the latest estimates by reliable groups such as the Center for Democratic Renewal (CDR) and the Southern Poverty Law Center, includes about 23,000 to 25,000 hard-core members. Some 150,000 sympathizers buy movement literature, send contributions to movement groups, or attend rallies, and another 450,000 people who don't purchase movement literature do read it."

29. W. Fitzhugh Brundage, *Lynching in the New South: Georgia and Virginia, 1880-1930* (Chicago: University of Illinois Press, 1993).

30. Roxanne Dunbar Ortiz, *An Indigenous People's History of the United States* (Boston, MA: Beacon Press, 2014).

31. Douglas A. Blackmon, *Slavery by Another Name: The Re-Enslavement of Black Americans from the Civil War to World War II* (New York: Doubleday, 2008).

32. Robin DiAngelo, *White Fragility: Why It's So Hard for White People to Talk About Racism* (Boston, MA: Beacon Press, 2018).

33. Robin DiAngelo, "White Fragility," *C-Span* video, 1:28:18, June 30, 2018, https://www.c-span.org/video/?447421-2/robin-diangelo-white-fragility.

34. Lorie A. Fridell, *Producing Bias-Free Policing: A Science-Based Approach* (Switzerland: Spring International Publishing, 2017), 10.

35. DiAngelo, *White Fragility*, 4. Speaking from my own experience I agree wholeheartedly with this observation.

36. DiAngelo, *White Fragility*, 5.

37. DiAngelo, *White Fragility*, 8.

38. DiAngelo, *White Fragility*, 18.

39. DiAngelo, *White Fragility*, 79.

40. DiAngelo, *White Fragility*, 28.

41. DiAngelo, *White Fragility*, 43.

42. Yuval Noah Harari, *21 Lessons for the 21ˢᵗ Century* (New York: Spiegel & Grau, 2018), 232.

HISTORY LESSONS

1. Holland, *Misogyny*, 39-40, 46, 53, 70-71, 74, 88. Holland's book offers the best explanation of the historical dynamics of misogyny that I have found. That honor killings still occur all over the world shows how difficult it is to change deeply-held cultural beliefs.

2. Holland, *Misogyny*, 73-75, 101. Some readers of the manuscript objected to this observation and some requested that it be downplayed, and this is, in part, why it is so difficult to deal with misogyny, because admitting the truth is the only way to address the issue.

3. Holland, *Misogyny*, 45-46, 96, 112-130, 198, 207, 274-275.

4. Holland, *Misogyny*, 6-7, 31, 68, 84, 93-94, 100-102, 137, 214, 241, 246.

5. Holland, *Misogyny*, 257-259.

6. Roy F. Baumeister, *Evil: Inside Human Violence and Cruelty* (New York: W. H. Freeman and Company, 1997), 120.

7. Stephanie Coontz, *A Strange Stirring: The Feminine Mystique and American Women at the Dawn of the 1960s* (New York: Basic Books, 2011), 1, 36, 38.

8. Peter H. Wood, *Strange New Land: Africans in Colonial America* (New York: Oxford University Press, 1996), 25. Peter Wood writes that, "By 1650, hereditary enslavement based upon color, not upon religion, was a bitter reality in the older Catholic colonies of the New World. In the Caribbean

and Latin America, for well over a century, Spanish and Portuguese colonizers had enslaved 'infidels': first Indians and then Africans."

9. Ta-Nehisi Coates, "The Case for Reparations," *The Atlantic*, June 2014, https://www.theatlantic.com/magazine/archive/2014/06/the-case-for-reparations/361631/. If this much history were only taught in schools, young people would grow up with much more appreciation for the lasting influence of overt racism.

10. Michael Kimmel, *Angry White Men: American Masculinity at the End of an Era* (New York: Perseus Books Group, 2013), 8.

11. Kimmel, *Angry White Men*, 9.

12. Michelle Alexander, *The New Jim Crow: Mass Incarceration in the Age of Colorblindness* (New York: Perseus, 2012 [paperback edition]), 9, "One in three black men is currently under control of the criminal justice system." Per Butler, *Chokehold*, 2-3, "The police kill, wound, pepper spray, beat up, detain, frisk, handcuff, and use dogs against blacks in circumstances in which they do not do the same to white people."

13. Butler, *Chokehold*, 33-34, 125, 130; Jeff Pegues, *Black and Blue: Inside the Divide Between the Police and Black America* (New York: Prometheus Books, 2017), 22-24. In a chapter titled "Broken Windows," Pegues presents a Department of Justice study of the Baltimore Police Department that shows a blatant mistreatment of minorities, especially African Americans.

14. Howard Rahtz, *Understanding the Use of Force* (Boulder, CO: Lynne Rienner Publishers, 2010), 34; Butler, *Chokehold*, 125, 130. Police statistics themselves demonstrate a component of racial bias in the perception of peace officers, both black and white, that makes it easier to pull a trigger when the suspect being confronted is black, and we need to fix this urgently to have any hope of proving that black lives matter as much as white lives do. Also see Fridell, *Producing Bias-Free Policing*, 15-18, 21, 25.

15. Kia Makarechi, "What the Data Really Says About Police and Racial Bias," *Vanity Fair*, July 14, 2016, https://www.vanityfair.com/news/2016/07/data-police-racial-bias.

16. Charles R. Epp, Steven Maynard-Moody, and Donald Haider-Markel, *Pulled Over: How Police Stops Define Race and Citizenship* (Chicago, IL: The University of Chicago Press, 2014), 159.

17. Paul Krugman, *The Conscience of a Liberal* (New York: W.W. Norton, 2007), 179. When I first discovered this bit of history, I found several references via Google in only a matter of minutes; now it seems harder, as if references to this racist legacy might better be swept aside. Other factors at work in the failure of Truman's attempt at universal health insurance included the bias against socialism and the perception that this was the first step on the road to communism.

18. Dayna Bowen Matthew, *Just Medicine: A Cure for Racial Inequality in American Health Care* (New York: New York University Press, 2015). Dayna Bowen Matthew makes a compelling case that the disparity in medical

treatment due to racial bias is staggering; while we will never know for sure how many citizens die from this social malady, it is mindboggling that we hear so little about it.

19. Check out the Equal Justice Initiative online at https://eji.org.

20. Ibram X. Kendi, *Stamped from the Beginning: The Definitive History of Racist Ideas in America* (New York: Basic Books, 2016).

21. Aziz Rana, *The Two Faces of American Freedom* (Cambridge, MA: Harvard University Press, 2010), 331, "Racial equality is understood as a specifically American project of integration, one that primarily consists of providing *worthy elements* within the black community with an equal opportunity to achieve professional and middle-class respectability" (italics mine). American history is rife with confirmation of Professor Rana's assertion.

22. Ibram X. Kendi, *How to Be an Antiracist* (New York: One World, 2019).

23. Kendi, *How to Be an Antiracist*, 131.

24. Kendi, *How to Be an Antiracist*, 22-23.

25. Douglas Murray, *The Madness of Crowds* (London, UK: Bloomsbury Continuum, 2019), 122.

26. By such reasoning, racism should have ended on April 9, 1865 at the Appomattox Court House in Virginia. All Murray has done is to demonstrate a serious lack of understanding of the subject of racism and how little value and urgency he places on the need to end racial prejudice. Hard-right conservatives often tend to treat racial bias as a cerebral tenet that can be alleviated or mitigated by a simple conscious change of mind, failing to comprehend that bias comes in the form of intuition, emanating from an emotionally-laden subconscious, where the storage of thousands of examples of implicit and explicit racism smolder in anticipation of being needed as sincere explanations of one's life experience when called upon to do so. That people who have spent a lifetime working tirelessly to put an end to the oppression felt by minorities because of implicit and explicit bias have been exaggerated beyond the need to do so, is in my view, beneath contempt.

27. Gordon Willard Allport, *The Nature of Prejudice* (Oxford, UK: Addison Wesley, 1954), 9.

28. Allport, *The Nature of Prejudice*, 9.

29. Allport, *The Nature of Prejudice*, 272, 404-405.

30. Ta-Nehisi Coates, *Between the World and Me* (New York: Random House, 2015).

31. Coates, *Between the World and Me*, 7.

32. Richard E. Nisbett, and Dov Cohen, *Culture of Honor: The Psychology of Violence in the South* (Boulder, CO: Westview Press, 1996).

33. Nisbett and Cohen, *Culture of Honor*, 5.

34. Bertram Wyatt Brown, *Southern Honor: Ethics and Behavior in the Old South* (New York: Oxford University Press, 2007), 53-55.

35. Ryan P. Brown, *Honor Bound: How a Cultural Ideal Has Shaped the American Psyche* (New York: Oxford University Press, 2016), 25. Here

are the top ten, beginning with number one: South Carolina, North Carolina, Alabama, Georgia, Arkansas, Mississippi, West Virginia, Virginia, Tennessee, and Texas.

36. Brown, *Honor Bound*, 29.
37. Brown, *Southern Honor*, 49.
38. Pinker, *The Better Angels*, 23.
39. Stephen Pinker, *The Blank Slate: The Modern Denial of Human Nature* (New York: Viking, 2002), 101.
40. Sapolsky, *Behave*, 31-44. We will soon explore this brain region in detail.
41. Put a few words about police officers going ballistic or out of control in the search field of YouTube, and you will be appalled by the number of examples.
42. *The Shootist*, directed by Don Siegel (Hollywood, CA: Paramount Pictures, 1976).
43. Alain de Botton, *Status Anxiety* (New York: Pantheon Books, 2004), 80.
44. Yuval Noah Harari, *Sapiens: A Brief History of Humankind* (New York: HarperCollins, 2015), 49. Harari points out that "at the individual level, ancient foragers were the most knowledgeable and skillful people in history."
45. Sapolsky, *Behave*, 25. Sapolsky points out that there is no brain "center" per se, but there is "a sub-sub-region of the motor cortex" that approximates a center.
46. Csikszentmihalyi, *The Evolving Self*, 47. As an example, helicopter gunners in Vietnam didn't get their hormones flowing until they landed after battles. Police officers often have a similar experience after stressful encounters. The fallout occurs when you get home.
47. Allport, *The Nature of Prejudice*, 148, 437, 509.
48. Sam Keen, *Faces of the Enemy: Reflections of the Hostile Imagination* (New York: Harper & Row, 1986), 28.
49. Greene, *Moral Tribes*, 350-353.

THE ROOTS OF POLICE RACISM

1. I have said "white people," but some will argue that this should apply to all people; however, the history and imbalance of power that still applies to our society makes the very idea of what is often referred to as reverse racism a moot point.
2. Ferguson, Missouri comes to mind because of so much media attention in recent years, but most large cities in America have communities that meet the criteria of being overpoliced because of the aggressive tactics of their local law enforcement agencies.
3. Jacey Fortin, "Arizona Prisons' Ban on Book About Racism in Criminal Justice Draws Challenge," *The New York Times*, May 22, 2019, https://www.nytimes.com/2019/05/22/us/arizona-bans-chokehold-book.html. Fortin reported on May 22, 2019 that the Arizona Department of Corrections had banned Paul Butler's book.

4. Norm Stamper, *To Protect and Serve: How to Fix America's Police* (New York: Nation Books, 2016), 245, 250.

5. Norm Stamper, *Breaking Rank: A Top Cop's Expose of the Dark Side of Policing* (New York: Nation Books, 2005); *Stamper, To Protect and Serve.*

6. Rahtz, *Understanding the Use of Force*, 33.

7. Bill Minutaglio, and Steven L. Davis, *Dallas 1963* (New York: Twelve, 2013), 102, 327. This book describes the political climate in Dallas from 1960 up to and just after the assassination of John F. Kennedy. I joined the Marines in March of 1960, and so—except from coming home on leave—I missed most of this period in Dallas history, and I must admit that the overt racism in Dallas during that period sounds much worse than I remember. On page 102, these authors report that in October 1961, the managing editor of the *Dallas Times Herald* resigned to become the public relations director for the KKK. Reading about the overt explicit racism in Dallas during this era, it becomes clear to me now how difficult it is to grow up in a culture where bigotry is the bias that binds—and how hard it is to overcome this indoctrination, because it essentially means breaking ideological ties with almost everyone you know.

8. Of course, this is contrary to the rules of jury selection. But in 1960s Texas, that's the way things were done. I was discharged after four years in the Marines in February 1964, so this must have occurred just before or after I arrived home.

9. From what I can gather from news reports, there are many parts of the country where similar laws and worse are still in place.

10. Angela J. Davis, ed., *Policing the Black Man: Arrest, Prosecution and Imprisonment* (New York: Pantheon, 2017), xv, xvi, 11, 173, 183. Butler, *Chokehold*, 33-34, cites ProPublica in showing that black police officers are more likely to shoot a black man than are white officers; see also Butler, *Chokehold*, 125, 130.

11. Sapolsky, *Behave*, 107-120.

12. Haidt, *The Righteous Mind*. There are many studies that can be found about how and why we are so prone to groupishness. In chapters 9, 10, and 11 of Haidt's work, you will find a good overview.

13. Christakis, *Blueprint*, 4, 266. Christakis observes that in-group favoritism is so powerful that children given randomly-assigned T-shirts of different colors favored the children wearing their color.

14. Haidt, *The Righteous Mind*, 134-138.

15. Jack Weatherford, *Savages and Civilization: Who Will Survive?* (New York: Crown Publishers, 1994), 256.

16. Baumeister, *Evil*, 68.

17. Lara Bazelon, "Seventeen Cases of Denied Innocence," *Slate*, January 10, 2018, https://slate.com/news-and-politics/2018/01/innocence-deniers-seventeen-cases-of-prosecutors-fighting-exoneration.html.

18. Shaila Dewan, "Prosecutors Block Access to DNA Testing for Inmates," *The New York Times*, May 17, 2009. See also Bryan Stevenson, *Just Mercy:*

A Story of Justice and Redemption (New York: Spiegel & Grau, 2015) for detailed case examples of prosecutorial denial.

19. Bessel A. van der Kolk, *The Body Keeps the Score: Brain, Mind, and Body in the Healing of Trauma* (New York: Penguin Books, 2014), 349. Van der Kolk cites as evidence the frequency of the publication of new research papers on the subject of trauma.

20. Dean Buonomano, *Brain Bugs: How the Brain's Flaws Shape Our Lives* (New York: W.W. Norton, 2011); Daniel Kahneman, *Thinking Fast and Slow* (New York: Farrar, Straus and Giroux, 2011). These books are just a couple of examples. Almost all the books published about human psychology mention studies about the importance of context. There have been so many studies that the field has been criticized for some studies using less-than-reliable conditions, but the sheer number of studies supports the prominence that context plays in our behavior. I have always found it disturbing that my behavior can be predicted given specific circumstances better than I could predict myself.

THE ELEPHANT ON YOUR BEAT:
OUR ORGANIC CEREBRAL ARCHITECTURE

1. Stamper, *To Protect and Serve*, 72.

2. Stamper, *Breaking Rank*, v.

3. Haidt, *The Righteous Mind*, 52-71. Another elephant metaphor for our emotions can be found in *The Elephant in the Brain: Hidden Motives in Everyday Life*, by Kevin Simler and Robin Hanson. The subtitle is the point of the book, showing how self-deceptive we are and how we so frequently misunderstand why we do what we do.

4. Sapolsky, *Behave*, 88.

5. Csikszentmihalyi, *The Evolving Self*, 48-51; Charles Darwin, *The Expression of the Emotions in Man and Animals: With an Introduction, Afterward and Commentaries by Paul Erkman* (London: Oxford University Press, 1998), 71; Friedman, *The Lives of Erich Fromm*, 100; Fromm, *The Anatomy of Human Destructiveness*, 129-147; Fromm, *The Sane Society*, 25-29; and Jaak Panksepp and Lucy Biven, *Affective Neuroscience: The Foundation of Human and Animal Emotions* (New York: Oxford University Press, 1998), 169. Whether we deny our animal nature by self-regard, arrogance, or self-deception, the result is the same, in that we begin our journey with a map that has the wrong coordinates.

6. Harold E. Russell, and Allan Beigel, *Understanding Human Behavior for Effective Police Work* (New York: Basic Books, 1990), 416.

7. Hayes, *September University*, 45-55.

8. Sapolsky, *Behave*.

9. Check out C-Span2 *Book TV* for Sapolsky's *Behave* lecture; it is worth watching more than once.

10. Sapolsky, *Behave*, 85.

11. Buonomano, *Brain Bugs*, 168; Sapolsky, *Behave*, 402. There has been a lot of criticism about framing studies, as some been shown to have been performed haphazardly at best, but there have been too many that confirm the validity of context to dismiss them.

12. Framing, anchoring, and priming offer effective strategies, especially in politics, because the language used can provide the context and set the whole tone and tenor of the conversation—and the same applies to courtroom testimony for jury consideration.

13. Lisa Feldman Barrett, *How Emotions Are Made: The Secret Life of the Brain* (New York: Houghton Mifflin Harcourt, 2017), 76. Barrett writes, "The U.S. Department of Justice analyzed shootings by Philadelphia police officers between 2007 and 2013 and found that 15 percent of the victims were unarmed. In half of these cases, an officer reportedly misidentified 'a nonthreatening object (e.g., a cell phone) or movement (e.g., tugging at the waistband)' as a weapon. Many factors may contribute to these tragedies, ranging from carelessness to racial bias, but it is also possible that some of the shooters actually perceive a weapon when none is present due to affective realism in a high-pressure and dangerous context. The human brain is wired for this sort of delusion, in part, because moment-to-moment interoception [the work of your silent partner] infuses us with affect, which we then use as evidence about the world." She adds an endnote of her own on page 76 to declare that she is not implying that affective realism is the primary cause of police shootings, but just that we are wired for prediction, for seeing what we expect to see.

14. Kevin Simler, and Robin Hanson, *The Elephant in the Brain: Hidden Motives in Everyday Life* (New York: Oxford University Press, 2018), 73-89.

15. Haidt, *The Righteous Mind*, 42, 65.

16. Siddhartha Mukherjee, *The Gene: An Intimate History* (New York: Scribner, 2016), 107, 403, 418.

17. Barrett, *How Emotions Are Made*, 225.

18. Barrett, *How Emotions Are Made*, 4-12. Barrett makes it clear that we are not as good as we think we are when it comes to intuiting the emotions of others by the expressions on their faces. But in police work, an attempt to read an expression is better than ignoring facial expressions altogether. If you see a flicker of steel that you think may be a weapon, a hostile facial expression of some type should be present in someone intending to shoot you. You say you don't have time to look at the face: You are wrong. If it is seeable, your silent partner has already looked, though things work out best if your silent partner is better trained.

19. Frans de Waal, *Mama's Last Hug: Animal Emotions and What They Tell Us about Ourselves* (New York: W.W. Norton, 2019), 51.

20. Barrett, *How Emotions Are Made*, 4-12, 76, 225. Barrett makes it clear that judging the emotions of others based on their facial expressions is unreliable. But I can't help but believe that through experience we are better

able to make an educated guess than to try to pay no attention to what we are seeing.

21. Panksepp and Biven, *Affective Neuroscience*, 215.

22. Dave Grossman, *On Killing: The Psychological Cost of Learning to Kill in War and Society* (New York: Back Bay Books, 2009), 317. Some military target training amounts to split-second shooting in which the speed of response and not the legitimacy of the target is the objective.

23. Stephen Pinker, *How the Mind Works*, (New York: W.W. Norton, 1997), 370, 416; Panksepp and Biven, *Affective Neuroscience*, 70-71. This is an excellent overview with graphic examples.

24. Sapolsky, *Behave*, 25, 38, 42-43, 59, 88. Sapolsky points out that the amygdala is "mostly about setting off alarms."

25. Sapolsky, *Behave*, 59. Sapolsky says this happens milliseconds before the frontal cortex is even aware of what one has seen.

26. Sebastian Junger, *War* (New York: Twelve, 2011).

27. Robert M. Sapolsky, *Why Zebras Don't Get Ulcers: The Acclaimed Guide to Stress, Stress-Related Diseases, and Coping* (New York: St. Martin's Press, 2004), 305, 342-344, 348-349.

28. Gregory Berns, *Iconoclast: A Neuroscientist Reveals How to Think Differently* (Boston, MA: Harvard Business Press, 2008), 69.

29. Hedges, *War Is a Force*, 3.

30. Hedges, *War Is a Force*, 10.

31. Colby Itkowitz, "Meet the 34-year-old neuroscientist developing a drug to prevent depression and PTSD," *Washington Post*, April 25, 2017, https://www.washingtonpost.com/news/inspired-life/wp/2017/04/25/meet-the-34-year-old-neuroscientist-developing-a-drug-to-prevent-depression-and-ptsd/?noredirect=on. Neuroscientist Rebecca Brachman is developing a drug that she hopes can prevent PTSD. This could have a huge impact for the armed forces and law enforcement organizations.

32. Becker, *The Denial of Death*, 178-179.

33. Sapolsky, *Behave*, 34; van der Kolk, *The Body Keeps the Score*, 69-70, 208-209.

34. Google the number of veterans dying each day from taking their own lives.

35. If you feel it is strange and way out of the ordinary that I'm bringing so many things to your attention that are not traditionally a part of police training, then my point is made.

36. Csikszentmihalyi, *Flow*, 52.

37. Sapolsky, *Behave*, 411, 560-563; Stephen Pinker, *The Stuff of Thought: Language as a Window into Human Nature* (New York: Viking, 2007), 344-346.

38. De Waal, *Mama's Last Hug*, 156.

39. Delattre, *Character and Cops*, 112.

40. Sapolsky, *Behave*, 453-454.

41. Debra Lieberman, and Carlton Patrick, *Objection: Disgust, Morality, and the Law* (New York, NY: Oxford University Press, 2018), 173.

42. George Lakoff, and Mark Johnson, *Metaphors We Live By* (Chicago, IL:

Chicago University Press, 1980), 5. These authors remind us that "The essence of metaphor is understanding and experiencing one kind of thing in terms of another."

43. Sapolsky, *Behave*, 555-562.

44. Edward O. Wilson, *The Origins of Creativity* (New York: Liveright Publishing, 2017), 161; Pinker, *The Stuff of Thought*, 238-278. Pinker offers a superb chapter on the use of metaphors.

45. George Lakoff, and Mark Johnson, *Philosophy in the Flesh: The Embodied Mind and Its Challenge to Western Thought* (New York: Basic Books, 1999), 13.

46. Lakoff and Johnson, *Philosophy in the Flesh*, 155, 190, 292, 300.

47. Lakoff and Johnson, *Philosophy in the Flesh*, 293-298.

48. Berns, *Iconoclast*, 58.

49. Sapolsky, *Behave*, 46, 59, 516-519, 528-534, 547, 559-560, 569, 622.

50. Stamper, *To Protect and Serve*, 232-233. Stamper also believes, as I do, that empathy can be strengthened by purposeful experience.

51. Robert M. Sapolsky makes it a point in his C-Span *Book TV* lecture to note that so much has been learned about these subjects only recently and the research continues.

52. Stamper, *To Protect and Serve*, 234.

53. Sapolsky, *Behave*, 18-19, 30, 38, 42, 45-64, 88, 91-92, 100, 132-134, 143-144, 557, 607, 614.

54. Sapolsky, *Behave*, 162-164. Adolescents experience increased dopamine in anticipation of novelty.

55. Sapolsky, *Behave*, 42, 45, 60, 78, 141-144, 148-153, 436.

56. Berreby, *Us and Them*, 262.

57. Sapolsky, *Behave*, 42.

58. Daniel J. Siegel, *Aware: The Science and Practice of Presence* (New York: TarcherPerigee, 2018), 307.

BRAIN CHEMISTRY

1. Sapolsky, *Behave*, 30, 64-77, 84, 103, 151, 275, 390, 555-556, 692. Synthesized in multiple brain regions, dopamine is a reward chemical highly subject to release upon anticipation of a forthcoming reward. See also Jaak Panksepp, and Lucy Biven, *The Archaeology of Mind: Neuroevolutionary Origins of Human Emotions* (New York: W.W. Norton, 2012), 109-136, 143.

2. Sapolsky, *Behave*, 64; Peter C. Whybrow, *The Well-Tuned Brain: Neuroscience and the Life Well Lived* (New York: W. W. Norton, 2015), 27, 46. Whybrow describes dopamine, serotonin and norepinephrine as the "brain's superhighway."

3. Sapolsky, *Behave*, 68.

4. Sapolsky, *Behave*, 70-71.

5. Sapolsky, *Behave*, 72-73.

6. Panksepp and Biven, *The Archaeology of Mind*, xi, 95, 109, 141. The authors identify seven basic affective systems in mammalian brains: Seeking

(expectancy), Fear (anxiety), Rage (anger), Lust (sexual excitement), Care (nurturance), Panic/Grief (sadness), and Play (social joy). The seeking system produces lots of dopamine-driven behaviors, from learning to being attracted to danger.

7. Sapolsky, *Behave*, 74. I cite Sapolsky here not specifically to make my claim, but simply as evidence about the nature of the reward delivery system.
8. Sapolsky, *Behave*, 74.
9. Sapolsky, *Why Zebras Don't Get Ulcers*, 338.
10. Sapolsky, *Why Zebras Don't Get Ulcers*, 343-334. Sapolsky says, give a rat cocaine and there is a thousand-fold increase in dopamine release. Fields, *Why We Snap*, 198-199, says there is a genetic component linked to sensation-seeking via dopamine.
11. Hayes, *September University*, 48-50; Panksepp and Biven, *The Archaeology of Mind*, 103, 109, 136, 141, 143.
12. Sapolsky, *Behave*, 108-116.We are not very far along in understanding the effects of oxytocin, but what has been learned to date is fascinating. There is lots of probable cause here. Stephen W. Porges, *The Polyvagal Theory: Neurophysiological Foundations of Emotions, Attachment, Communication, Self-regulation* (New York: W.W. Norton, 2011), 175, 176. Stephen W. Porges' wife Sue Carter has been instrumental in research about the effects of oxytocin and vasopressin.
13. Patricia S. Churchland, *Touching a Nerve: Our Brains, Our Selves* (New York: W.W. Norton, 2013), 101. Churchland cautions that not enough is known yet about oxytocin to be sure we understand it. At this point, it looks to me as if we are chemically cocktailed for tribalistic behavior.
14. Csikszentmihalyi, *The Evolving Self*, 59.
15. Sapolsky, *Behave*, 102-106.
16. Robert M. Sapolsky, *The Trouble with Testosterone* (New York: Touchstone, 1997), 155.
17. Sapolsky, *Behave*, 155. Sapolsky reminds us testosterone doesn't cause aggression: It just exaggerates the aggression that is already there.
18. Sapolsky, *Behave*, 102-103.
19. There is ample probable cause to study the biological implications for sexual dominance, especially when it comes to alpha males.
20. Sapolsky, *Behave*, 134, 692; van der Kolk, *The Body Keeps the Score*, 33, 155-156, 264.
21. Van der Kolk, *The Body Keeps the Score*, 33-34.
22. Porges, *The Polyvagal Theory*, 149-150; van der Kolk, *The Body Keeps the Score*, 30, 61, 156, 164, 225.
23. Wilson, *The Origins of Creativity*, 117.
24. Jeff Wise, *Extreme Fear: The Science of Your Mind in Danger* (New York: Palgrave Macmillan, 2009), 20, 35.
25. Wise, *Extreme Fear*, 50-51, 76.
26. Nisbett and Cohen, *Culture of Honor*, 13, 28, 30-32.
27. Fields, *Why We Snap*, 39.

28. Fields, *Why We Snap*, 40-43
29. Fields, *Why We Snap*, 47.
30. Fields, *Why We Snap*, 57-58, 341.
31. Panksepp and Biven, *Affective Neuroscience*, 187.
32. Panksepp and Biven, *Affective Neuroscience*, 204.

THE TAX OF HYPERVIGILANCE

1. Van der Kolk, *The Body Keeps the Score*, 51-74.
2. Kevin M. Gilmartin, *Emotional Survival for Law Enforcement: A Guide for Officers and Their Families* (Tucson, AZ: E-S Press, 2002), 38.
3. Stamper, *Breaking Rank*, 187.
4. Sapolsky, *Behave*, 34-40.
5. Van der Kolk, *The Body Keeps the Score*, 63-64. Section five in this book offers more advice on these processes.
6. Gilmartin, *Emotional Survival for Law Enforcement*.
7. Edgar Sandoval, and Ashley Southall, "Two More N.Y. Police Officers Die by Suicide, Bringing Total to 9 This Year," *The New York Times*, August 13, 2019, https://www.nytimes.com/2019/08/13/nyregion/nypd-officer-suicide.html.
8. Gilmartin, *Emotional Survival for Law Enforcement*, 42.
9. Delattre, *Character and Cops*, 492-494. Delattre discusses the suicide rate of war veterans in a chapter titled "From War Veterans to Peace Officers."
10. Gilmartin, *Emotional Survival for Law Enforcement*, 98.
11. Try a YouTube search with an assortment of words about police behavior. Keep adding innovative words by changing the context and you will be appalled at what you see. A big part of my presentation is for the express purpose of keeping you from adding to these videos.
12. Marc Bekoff, "Social Dominance Is Not a Myth: Wolves, Dogs, and," *Psychology Today*, February 15, 2012, https://www.psychologytoday.com/ca/blog/animal-emotions/201202/social-dominance-is-not-myth-wolves-dogs-and.
13. De Waal, *Mama's Last Hug*, 177.
14. Mlodinow, *Subliminal*, 111-125. This is a fascinating discussion about body language.
15. There was so much initial enthusiasm over the discovery of mirror neurons that there has since been a backlash in academia; now their importance is being downplayed with equal fervor. However, they remain an important discovery, especially when we examine the notion of empathy and relating to others.
16. Hayes, *September University*, 104-107.
17. Panksepp and Biven, *Affective Neuroscience*, 169.
18. Conniff, *The Ape in the Corner Office*, 89.
19. Simler and Hanson, *The Elephant in the Brain*, 111-127. These authors do an excellent job of stating the importance of understanding body language.

20. Sapolsky, *Behave*, 3.
21. Sapolsky, *Behave*, 66, "Punishing norm violations is satisfying."
22. Frans de Waal, *Our Inner Ape* (New York: Riverhead Books, 2005), 187. De Waal says, "We know now that emotional contagion resides in parts of the brain so ancient that we share them with animals as diverse as rats, dogs, elephants, and monkeys."
23. De Waal; *Our Inner Ape*, 120; Mlodinow, *Subliminal*, 110, 116, 119-123, 130-131, 134; Panksepp and Biven, *Affective Neuroscience*, 169; Sapolsky; *Behave*, 421-426.
24. Erich Fromm observed that we make some assumptions about our simian cousins' behavior based on their conduct in zoo cages. If we were to assume the same degree of innate aggressiveness that chimpanzees exhibit in their natural habitat, he says, we would experience a more peaceful world. But here is the thing: Fromm points out that we don't live in the natural habitat conditions we evolved in any more than zoo animals do. Now, as it turns out Fromm was wrong at least in matters of degree, as E. O. Wilson points out. Jane Goodall's field work suggests that hunter-gatherers and early farmers had about the same death rates from violence as chimpanzees, but that nonlethal violence among chimpanzees may be between a hundred and a thousand times more violent than humans. And yet, Fromm's observation about the stress aspect is profound. We too are primates and we create social and economic cages we call communities of culture and the higher the stress, the greater the need for a police presence, the areas where there is little trust of and by law enforcement are very much in character like the cages in zoos for animals. So, my point is that our communities can be so out of sync with the way we have lived for 99.999 percent of our time on the planet that our behavior can be comparable to that of caged animals. See also Csikszentmihalyi, *The Evolving Self*, 48-51; Dean Falk, *Braindance: New Discoveries About Human Origins and Brain Evolution* (New York: Henry Holt and Company, 1992), 204-220; Friedman, *The Lives of Erick Fromm*, 100; Fromm, *The Sane Society*, 25-29; and Fromm, *The Anatomy of Human Destructiveness*, 129-147.
25. Philip Zimbardo, *The Lucifer Effect: Understanding How Good People Turn Evil* (New York: Random House, 2007), 363. Zimbardo cites more than 50 blows while two dozen officers watched.
26. Matt Taibbi, *The Divide: American Injustice in the Age of the Wealth Gap* (New York: Spiegel & Grau, 2014).
27. Zimbardo, *The Lucifer Effect*, 317.
28. Abigail Marsh, *The Fear Factor: How One Emotion Connects Altruists, Psychopaths, and Everyone In-Between* (New York: Basic Books, 2017), 5-6, 82-100, 131-141, 150-153, 198-199. It's important to realize that size alone may not be an accurate indicator of effect because altruists also have enlarged amygdalas and the amygdalas of psychopaths are smaller than normal.
29. Stamper, *To Protect and Serve*, 77.

30. Taibbi, *The Divide*. Taibbi chronicles the incident and aftermath.

31. It is, however, not lost on me that as many times as I used a chokehold in making arrests what happened with Eric Garner could have also happened because of my actions, although I can't imagine not responding to repeated pleas about not being able to breathe. Both politics and policy play a role here when one considers making a physical arrest instead of a summons to appear in court from selling cigarettes one at a time.

32. Cass R. Sunstein, *Conformity: The Power of Social Influences* (New York: New York University Press, 2019), 25.

33. A few days after the incident my wife answered a knock at the door and the two FBI agents were there to encourage me to apply to become an FBI agent, but I didn't have the college hours required at the time, so I didn't apply.

34. Check out Chip Huth and Dean Crisp, both on TEDx.

INFLUENCING YOUR LIMBIC SYSTEM

1. Porges, *The Polyvagal Theory*, 59, "The polyvagal theory proposes that the evolution of the mammalian autonomic nervous system provides the neurophysiological substrates for adaptive behavioral strategies. It further proposes that physiological state limits the range of behavior and psychological experience. The theory links the evolution of the autonomic nervous system to affective experience, emotional expression, facial gestures, vocal communication, and contingent social behavior." There are several lectures by Stephen Porges on YouTube that are very insightful about polyvagal theory. In my view, there is much to learn about how our perception and assessment of risk works.

2. Porges, *The Polyvagal Theory*, 137, 153-154, 160.

3. Porges, *The Polyvagal Theory*, 14.

4. Porges makes this point clear at every opportunity.

5. Porges, *The Polyvagal Theory*, 195, "In safe environments, our autonomic state is adaptively regulated to dampen sympathetic activation and to protect the oxygen-dependent central nervous system from the metabolically conservative reactions of the dorsal complex."

6. Porges, *The Polyvagal Theory*, 247.

7. Porges, *The Polyvagal Theory*, 124-125, 204, 249, 265.

8. I don't know where I first heard about this observation; it must have been something I read. I've spent a lot of time trying to find a source but haven't had any luck. That said, it seems self-evident.

9. Van der Kolk, *The Body Keeps the Score*, 209.

10. Normally the headquarters station downtown and the Southwest station in Oak Cliff would be on separate radio channels, but in the case of a manhunt multiple channels may be involved.

11. E. R. Walt, *Holloway's Raiders: A History of the Dallas Police Department's Deadly Shotgun Squads* (West Conshohocken, PA: Infinity Publishing,

2016), 281-295. E. R. Walt's book is a history of the Dallas Police Department's shotgun squads.

12. Walt, *Holloway's Raiders*, 284-285. There was an embarrassing incident involving the accounting department in which Floyd Knight's widow was docked $27.74 because he was killed before finishing his shift. The backlash earned the DPD a "Fickle Finger of Fate" on *Rowan & Martin's Laugh-In*. The episode lives on via YouTube at https://www.youtube.com/watch?v=EqlNbXK-Bu4&list=PLYSJjOQbyvz_xC96fA3X1jIBU9kOYxwqx&index=20&t=0s.

13. Grossman, *On Killing*, xviii, xxxi, 1-4, 30-31, 37-40, 58-59, 86.

14. Grossman, *On Killing*, 310-315.

15. United States Department of Justice, "Investigation of the Ferguson Police Department," Civil Rights Division, March 4, 2015, https://www.justice.gov/sites/default/files/opa/press-releases/attachments/2015/03/04/ferguson_police_department_report.pdf.

16. United States Department of Justice, "Investigation of the Ferguson Police Department."

17. Grossman, *On Killing*, 158, 160-164, 189-190, 211-212.

18. William Ian Miller, *The Anatomy of Disgust* (Cambridge, MA: Harvard University Press, 1997), 206-234.

19. Miller, *The Anatomy of Disgust*, 206.

20. Clearly a bias can exist that falls short of being overtly, explicitly racist. For example, simply seeing black men as being more dangerous, because of the way they are characterized in entertainment media is a less-explicit bias, but the result is the same as if it were explicit racism, and if, metaphorically, the line in one's mind enters the territory of disgust, then the result is the same. The evidence is overwhelming that racism is a system and not an occurrence or an event. Once we accept this, the subtleties of racism become clearer.

21. Alexis Artwohl, and Loren W. Christensen, *Deadly Force Encounters: What Cops Need to Know to Mentally and Physically Prepare for a Gunfight* (Boulder, CO: Paladin Press, 1997), 38.

22. Artwohl and Christensen, *Deadly Force Encounters*, 51.

23. There is enough probable cause in the area of deadly police force and the autonomic nervous system that you might consider setting up a Google Alert when new books and papers are published on the subject. The ability to do this is like having an assistant on the constant lookout for information that you need to do your job. You can get notifications when the authors you like to read publish new books and articles, and if you are a detective you can even set up alerts for subjects pertinent to a criminal investigation. It's like having a partner that never sleeps.

24. Allport, *The Nature of Prejudice*, 488-492.

25. Allport, *The Nature of Prejudice*, 436.

26. Barrett, *How Emotions Are Made*, 151.

27. De Waal, *Mama's Last Hug*, 256.

28. Barrett, *How Emotions Are Made*, 154.

29. Allport, *The Nature of Prejudice*, 8.

30. *Comes a Horseman*, directed by Alan J. Pakula, 1978 (Los Angeles: Chartoff-Winkler Productions).

31. This is not the same example, but the point it makes is similar: Alanna Vagianos, "Why Women Surgeons Around the World Are Recreating This Magazine Cover," *Huffington Post*, April 11, 2017, https://www.huffingtonpost.com/entry/women-around-the-world-re-created-this-magazine-cover-to-show-what-a-surgeon-looks-like_us_58ed0958e4b0c89f9121ef24.

32. A considerable number of the books in this bibliography make this argument in myriad ways.

33. Matthew, *Just Medicine*.

34. For an up-to-date description, along with current news about the IAT, do a Google search for IAT and Harvard University, and you will likely still be able to find a page where visitors are invited to take the tests.

35. Bloom, *Just Babies*, 125. Paul Bloom observes, "It is one of the more interesting discoveries of psychology that even the least racist people in the world have unconscious racial biases. A black face, flashed on a computer screen too fast to consciously perceive, tends to trigger thoughts of aggression among white subjects; they are more likely to complete a word fragment like 'HA_E' as 'HATE.'"

36. Henry David Thoreau, *The Portable Thoreau*, ed. Carl Bode (New York: Penguin Books, 1947), 109-137.

37. Nicholas Wade, *Before the Dawn: Recovering the Lost History of Our Ancestors* (New York: The Penguin Press, 2006). This controversial book is a great place to start to explore the findings of human savagery suggested by the fossil record of prehistory. This argument is not settled and will likely remain unsettled. It's also very likely that enough differences existed in prehistorical tribes to make all sorts of cases for peace and all-out war.

38. Pinker, *The Better Angels*. Pinker offers a compelling history that shows a gradual decline in violence.

39. Pinker, *The Better Angels*. A very good book to reread every time you become thoroughly discouraged with the social trajectory of human culture with regard to violence and war.

40. Allport, *The Nature of Prejudice*; Berreby, *Us and Them*; Jonathan Kahn, *Race on the Brain: What Implicit Bias Gets Wrong about the Struggle for Racial Justice* (New York: Columbia University Press, 2017); Keen, *Faces of the Enemy*; Kendi, *Stamped from the Beginning*; Ian Haney Lopez, *Dog Whistle Politics: How Coded Racial Appeals Have Reinvented Racism and Wrecked the Middle Class* (New York: Oxford University Press, 2014); Stephen Pinker, *Enlightenment Now: The Case for Reason, Science, Humanism, and Progress* (New York: Viking, 2018), 215-216; Howard J. Ross, *Everyday Bias: Identifying and Navigating Unconscious Judgments in Our Daily Lives* (Lanham, Maryland: Rowman & Littlefield, 2014); and Sapolsky, *Behave*. As previously noted, explicit bias is a conscious

acknowledgment of learned prejudice, sometimes openly expressed or often felt, but kept private, while implicit bias is something you assume subconsciously, but don't know that you know.

41. Sapolsky, *Behave*, 328-344.
42. It feels like the truth, because our subconscious is duty-bound to "peg" reality for us—and our frontal cortex feels compelled to explain our behavior and put the best face on it.
43. Ross, *Everyday Bias*.
44. Sapolsky, *Behave*, 116-117, 135, 389, 614.
45. David Eagleman, *Incognito: The Secret Lives of the Brain* (New York: Random House, 2011), 126. For this reason, it's important to remember you're always in danger of confusing the past with the present.
46. Sapolsky, *Behave*, 391-392.
47. Sapolsky, *Behave*, 392.
48. There is lots of information online on this subject, including books, papers and videos of psychological research.
49. Jill Ballante, and Chuck Hadad, "Study: White and black children biased toward lighter skin," *CNN*, May 14, 2010, http://www.cnn.com/2010/US/05/13/doll.study/index.html. Google "black and white doll studies," and you will find research articles and YouTube videos showing that children, both black and white, intuit an early preference for white over black.
50. Margaret Hagerman, *White Kids: Growing Up with Privilege in a Racially Divided America* (New York: New York University Press, 2018). This work follows students through two years of interviews, with follow-ups showing that, for the most part, racist attitudes learned early do not change much over time.
51. Barrett, *How Emotions Are Made*, xii, 27, 31, 82, 118, 126, 132, 141, 241.
52. Barrett, *How Emotions Are Made*, 27-31, 153.
53. Berns, *Iconoclast*, 76; Sapolsky, *Behave*, 27. Sapolsky reminds us that, "Emotions filter the nature and accuracy of what is remembered."
54. Berns, *Iconoclast*, 76, 143, 152-153.
55. Berns, *Iconoclast*, 78-79.
56. Sapolsky, *Behave*, 403.
57. Sapolsky, *Why Zebras Don't Get Ulcers*, 362-263. Sapolsky questions the notion that we human beings truly have ranks, noting that we belong to numerous ranking systems at the same time. I'm sympathetic in that I do suspect there are people among us who are not much affected by rank. But for police officers, I believe it is a different story. A simple call to 911 is a request for some dominance, and upon the arrival of the police at the scene, this ranking will play out.

USING FORCE APPROPRIATELY

1. Rahtz, *Understanding the Use of Force*, 47.
2. I arrested a couple of high school football coaches once with a partner;

I don't recall the nature of the call or the reason for the arrest, but I do remember that the coach I arrested flinched when I moved to handcuff him, and I responded by choking him down. His reaction, and my own, have stayed with me to this day, since I almost immediately realized the reaction I'd taken for resistance was very likely involuntary, from an inability to readily accept the reality of what was happening to him.

3. Rahtz, *Understanding the Use of Force*, 136.

4. Matt Stroud, *Thin Blue Lie: The Failure of High-Tech Policing* (New York: Metropolitan Books, 2019), 11, 212-214. Stroud explains that tasers do not reduce the use of firearms in policing, which is a common expectation, and in many cases they are lethal. This subject is worthy of further study.

5. Rahtz, *Understanding the Use of Force*, 50. I can find no measurable results in whether eliminating nightsticks has been effective or ineffective. Rahtz mentions one incident where the elimination of nightsticks or batons led to officers carrying metal flashlights which resulted in a death when a flashlight was used as a nightstick.

6. Panksepp and Biven, *Affective Neuroscience*, 215.

7. Sapolsky, *Behave*, 432. My take on this is simply that this subject is worthy of further study.

8. John Bargh, *Before You Know It: The Unconscious Reasons We Do What We Do* (New York: Touchstone, 2017), 272. He references Marcelo Medoza, Barbara Poblete, and Carlos Castillo, "Twitter Under Crisis: Can We Trust What We RT?" Paper presented at *Social Media Analytics*, January 2010, http://snap.stanford.edu/soma2010/papers/soma2010_11.pdf; and B. D. Stewart, and B. K. Payne, "Bringing Automatic Stereotyping Under Control: Implementation Intentions as Efficient Means of Thought Control," *Personality and Social Psychology Bulletin*, 34: 1332-1345, on this topic.

9. Fields, *Why We Snap*, 179.

10. Two books, both by Lt. Col Dave Grossman, are especially helpful in preparing you for life-threatening events: *On Combat: The Psychology and Physiology of Deadly Conflict in War and Peace*, and *On Killing: The Psychological Cost of Learning to Kill in War and Society*. Grossman offers exceptionally good advice about how the parasympathetic nervous system operates.

11. Rahtz, *Understanding the Use of Force*, 49.

12. Google "Black Lives Matter" for applicable URLs. This is another subject to keep abreast of because the Black Lives Matter movement amounts to a constant call for paying attention to police behavior and there is nothing to be gained by police officers and department spokesman arguing against these efforts. The only way to make progress here is with statistics that prove law enforcement behavior reinforces the declaration that black lives matter.

13. I realize this is a dangerous assumption on my part and I would not recommend that you take my experience in this incident as a need to read the mind of a suspect pointing a gun at you, because it might be the last thing you see. I would only remind you of the need for mindfulness.

14. After this incident was reported in our local newspaper, several people asked me if I was afraid, or in fear of my life. My answer was no, I was aware of the danger, but I was furious that this individual had broken into my home.

MEMO TO MANAGEMENT

1. Gilmartin, *Emotional Survival for Law Enforcement*.
2. Davis, *Policing the Black Man*, 173.
3. Robbin Shipp, Esq., and Nick Chiles, *Justice While Black: Helping African American Families Navigate and Survive the Criminal Justice System* (Chicago, IL: Bolden, 2014).
4. Kristian Williams, *Our Enemies in Blue: Police and Power in America* (Oakland, CA: AK Press, 2015). This is the third edition.
5. Williams, *Our Enemies in Blue*, 527-546.
6. D. Watkins, *The Beast Side: Living (and Dying) While Black in America* (New York: Hot Books, 2015), 126-127.
7. Carl Rowan, *The Coming Race War in America: A Wake-up Call* (New York: Little, Brown and Company, 1996), 282-287.
8. Rowan, *The Coming Race War*, 282-283.
9. Rowan, *The Coming Race War*, 10-12, 14-15, 36, 283-284, 291, 295. *The Turner Diaries* is a 1978 novel by William Luther Pierce under the pseudonym Andrew Macdonald. The book, which became an instant hit with hate groups, depicts a violent revolution incited by a war about race.
10. Rowan, *The Coming Race War*, 292-293.
11. Rowan, *The Coming Race War*, 298.
12. Carol Anderson, *White Rage: The Unspoken Truth of Our Racial Divide* (New York: Bloomsbury, 2017), 6.
13. Matthew Horace, and Ron Harris, *The Black and the Blue: A Cop Reveals the Crimes, Racism, and Injustice in America's Law Enforcement* (New York: Hachette Books, 2018).
14. Horace and Harris, *The Black and the Blue*, 213.
15. Stamper, *To Protect and Serve*, 45.
16. Horace and Harris, *The Black and the Blue*, xv.
17. Deray Mckesson, *On the Other Side of Freedom: The Case for Hope* (New York: Viking, 2018), 45.
18. Mckesson, *On the Other Side of Freedom*, 47.
19. Mckesson, *On the Other Side of Freedom*, 75.
20. Christakis, *Blueprint*, 272. Christakis notes that political polarization in America has been exacerbated by the loss of the former Soviet Union as a common enemy.
21. Berreby, *Us and Them*, 93-116.
22. Butler, *Chokehold*, 81. The stop-and-frisk statistics are indeed telling.
23. Lawrence O'Donnell, *Deadly Force: A Police Shooting and My Family's Search for the Truth* (New York: William Morrow, 1983), viii.

24. O'Donnell, *Deadly Force*, ix.

25. O'Donnell, *Deadly Force*, 138. We had an incident in Dallas in October 1967 in which a Dallas officer named Ray Blades, someone whom I had worked with as a partner on occasion, was caught burglarizing a store in the Oak Cliff section of Dallas. We were so incensed that for months, that I'm aware of, and maybe years, police officers stopped Blades every time they saw him and arrested him whenever possible because of the embarrassment he had brought to the department. In O'Donnell's case I can imagine the burglar who was caught and arrested saying before a judge, "Your honor, my partner in crime was a Boston police sergeant but they let him go. Why me?"

26. Tom Jackman, "New Orleans Police Pioneer New Way to Stop Misconduct, Remove 'Blue Wall of Silence,'" *Washington Post*, January 24, 2019, https://www.washingtonpost.com/crime-law/2019/01/24/new-orleans-police-pioneer-new-way-stop-misconduct-remove-blue-wall-silence/.

27. Albert Fox Cahn, "How bodycams distort real life," *The New York Times*, August 8, 2019, https://www.nytimes.com/2019/08/08/opinion/bodycams-privacy.html. This piece by Albert Fox Cahn calls attention to the fact that bodycams distort reality by taking the perspective of the viewer and this is easy to understand, but one view is better than none.

28. Tom Jackman, "Federal task force bans body cameras, so Atlanta police pull out. Others may follow," *Washington Post*, June 14, 2019, https://www.washingtonpost.com/crime-law/2019/06/14/federal-task-forces-ban-body-cameras-so-atlanta-police-pull-out-others-may-follow/. Unfortunately, Justice Department officers do not currently allow bodycams.

29. Charles M. Blow, *Fire Shut Up in My Bones: A Memoir* (New York: Mariner Books, 2015), 175. Charles M. Blow is my favorite newspaper columnist. He argues that poetic justice resides in the fact that racism compromises, diminishes, and deflates the stature of racists. See Charles M. Blow, "On Race: The Moral High Ground," *New York Times*, May 31, 2018, https://www.nytimes.com/2018/05/31/opinion/roseanne-valerie-jarrett-race-trump.html.

30. Michelle Lou, and Brandon Griggs, "A proposed Tennessee law would make it a felony for police officers to disable their body cams," *CNN*, February 27, 2019, https://www.cnn.com/2019/02/27/us/tennessee-body-cam-felony-trnd/index.html.

31. Robert A. Burton, *On Being Certain: Believing You Are Right Even When You're Not* (New York: St. Martin's Press, 2008), 218.

32. Delattre, *Character and Cops*, 311.

33. Jill Leovy, *Ghettoside: A True Story of Murder in America* (New York: Spiegel & Grau, 2015), 25. As complaints accumulated against them, they became less transferable to other districts.

34. *USA Today* has created an online searchable database of police officers found unfit for duty.

35. Sapolsky, *Behave*. This book is an excellent introduction to the psychology of human behavior and on myriad matters which are very important to police work.

36. David J. Thomas, *The State of American Policing: Psychology, Behavior, Problems and Solutions* (Santa Barbara, CA: Praeger, 2019), 113. Thomas says the "I was in fear of my life" is used so often in suspicious circumstances that those in minority communities find it difficult to believe.

37. Alan Blinder, "Michael Slager, Officer in Walter Scott Shooting, Gets 20-Year Sentence," *New York Times*, December 7, 2017, https://www.nytimes.com/2017/12/07/us/michael-slager-sentence-walter-scott.html.

38. Tasha Tsiperas, " 'This is a start,' says Jordan Edwards' mother after ex-cop Roy Oliver gets 15 years for murdering 15-year-old," *The Dallas Morning News*, August 30, 2018, https://www.dallasnews.com/news/courts/2018/08/29/defense-hopes-show-jury-real-roy-oliver-seeking-mercy-ex-cop-murdered-jordan-edwards.

39. If you have ever hunted moose or deer, the excitement of seeing your quarry takes on a new perspective when there are severe penalties for shooting an animal whose antlers don't meet regulation requirements. Using an animal comparison may seem inappropriate for obvious reasons, but the awareness aspect is precisely the same: A compelling need to pay attention to what you are looking at only works if it is manifest. And another hunting example is applicable. If you have ever gone hunting and created an image of the animal you are hunting out of trees and brush, because we frequently see what we expect to see, and if you can make a deer out of a tree stump, you can make a gun out of a cell phone.

40. Jake Bleiberg, "Slain man's brother, judge, hug ex-cop sentenced to 10 years," *AP News*, October 2, 2019, https://www.apnews.com/1efb02d5b6d2431db247214c6fa71488.

41. Stamper, *Breaking Rank*, 93.

42. Stamper, *Breaking Rank*, 261.

43. Stamper, *To Protect and Serve*, 67.

44. Stamper, *To Protect and Serve*, 77.

45. Panksepp, and Biven, *The Archaeology of Mind*, 176.

46. Gavin De Becker, *The Gift of Fear: Survival Signals That Protect Us from Violence* (New York: Dell Publishing, 1997).

47. Zachary Siegel, "Is the Psychology of Deadly Force Ready for the Courts?" *Scientific American*, December 20, 2018, https://www.scientificamerican.com/article/is-the-psychology-of-deadly-force-ready-for-the-courts/.

48. "Laquan MacDonald shooting video," YouTube video, 1:55, posted by "Chicago Sun-Times," August 24, 2018, https://www.youtube.com/watch?v=xaXuT9sxCnI.

49. Mark Guarino, and Mark Berman, "Chicago police officer Jason Van Dyke convicted of second-degree murder for killing Laquan MacDonald," *Washington Post*, October 5, 2018, https://www.washingtonpost.com/news/post-nation/wp/2018/10/05/chicago-police-officer-jason-van-dyke-convicted-of-second-degree-murder-for-killing-laquan-mcdonald/?noredirect=on&utm_term=.ec6952bb49fe.

50. In my view, while a common psychological defense of police officers might

bring much-needed attention to the mental health conditions of police officers, this subject is so complex that the appearance of pseudoscience could make the politicization worse and set the reputation of law enforcement back even further, if defense strategies become a regular news feature. In any event, my hope is that more of the work of biological scientists can be brought to bear to study what is occurring when mistakes cost the lives of innocent people and the lives of peace officers.

POLITICS AND POLICE

1. Ashley Southal, "Daniel Pantaleo, Officer Who Held Eric Garner in Chokehold, Is Fired," *The New York Times*, August 19, 2019, https://www.nytimes.com/2019/08/19/nyregion/daniel-pantaleo-fired.html. On August 19, 2018, Officer Daniel Pantaleo was fired from the NYPD by Commissioner James P. O'Neill for violating the department policy on chokeholds in the case of Eric Garner. The Police Benevolent Association president Patrick J. Lynch said in a statement, "We will uphold our oath, but we cannot and will not do so by needlessly jeopardizing our careers or personal safety." The only thing accomplished in a public statement like this is to increase the feelings of us versus them between the police and the public. This is another example of a missed opportunity to assure the public that the police are on their side.

2. Bill Bishop, with Robert G. Cushing, *The Big Sort: Why the Clustering of Like-Minded America is Tearing Us Apart* (New York: Houghton Mifflin, 2008). *The Big Sort* shows how we are geographically coming together and apart at the same time.

3. There is so much research going on in this field that a Google search for papers and books is the best way to get the latest information.

4. A Google search is recommended here as well for books and papers because this is increasingly a hot topic.

5. Eberhardt, *Biased*, 68, 70, 73, 76, 78, 83, 101-103. Eberhardt cites studies that not only support the fact that lethal force is used more often on black men, but that so is just about every other abuse resulting from implicit and explicit racism, from excessive stops and searches to just being more disrespectful of black people during routine police stops. This point of contention has inspired statistical war games in which truth is easily obscured by ideology. I've read defensive statements by police spokesman who claim that black men simply commit more crimes than white men, thus that explains the disparity, but this argument falls flat in view of the mounting evidence.

6. Cheryl Dorsey, *Black and Blue: The Creation of a Social Advocate* (Los Angeles, CA: Dorsey, 2018), 228.

7. Ellie Bufkin, " 'Zero tolerance for resisting police': Barr slams law enforcement protesters," *Washington Examiner*, August 14, 2019, https://www.washingtonexaminer.com/news/zero-tolerance-for-resisting-police-

barr-slams-law-enforcement-protesters.

8. That these books appear popular because of 4 stars on Amazon is simply evidence of a bias about law enforcement that in my view is evidence of a superficial understanding of the subject.

9. Heather Mac Donald, *The War on Cops: How the New Attack on Law and Order Makes Everyone Less Safe* (New York: Encounter Books, 2016), 59.

10. Mac Donald, *The War on Cops*, 17; The Editorial Board, "The Meaning of the Ferguson Riots," *The New York Times*, November 25, 2014, https://www.nytimes.com/2014/11/26/opinion/the-meaning-of-the-ferguson-riots.html.

11. David Clarke, Jr., *Cop Under Fire: Moving Beyond Hashtags of Race, Crime and Politics for a Better America* (Franklin, TN: Worthy Publishing, 2017), 35.

12. Clarke, *Cop Under Fire*, 35. This is pure political partisan exaggeration for the simple purpose of appealing to one faction while alienating others, and when peace officers do this there is no upside.

13. Clarke, *Cop Under Fire*, 119.

14. Greg Lukianoff, and Jonathan Haidt, *The Coddling of the American Mind: How Good Intentions and Bad Ideas are Setting Up a Generation for Failure* (New York: Penguin, 2018), 88-89, 126.

15. Lukianoff and Haidt, *The Coddling of the American Mind*. The point of this book is that we have reached a point in which college students have become so intolerant of opposing views that they would rather shout people down than listen to opinions that they don't agree with. This is a growing concern for law enforcement, and it needs to be handled carefully.

16. Clarke, *Cop Under Fire*. This book is a disgrace to the honorable field of law enforcement, and David Clarke is an iconic example of the kind of individual who should not under any circumstance be allowed to serve as a peace officer.

17. Barack H. Obama, *The Audacity of Hope: Thoughts on Reclaiming the American Dream* (New York: Crown Publishing Group, 2006), 55.

18. Clarke, *Cop Under Fire*, 230.

19. You can search the keywords and listen to or read Trump's speech where he suggests there is no need for the police to worry about roughing people up. His crowd answered with laughter.

20. In writing this book, I have read, and read about, so many books and reports with documented cases of abuses of police behavior, so many of which are so horrendous and mind numbing that it's hard to keep going. The examples listed in the books in this bibliography are enough to permanently disabuse one of positive notions about law enforcement that it will take an enormous effort for police departments to renew the faith in law enforcement of those of us who have read them.

21. Mark Berman, "Trump tells police not to worry about injuring suspects during arrests," *The Washington Post*, July 28, 2017, https://www.washingtonpost.com/news/post-nation/wp/2017/07/28/trump-tells-police-not-to-worry-about-injuring-suspects-during-arrests/?utm_term=.4fea0acc6d10.

22. Both letters are available online by searching for the respective organizations.

23. Thoreau, *The Portable Thoreau*.

24. Thoreau, *The Portable Thoreau*, 136-137.

25. Donna Zuckerberg, *Not All Dead White Men: Classics and Misogyny in the Digital Age* (Cambridge, MA: Harvard University Press, 2018).

26. Charlie May, "FBI investigated white supremacists infiltrating law enforcement agencies: A report," *Salon.com*, January 31, 2017, https://www.salon.com/2017/01/31/fbi-investigating-white-supremacists-infiltrating-law-enforcement-agencies-report/.

27. Dorsey, *Black and Blue*, 133. Retired LAPD Sgt. Cheryl Dorsey says the KKK is making its presence known in policing.

28. *The New York Times* has numerous reports on the subject of prosecutorial abuse: January 4, 2014, "Rampant Prosecutorial Misconduct"; January 17, 2018, "Prosecutors Had the Wrong Man. They Prosecuted Him Anyway"; June 18, 2018, "What Happens When Prosecutors Break the Law?" These stories are only the tip of the iceberg. This is another subject where a Google alert can help with keeping you updated about the quest for justice.

29. Jeffrey Ian Ross, and Stephen C. Richards, *Beyond Bars: Rejoining Society After Prison* (New York: Penguin, 2009), 150-153. While in prison, credit card and consumer debt continue to grow interest, and upon release from prison, one is for all practical purposes broke, unemployable, ineligible for credit and in many cases in arrears on child support.

30. Charles Hayes, *Existential Aspirations: Reflections of a Self-taught Philosopher* (Wasilla, AK: Autodidactic Press, 2010a), 65-67.

31. Danielle Sered, *Until We Reckon: Violence, Mass Incarceration, and A Road to Repair* (New York: The New Press, 2019), 89.

32. Tamler Sommers, *Why Honor Matters* (New York: Basic Books, 2018), 157.

33. Alexander, *The New Jim Crow*, 138.

34. Dmitry Orlov, *Reinventing Collapse: The Soviet Example and American Prospects* (Gabriola Island, BC, Canada: New Society Publishers, 2008), 42-43.

35. David Couper, *Arrested Development: A Veteran Police Chief Sounds Off About Protest, Racism, Corruption and the Seven Steps Necessary to Improve Our Nation's Police* (Blue Mounds, WI: New Journey Press, 2012), 157; David Couper, *Telling It Like It Is: Couper On Cops* (Blue Mounds, WI: New Journey Press, 2017), 112.

36. Couper, *Arrested Development*, 13.

37. Couper, *Arrested Development*, 72.

38. Couper, *Arrested Development*, 90.

39. Couper, *Arrested Development*, 159.

40. Couper, *Telling It Like It Is*, 30.

41. David C. Couper, *Improving Police* (blog). October 15, 2019, https://improvingpolice.wordpress.com/.

ROLL CALL

1. Delattre, *Character and Cops*, 158. Delattre mentions William James' recommendation about making a habit as quickly as possible, and this is the time to do it.
2. Stephen D. Brookfield, *Teaching for Critical Thinking: Tools and Techniques to Help Students Question Their Assumptions* (San Francisco: Jossey-Bass, 2012), 11, 71.
3. Jane Jacobs, *Dark Age Ahead* (New York: Random House, 2004), 131-132.
4. Martin Buber, *I and Thou* (New York: Touchstone, 1970).
5. Buber, *I and Thou*, 103.
6. Chris Hayes, *A Colony in a Nation* (New York: W.W. Norton, 2017). No relation to me.
7. John F. Schumaker, *The Age of Insanity: Modernity and Mental Health* (Westport, CT: Praeger Publishers, 2001), 176.
8. William Easterly, *The Tyranny of Experts: Economists, Dictators and the Forgotten Rights of the Poor* (New York: Basic Books, 2013), 7. He further points out that the absence of technical solutions is a symptom and not the cause of poverty.
9. Schumaker, *The Age of Insanity*, 176.
10. Inspector Edward Preston.
11. John Stuart Mill, "On Liberty," in *Great Books of the Western World*, ed. Robert Maynard (Chicago, IL: Encyclopedia Britannica, 1952), 43: 271.
12. Mill, "On Liberty," 43: 273.
13. Abraham H. Maslow, *Motivation and Personality* (New York: Harper and Row, 1954).
14. Richard Wrangham, *The Goodness Paradox: The Strange Relationship Between Virtue and Violence in Human Evolution* (New York: Pantheon Books, 2019), 280.
15. Cornel West, *Race Matters* (Boston: Beacon Press, 1993), 15. I get this feeling especially when reading *Dallas 1963*, the book that covers the time from 1960 up to the assassination of JFK. I joined the Marines on my 17th birthday and it's so easy to forget how some things have changed and others have remained the same.
16. Charles D. Hayes, "Police Authority and Racism," *LA Progressive*, August 1, 2009, https://www.laprogressive.com/police-racist-abuse/.
17. At the time of publication, the opioid epidemic is mostly in white neighborhoods. Google it and set up an alert for your geographic region because, regardless of your duties in law enforcement, this is very likely information that will prove useful to you.
18. Milton Friedman, and Thomas Szasz, *On Liberty and Drugs: Essay of the Free Market and Prohibition* (Washington, D.C. The Drug Policy Foundation, 1992), 70. "The case for prohibiting drugs is exactly as strong and as weak as the case for prohibiting people from overeating," say Friedman and Szasz. "We all know that overeating causes more deaths than drugs do." Of course, this was long before the opioid crisis.

19. *The Constitution of the United States*, National Archives, 2019, https://www.archives.gov/founding-docs/constitution.
20. Butler, *Chokehold*, 171.
21. Charles Murray, *Coming Apart: The State of White America 1960-2010* (New York: Crown Forum, 2012), 181.
22. Alexandra Natapoff, *Punishment Without Crime: How Our Massive Misdemeanor System Traps the Innocent and Makes America More Unequal* (New York: Basic Books, 2018), 208-209.
23. Thomas Abt, *Bleeding Out: The Devastating Consequences of Urban Violence—and a Bold New Plan for Peace in the Streets* (New York: Basic Books, 2019), 120. Abt writes, "Criminologists have demonstrated that policing works best when focused on high-activity places. When there are more officers in an area, would-be shooters worry more about getting arrested and refrain from violence." It is my conclusion that so-called "hot-spot attention" works best if the officers involved focus on violence and not petty offenses. Making the community residents feel safe should be the priority.
24. United States Department of Justice, "Investigation of the Ferguson Police Department."
25. Kathleen Hall Jamieson, *Cyber War: What We Don't, Can't, and Do Know* (New York: Oxford University Press, 2018), 86-91. Every police department in America should be hyperaware of this threat.
26. Stroud, *Thin Blue Lie*, 76. Politics indeed. Stroud explains that the Broken Windows ideology was a refutation of and a backlash to a study by the Johnson Administration, "The Challenge of Crime in a Free Society." This study will be discussed in the Epilogue.
27. Howard Rahtz, *Race, Riots, and the Police* (Boulder, CO: Lynne Rienner Publishers, 2016), 166-167. Rahtz goes on to remind us of the danger officers face in revenue-enhancement traffic stops, adding that "The relationship of aggressive policing to crime control and public safety is nebulous at best."
28. Issa Kohler Hausmann, *Misdemeanorland: Criminal Courts and Social Control in an Age of Broken Windows Policing* (Princeton, NJ: Princeton University Press, 2018), 7-8, 11.
29. Hayes, *A Colony in a Nation*, 64.
30. Kris Van Cleave, "Deaths at red lights have surged since 2012, AAA study finds," *CBS News*, August 29, 2019, https://www.cbsnews.com/news/aaa-study-deaths-at-red-lights-have-surged-2019-08-29/.
31. Hausmann, *Misdemeanorland*, 25. Hausmann writes about the origins of Broken Windows Policing and states that it was developed from the work of political scientists James Q. Wilson and George L. Kelling and an article they wrote in 1982.
32. Hausmann, *Misdemeanorland*, 27.
33. Jerry Z. Muller, *The Tyranny of Metrics* (Princeton, NJ: Princeton University Press, 2018), 125-129. Muller calls our attention to the fascination with

metrics depicted in David Simon's television series *The Wire*, which in my view is one of the best shows of its kind in existence.

34. Hayes, *A Colony in a Nation*, 174.
35. Sue Rahr, and Stephen K. Rice, "From Warriors to Guardians: Recommitting American Police Culture to Democratic Ideals," *New Perspectives in Policing Bulletin* (Washington, DC: U.S. Department of Justice, National Institute of Justice, 2015), NCJ 248654, https://www.ncjrs.gov/pdffiles1/nij/248654.pdf.
36. Plato, "The Dialogues," in *Great Books of the Western World*, trans. by Benjamin Jowett (Chicago, IL: Encyclopedia Britannica, 1952) 7: 301.
37. Plato, "The Dialogues," 7: 319-320.
38. Plato, "The Dialogues," 7: 339.
39. Delattre, *Character and Cops*, 18.
40. Walter Lippmann, *Public Opinion* (New York: Simon and Schuster, 1922).
41. Sapolsky, *Behave*, 403.
42. Rahtz, *Understanding the Use of Force*, 35.
43. Rahtz, *Understanding the Use of Force*, 39.
44. Sered, *Until We Reckon*, 235.
45. Hari, *Chasing the Scream*.
46. Robert Ardrey, *The Territorial Imperative: A Personal Inquiry into the Animal Origins of Property and Nations* (New York: Dell Publishing, 1966), 217.
47. Wilson, *The Origins of Creativity*, 125.
48. An existential education is to become so well-versed in the humanities that you can dissipate your own existential angst that comes part and parcel with the human condition without the need to find fault with other people for keeping you from getting what you consider your due in life.
49. Fuller, *Somebodies and Nobodies*, 2, 5-6. Fuller says, "rankism is the mother of all isms, that racism, sexism, and ageism are subspecies of rankism and that the accompanying indignity festers causing angst and resentment."
50. Paul J. Zak, *The Moral Molecule: How Trust Works* (New York: Plume, 2013).
51. Delattre, *Character and Cops*, 230-231. A grave danger here is that these feelings of dominance very often become self-justifying, or what Delattre refers to as "Noble Cause Corruption and Excusable Wrongdoing."
52. Fields, *Why We Snap*.
53. Radley Balko, *Rise of the Warrior Cop: The Militarization of America's Police Forces* (New York: Public Affairs, 2014), 334.
54. Balko, *Rise of the Warrior Cop*, xv.
55. Balko, *Rise of the Warrior Cop*, 35.
56. Thomas, *The State of American Policing*, 140. Thomas says the transition toward militarization began when the 6-shot revolver was replaced with semiautomatic pistols which held 15 rounds.
57. There are lots of studies being conducted in this arena. Put words like "watching eyes effects" and "illusions of being observed" in Google for the latest information.

58. This thread reminds me of the reality television shows that feature live police action like *Live PD*. While I can see value in watching these programs for training purposes, I personally find them distasteful as entertainment.

59. Malcolm Gladwell, *Talking to Strangers: What We Should Know About the People We Don't Know* (New York: Little Brown and Company, 2019), 1-13, 313-342.

60. There is ample probable cause here to research how the facial expressions of the mentally ill or people with developmental disorders might not typically conform to what we are accustomed to seeing. In addition, the assumptions we make about body language and facial expressions are not always accurate. Joe Navarro, a former FBI agent who now writes and speaks about body language and facial expressions states that many behaviors that people ascribe to dishonesty are in fact self-soothing behaviors which occur in response to stress, e.g., crossing the arms, touching the face, covering the mouth, in a talk available from WIRED, "Former FBI Agent Explains How to Read Body Language | Tradecraft | WIRED," YouTube Video, 14:43, May 21, 2019, https://www.youtube.com/watch?v=4jwUXV4QaTw. Navarro has also written a number of books on the topic, including *Clues to Deceit: A Practical List*.

TENDING TO COMMUNITY

1. Stamper, *Breaking Rank*, 353.

2. Cass R. Sunstein, *On Freedom* (Princeton, NJ: Princeton University Press, 2019), 2, 29.

3. David Sloan Wilson, *This View of Life: Completing the Darwinian Revolution* (New York: Pantheon Books, 2019), 117-119.

4. Stamper, *Breaking Rank*, 353.

5. Indeed, if the work of many of those in academia becomes too publicly popular it frequently threatens their standing.

6. Jeff Schmidt, *Disciplined Minds: A Critical Look at Salaried Professionals and the Soul-Battering System that Shapes their Lives* (Boston, MA: Rowan & Littlefield, 2000), 250-251.

7. Schmidt, *Disciplined Minds*, 12-15.

8. This should not, however, be considered a one-sided argument; many college and university professors would be eager to assist law enforcement agencies if asked.

9. Schmidt, *Disciplined Minds*, 250-251.

10. William Luke Hunt, *The Retrieval of Liberalism in Policing* (New York: Oxford University, 2019), 30-36.

11. Hunt, *The Retrieval of Liberalism*. Even the retail price of this book shows that it is only expected to be read by a small cadre of academics.

12. Schmidt, *Disciplined Minds*, 33.

13. Schmidt, *Disciplined Minds*, 33.

14. Dorsey, *Black and Blue*, 5, 252. Retired Los Angeles police sergeant Cheryl

Dorsey calls this "contempt of cop." It is in my view evidence of an enlarged amygdala—an overexposure to stress in which one becomes hypersensitive to insult.

15. Taylor, *Brainwashing*.
16. Fields, *Why We Snap*, 243.
17. Fields, *Why We Snap*, 249.
18. The current percentage of women in law enforcement is somewhere in the vicinity of 10 to 15 percent.
19. Taylor, *Brainwashing*, 168.
20. Churchland, *Touching a Nerve*, 101. Churchland writes, "When animals are in high alert against danger, when they are preparing to fight or flee, stress hormones are high and oxytocin levels are low. When the threat has passed, and you are among friends, hugging and chatting, stress hormones back off and oxytocin levels surge."
21. Taylor, *Brainwashing*, 28.
22. Zak, *The Moral Molecule*, 83.
23. Zak, *The Moral Molecule*, 84.
24. Zak, *The Moral Molecule*, 187.
25. David Simon, *Homicide: A Year on the Killing Streets* (New York: Picador, 1991), 47.
26. Fields, *Why We Snap*, 198-199.
27. Panksepp and Biven, *The Archaeology of Mind*, 155. Panksepp and Biven also point out the role testosterone plays in dominance, particularly among males.
28. Stamper, *To Protect and Serve*, 220.
29. Stamper, *To Protect and Serve*, 221-225.
30. Stamper, *Breaking Rank*, 117.
31. Delattre, *Character and Cops*, 271.
32. Such biases show up under many different guises. In a June 2017 report, Vera Bergengruen of the McClatchy Washington Bureau reported that in every branch of our military service organizations, black men face harsher military punishments than white men.
33. Adam Plantinga, *Police Craft: What Cops Know About Crime, Community and Violence* (Fresno, CA: Quill Driver Books, 2018), 218-221.
34. Nick Selby, Ben Singleton, and Ed Flosi, *In Context: Understanding Police Killings of Unarmed Civilians* (St. Augustine, FL: Contextual Press, 2016), 72. This book does seem to me to be an attempt to be objective, but it was published in 2016, and although it mentions the DOJ Report on the Ferguson Police Department in 2015, it does not report on the findings and that to me is disappointing.
35. Pinker, *Enlightenment Now*, 215-216.
36. Pinker, *Enlightenment Now*, 175.
37. Logan Struther, Charles Menifield, and Geiguen Shin, "We gathered data on every confirmed, line-of-duty killing of a civilian in 2014 and 2015. Here's what we found," *The Washington Post*, August 29, 2018, https://www.

washingtonpost.com/news/monkey-cage/wp/2018/08/29/we-gathered-data-on-every-confirmed-line-of-duty-police-killing-of-a-civilian-in-2014-and-2015-heres-what-we-found/?utm_term=.0183ddf25f99.

38. Scottie Andrew, "Police Are Three Times More Likely To Kill Black Men, Not A Problem Confined to A Single Region," *Newsweek*, July 23, 2018, https://www.newsweek.com/black-men-three-times-likely-be-killed-police-1037922.

39. Butler, *Chokehold*, 2.

40. Fields, *Why We Snap*, 38-43.

41. Martinez, *Creating Freedom*, 57.

42. Robert C. Solomon, *A Passion for Justice: Emotions and the Origins of the Social Contract* (New York: Addison-Wesley, 1990), 3.

43. Solomon, *A Passion for Justice*, 32-33.

44. Solomon, *A Passion for Justice*, 54.

45. Solomon, *A Passion for Justice*, 71.

46. Solomon, *A Passion for Justice*, 70.

47. Solomon, *A Passion for Justice*, 73.

48. Rahr and Rice, "From Warriors to Guardians"; Stamper, *To Protect and Serve*, 231.

49. Stamper, *To Protect and Serve*, 231.

50. Stamper, *Breaking Rank*, 387.

51. Solomon, *A Passion for Justice*, 94-95

52. Solomon, *A Passion for Justice*, 98.

53. Solomon, *A Passion for Justice*, 138-144.

54. Solomon, *A Passion for Justice*, 145.

55. Solomon, *A Passion for Justice*, 152.

56. Solomon, *A Passion for Justice*, 225.

57. Solomon, *A Passion for Justice*, 243.

58. Solomon, *A Passion for Justice*, 243.

59. Solomon, *A Passion for Justice*, 245.

60. Stevenson, *Just Mercy*, 18.

LEARNING CODE 3

1. Mattis, *Call Sign Chaos*, 42.

2. Sapolsky, *Behave*, 605.

3. Brookfield, *Teaching Critical Thinking*, 20.

4. Thomas, *The State of American Policing*, 173.

5. Stamper, *Breaking Rank*, 387.

6. Shortly after I published *Self-University*, adult educator Peter Jarvis came to Anchorage and he audited some university courses. One of the professors at Alaska Pacific University gave him a copy of my book and I was invited to sit in a class over several days. I participated in the discussion that Peter Jarvis conducted, and he offered to enroll me in his doctoral program in the UK. A local professor asked him how he would do that, being that I did

not have a college degree, and he said he would do it the same way Harvard does on occasion.

7. Peter Jarvis, *Paradoxes of Learning: On Becoming an Individual in Society* (San Francisco, CA: Jossey Bass, 1992), 9.

8. Scotty Barry Kaufman, "Who Created Maslow's Iconic Pyramid?" *Scientific American,* Beautiful Minds blog, April 23, 2019, https://blogs. scientificamerican.com/beautiful-minds/who-created-maslows-iconic-pyramid/. In this piece, Kaufman speculates about where Abraham Maslow's Hierarchy of Needs really came from, suggesting that others were making similar arguments. My experience studying myriad subjects and reading voraciously is that it is a very common occurrence for many people far removed from one another to be thinking and making very similar arguments and this happens so often that it's very difficult to conclude that one person necessarily influenced another. All it takes to appreciate this is to become interested enough to get caught up in the pursuit of knowledge.

9. There are two documentaries on PBS, *Slavery by Another Name* and *Reconstruction: America After the Civil War,* which offer a good way to begin this historical inquiry. Some of the incidents in the films are hard to watch without taking time outs.

10. Here is an April 2019 nonpartisan exploration of the racial divide by the Pew Research Center that shows clearly a deep divide in black versus white attitudes about race in America. It is worth examining in detail: Juliana Menasce Horowitz, Anna Brown, and Kiana Cox, "Race in America 2019," *Pew Research Center,* April 9, 2019, https://www.pewsocialtrends. org/2019/04/09/race-in-america-2019/.

11. David Brooks, *The Second Mountain: The Quest for a Moral Life* (New York: Random House, 2019), xvi.

12. Brooks, *The Second Mountain,* 28, 36-37.

CONTEMPLATION AND SELF-REFLECTION

1. Ralph Waldo Emerson, *Emerson: Essays and Lectures* (New York: The Library of America, 1983), 297-298.

2. Emerson, *Emerson,* 298.

3. Eberhardt, *Biased,* 6.

4. Eberhardt, *Biased,* 12.

5. Eberhardt, *Biased,* 74-78.

6. "Project Implicit," Harvard University, accessed May 13, 2019, https:// implicit.harvard.edu/implicit/takeatest.html.

7. "Citizens Police Data Project," Invisible Institute, accessed September 9, 2019, http://invisible.institute/police-data. For example, this organization is dedicated to holding police officers accountable to the public they serve.

8. Chris Evatt, *The Myth of Free Will* (Sausalito, CA: Café Essays, 2010).

9. Sapolsky, *Behave,* 586-613, offers a fascinating discussion of this subject.

HONOR REVISITED: A TRUE-BLUE BIAS

1. Sapolsky, *Behave*, 266-273, 328-321.
2. Ernest Becker, *Escape from Evil* (New York: The Free Press, 1975), 14.
3. For all recorded history we have known of our tribalistic predilections, but it was only recently learned that oxytocin, the bonding chemical that brings us together, also predisposes us to come together to reject outsiders.
4. Robert Winston, *Human Instinct: How Our Primeval Impulses Shape Our Modern Lives* (New York: Bantam Press, 2002), 5. I take his notion that they were not subject to low-level stress to mean they were more accustomed to more of the kind of stress that represented real danger.
5. Abraham H. Maslow, *The Farther Reaches of Human Nature* (New York: Penguin Press, 1971).
6. Otto Rank, *Beyond Psychology* (New York: Dover, 1941), 13. Rank made this observation in the 1930s. He was a colleague of Sigmund Freud who later became a harsh critic of Freud.
7. Francis Fukuyama, *Identity: The Demand for Dignity and the Politics of Resentment* (New York: Farrar, Straus and Giroux, 2018), 49.
8. Fukuyama, *Identity*, 42-44.
9. Paul Shepard, *Coming Home to the Pleistocene* (Washington, DC: Island Press, 1998), 34. He further stated that "The health of a society is a measure of its freedom from stress, individual suffering, psychopathology, tyranny, and ecological dysfunction as a result of straying from the basic ancestral form."
10. De Waal, *Our Inner Ape*, 247.
11. Shepard, *Coming Home*, 72-73. Numerous studies suggest hunter/gatherer societies only required three or four hours a day of what we would call work. The phrase "nasty, brutish and short" is a quote from Thomas Hobbes' *Leviathan*.
12. Shepard, *The Only World We've Got* (San Francisco, CA: Sierra Club Books, 1996), 193.
13. Shepard, *The Only World We've Got*, 193.
14. Christopher Ryan, *Civilized to Death: The Price of Progress* (New York: Avid Reader Press, 2019), 168.
15. James Forman, Jr., *Locking Up Our Own: Crime and Punishment in Black America* (New York: Farrar, Straus and Giroux, 2017), 185-215. Yale law professor James Forman, Jr. describes Attorney General Eric Holder's efforts to protect black citizens by using pretext traffic stops in Washington, DC. Though born of good intentions to get guns off the street, I don't know how anyone can read this account and not see that the results are more harm than good.
16. John F. Pfaff, *Locked In: The True Causes of Mass Incarceration and How to Achieve Real Reform* (New York: Basic Books, 2017), 163.
17. Matt Ferner, "If You Want to Totally Change America's Criminal Justice System, You Need a Plan," *Huffington Post*, May 29, 2018, https://www.huffingtonpost.com/entry/fair-just-prosecution-criminal-justice-reform_us_5aff5a94e4b0463cdba1e59d.

18. Barrett, *How Emotions Are Made*, 235. Barrett writes, "Want to increase the likelihood of a conviction in a murder trial? Show the jury some gruesome photographic evidence. Tip the body budgets out of balance, and chances are they'll attribute their unpleasant affect to the defendant: I feel bad, therefore you must have done something bad, you are a bad person."

19. Adam Benforado, *Unfair: The New Science of Criminal Injustice* (New York: Crown Publishers, 2015), 39.

20. Leovy, *Ghettoside*. Leovy makes numerous references to a century ago when, in some communities, the murder of blacks by blacks was treated as being acceptable enough to result in lighter sentences for the accused.

21. Plato, "The Dialogues," 7: 346-349.

22. Sommers, *Why Honor Matters*, 185.

23. David M. Kennedy, *Don't Shoot: One Man, A Street Fellowship, and the End of Violence in Inner-City America* (New York: Bloomsbury, 2011), 16-20.

24. Kennedy, *Don't Shoot*, 22. Kennedy's book offers a multitude of strategies for dealing with crime in inner cities.

25. Alan Page Fiske, and Tage Shakti Rai, *Virtuous Violence* (Cambridge, UK: Cambridge University Press, 2015), 1-12. Their thesis is that people are morally motivated to act to affect relations with others.

26. Kwame Anthony Appiah, *The Honor Code: How Moral Revolutions Happen* (New York: W.W. Norton, 2010), 187.

27. Kennedy, *Don't Shoot*, 148.

28. Becker, *The Denial of Death*, 5-6.

29. Yuval Noah Harari, *Homo Deus: A Brief History of Tomorrow* (New York: HarperCollins, 2017), 330.

30. Harari, *Homo Deus*, 331.

31. Harari, *Homo Deus*, 309-350.

32. Shepard, *Coming Home*, 72. It is indeed ironic that our hunter and gatherer ancestors had much more leisure time than modern man. Perhaps someday by necessity we will come full circle regarding our time spent for labor.

33. Daniel Markovits, *The Meritocracy Trap: How America's Foundational Myth Feeds Inequality, Dismantles the Middle Class, and Devours the Elite* (New York: Penguin Press, 2019), 207. Discussing the plight of African Americans who have been incarcerated, Markovits writes, "Where prior convictions preclude subsequent employment, meritocratic inequality performs an astonishing inversion of the American race order. When leisure constituted status, racial subordination was imposed, under slavery, through legally compelled labor. Now that industry constitutes status, racial subordination is imposed through legally enforced idleness."

34. Sebastian Junger, *Tribe: On Homecoming and Belonging* (New York: Twelve, 2016), xvii.

35. Junger, *Tribe*, 66.

36. Kennedy, *Don't Shoot*, 207.

37. Edward O. Wilson, *Consilience: The Unity of Knowledge* (New York: Alfred A. Knopf, 2002), 52.

38. Stephanie M. Conn, *Increasing Resilience in Police and Emergency Personnel: Strengthening Your Mental Armor* (New York: Routledge, 2018), 170.

39. Conn, *Increasing Resilience*, 116.

EPILOGUE

1. President's Commission on Law Enforcement and Administration of Justice, *The Challenge of Crime in a Free Society* (Washington, DC: United States Government Printing Office, 1967), https://www.ncjrs.gov/pdffiles1/nij/42.pdf.

2. President's Commission on Law Enforcement and Administration of Justice, *The Challenge of Crime*, 295.

3. Given the controversy that a report like this would generate, it must have received a lot of media attention, but it does not surprise me that I have no memory of this report being passed on to rank and file police officers or discussed in our detail meetings prior to shift. Although, at the time, given my own attitude and educational level I would have likely scoffed at the idea that these professionals knew more than I did about what needed to be done, I couldn't have been more wrong. It is also not surprising that a report offering so many recommendations for overhauling policing was beyond the authority, administrative, and financial capability of local police departments to make many of the changes, especially regarding funding, but the fact that this study was regarded as too political to take seriously by many departments was unfortunate for inner cities and communities all over America because the need is still profound, but then it's naive using 1967 as a benchmark because our ancestors knew what needed to be done during Reconstruction.

4. Oscar Wilde, "A Few Maxims for the Instruction of the Over-Educated," Wikisource, (November 17, 1894) 2015, https://en.wikisource.org/wiki/A_Few_Maxims_For_The_Instruction_Of_The_Over-Educated.

5. *Morning Joe,* "Writer calls for making conservatism unappealing to racists," MSNBC, September 5, 2019, https://www.msnbc.com/morning-joe/watch/writer-calls-for-making-conservatism-unappealing-to-racists-68254277799.

6. Kathleen Belew, *Bring the War Home: The White Power Movement and Paramilitary America* (Cambridge, MA: Harvard University Press, 2018). This book offers an intricate and detailed history of how the feelings of having been betrayed by their government during the Vietnam War, combined with rising inequality, technological employment displacement and immigration, helped to create a formidable white power movement in America.

7. Alexander, *The New Jim Crow*. The Jim Crow laws were not overturned until a couple of years before I became a police officer in 1966, but as Michelle Alexander makes crystal clear, the discrimination continued by other means.

8. Baratunde Thurston, "How to deconstruct racism, one headline at a time," filmed April 2019, in Vancouver, BC, TED video, 16:44, https://www.ted.com/talks/baratunde_thurston_how_to_deconstruct_racism_one_headline_at_a_time?language=en, is a perspective by Baratunde Thurston that drives the point home about the disparity in the way African Americans are treated by the white public at large and the police. This will take nearly 17 minutes of your time, but it is worth considering.

9. "We asked 155 police departments about their racial bias training. Here's what they told us," *CBS News*, August 7, 2019, https://www.cbsnews.com/news/racial-bias-training-de-escalation-training-policing-in-america/.

10. John Gramlich, "Black and white officers see many key aspects of policing differently," *Pew Research Center*, January 12, 2017, https://www.pewresearch.org/fact-tank/2017/01/12/black-and-white-officers-see-many-key-aspects-of-policing-differently/.

11. Justin Hansford, "5 Years After Ferguson, We're Losing the Fight Against Police Violence," *The New York Times*, August 9, 2019, https://www.nytimes.com/2019/08/09/opinion/ferguson-anniversary-police-race.html.

12. Richard Rorty, *Achieving Our Country* (Cambridge, MA: Harvard University Press, 1998), 81-91.

13. Chuck Todd, "Meet the Press – August 11, 2019," *NBC News*, August 11, 2019, https://www.nbcnews.com/meet-the-press/meet-press-august-11-2019-n1041196.

14. Charles M. Blow, "Denying Racism Supports It," *The New York Times*, July 21, 2019, https://www.nytimes.com/2019/07/21/opinion/trump-racism.html.

15. "72 Philadelphia cops pulled off street amid probe into racist Facebook posts," *Washington Post*, June 20, 2019, https://www.washingtonpost.com/nation/2019/06/20/philadelphia-cops-pulled-off-street-amid-probe-into-racist-facebook-posts/.

16. Kendi, *How to Be An Antiracist* (New York: One World, 2019), 23.

17. "The Antiracist Research and Policy Center," American University, accessed September 9, 2019, https://www.american.edu/centers/antiracism/.

BIBLIOGRAPHY

Abt, Thomas. *Bleeding Out: The Devastating Consequences of Urban Violence—and a Bold New Plan for Peace in the Streets*. New York: Basic Books, 2019.

Alexander, Michelle. *The New Jim Crow: Mass Incarceration in the Age of Colorblindness*. New York: The New Press, 2010.

Allman, William F. *The Stone Age Present: How Evolution Has Shaped Modern Life: From Sex, Violence and Language to Emotions, Morals, and Communities*. New York: Simon & Schuster, 1994.

Allport, Gordon Willard. *The Nature of Prejudice*. Reading, MA: Addison-Wesley, 1979.

Anderson, Carol. *White Rage: The Unspoken Truth of Our Racial Divide*. New York: Bloomsbury, 2017.

Anderson, Walter Truett. *Reality Isn't What It Used to Be: Theatrical Politics, Ready-to-Wear Religion, Global Myths, Primitive Chic, and Other Wonders of the PostModern World*. San Francisco: Harper & Row, 1990.

———, editor. *The Truth About the Truth: De-confusing and Re-constructing the Postmodern World*. New York: Tarcher/Putnam, 1995.

———. *All Connected Now: Life in the First Global Civilization*. Cambridge, MA: Westview Press, 2001.

Andreasen, Nancy C. *The Creating Brain: The Neuroscience of Genius*. New York: Dana Press, 2005.

Andrew, Scottie. "Police Are Three Times More Likely To Kill Black Men, Not A Problem Confined to A Single Region." *Newsweek*, July 23, 2018. https://www.newsweek.com/black-men-three-times-likely-be-killed-police-1037922.

Appiah, Kwame Anthony. *The Ethics of Identity*. Princeton, NJ: Princeton University Press, 2005.

———. *Cosmopolitanism: Ethics in a World of Strangers*. New York: W.W Norton, 2006.

———. *Experiments in Ethics*. Cambridge, MA: Harvard University Press, 2008.

———. *The Honor Code: How Moral Revolutions Happen*. New York: W.W. Norton, 2010.

———. *The Lies That Bind: Rethinking Identity*. New York: W.W. Norton, 2018.

Ardrey, Robert. *The Territorial Imperative: A Personal Inquiry into the Animal Origins of Property and Nations*. New York: Dell Publishing, 1966.

Arendt, Hannah. *Between Past and Future: Eight Exercises in Political Thought*. New York: Penguin Books, 1968.

Ariely, Dan. *Predictably Irrational: The Hidden Forces That Shape Our Decisions*. New York: Harper Collins, 2008.

Artwohl, Alexis, and Loren W. Christensen. *Deadly Force Encounters: What Cops Need to Know to Mentally and Physically Prepare for a Gunfight*. Boulder, CO: Paladin Press, 1997.

Auguet, Roland. *Cruelty and Civilization: The Roman Games*. New York: Routledge, 1994.

Baird, Robert, M., and Stuart E. Rosenbaum, editors. *Bigotry, Prejudice and Hatred: Definitions, Causes & Solutions*. Buffalo, New York: Prometheus Books, 1992.

Ballante, Jill, and Chuck Hadad. "Study: White and black children biased toward lighter skin." *CNN*, May 14, 2010. http://www.cnn.com/2010/US/05/13/doll.study/index.html.

Balko, Radley. *Rise of the Warrior Cop: The Militarization of America's Police Forces*. New York: Public Affairs, 2014.

Banaji, Mahzarin R., and Anthony G. Greenwald. *Blindspot: Hidden Biases of Good People*. New York: Bantam Books, 2016.

Baptist, Edward E. *The Half Has Never Been Told: Slavery and the Making of American Capitalism*. New York: Basic Books, 2014.

Bargh, John. *Before You Know It: The Unconscious Reasons We Do What We Do*. New York: Touchstone, 2017.

Barkan, Steven E. *Race, Crime and Justice: The Continuing American Dilemma*. New York: Oxford University Press, 2019.

Barkow, Jerome H., Leda Cosmides, and John Tooby, editors. *The Adapted Mind: Evolutionary Psychology and the Generation of Culture*. New York: Oxford University Press, 1992.

Barrett, Lisa Feldman. *How Emotions Are Made: The Secret Life of the Brain*. New York: Houghton Mifflin Harcourt, 2017.

Baumeister, Roy F. *Evil: Inside Human Violence and Cruelty*. New York: W.H. Freeman and Company, 1997.

Bazelon, Lara. "Seventeen Cases of Denied Innocence." *Slate*, January 10, 2018. https://slate.com/news-and-politics/2018/01/innocence-deniers-seventeen-cases-of-prosecutors-fighting-exoneration.html.

Becker, Ernest. *Beyond Alienation: A Philosophy of Education for the Crisis of Democracy*. New York: George Braziller, 1967.

–––. *The Denial of Death*. New York: The Free Press, 1973.

–––. *Escape from Evil*. New York: The Free Press, 1975.

Bekoff, Marc. "Social Dominance Is Not a Myth: Wolves, Dogs, and." *Psychology Today*, February 15, 2012. https://www.psychologytoday.com/ca/blog/animal-emotions/201202/social-dominance-is-not-myth-wolves-dogs-and.

Belew, Kathleen. *Bring the War Home: The White Power Movement and Paramilitary America*. Cambridge, MA: Harvard University Press, 2018.

Benforado, Adam. *Unfair: The New Science of Criminal Injustice*. New York: Crown Publishers, 2015.

Berger, Jonah. *Invisible Influence: The Hidden Forces that Shape Behavior*. New York: Simon & Schuster, 2016.

Berman, Mark. "Trump tells police not to worry about injuring suspects during arrests." *The Washington Post*, July 28, 2017. https://www.washingtonpost.com/news/post-nation/wp/2017/07/28/trump-tells-police-not-to-worry-about-injuring-suspects-during-arrests/?utm_term=.4fea0acc6d10.

Berns, Gregory. *Iconoclast: A Neuroscientist Reveals How to Think Differently*. Boston, MA: Harvard Business Press, 2008.

Berreby, David. *Us and Them: Understanding Your Tribal Mind*. New York: Little Brown and Company, 2005.

Bishop, Bill, with Robert G. Cushing. *The Big Sort: Why the Clustering of Like-Minded America is Tearing Us Apart*. New York: Houghton Mifflin, 2008.

Blackmon, Douglas A. *Slavery by Another Name: The Re-Enslavement of Black Americans from the Civil War to World War II*. New York: Doubleday, 2008.

Bleiberg, Jake. "Slain man's brother, judge, hug ex-cop sentenced to 10 years." *AP News*, October 2, 2019. https://www.apnews.com/1efb02d5b6d2431db247214c6fa71488.

Blinder, Alan. "Michael Slager, Officer in Walter Scott Shooting, Gets 20-Year Sentence." *New York Times*, December 7, 2017. https://www.nytimes.com/2017/12/07/us/michael-slager-sentence-walter-scott.html.

Bloom, Paul. *Just Babies: The Origins of Good and Evil*. New York: Crown Publishing, 2013.

–––. *Against Empathy: The Case for Rational Compassion*. New York: HarperCollins, 2016.

Blow, Charles M. "Denying Racism Supports It." *The New York Times*, July 21, 2019. https://www.nytimes.com/2019/07/21/opinion/trump-racism.html.

–––. *Fire Shut Up in My Bones: A Memoir*. New York: Mariner Books, 2015.

–––. "On Race: The Moral High Ground." *New York Times*, May 31, 2018. https://www.nytimes.com/2018/05/31/opinion/roseanne-valerie-jarrett-race-trump.html

Bohm, David, and Mark Edwards. *Changing Consciousness: Exploring the Hidden Source of the Social, Political, and Environmental Crises Facing Our World*. San Francisco: Harper, 1991.

Bonilla-Silva, Eduardo. *Racism without Racists: Color-Blind Racism and the Persistence of Racial Inequality in America*. Lanham, MD: Rowman and Littlefield Publishers, Inc., 2014.

Bowe, John. *Nobodies: Modern American Slave Labor and the Dark Side of the New Global Economy*. New York: Random House, 2007.

Bowman, James. *Honor: A History*. New York: Encounter Books, 2006.

Brodie, Richard. *Virus of the Mind: The New Science of the Meme*. Seattle: Integral Press, 1996.

Brookfield, Stephen D. *Teaching for Critical Thinking: Tools and Techniques to Help Students Question Their Assumptions*. San Francisco: Jossey-Bass, 2011.

———. *Teaching for Critical Thinking: Tools and Techniques To Help Students Question Their Assumptions*. San Francisco: Jossey-Bass, 2012.

Brooks, David. *The Second Mountain: The Quest for a Moral Life*. New York: Random House, 2019.

Brown, Bertram Wyatt. *Southern Honor: Ethics and Behavior in the Old South*. New York: Oxford University Press, 2007.

Brown, Ryan P. *Honor Bound: How a Cultural Ideal Has Shaped the American Psyche*. New York: Oxford University Press, 2016.

Brundage, W. Fitzhugh. *Lynching in the New South: Georgia and Virginia, 1880-1930*. Chicago: University of Illinois Press, 1993.

Buber, Martin. *I and Thou*. New York: Touchstone, 1970.

Bufkin, Ellie. " 'Zero tolerance for resisting police': Barr slams law enforcement protesters." *Washington Examiner*, August 14, 2019. https://www.washingtonexaminer.com/news/zero-tolerance-for-resisting-police-barr-slams-law-enforcement-protesters.

Buonomano, Dean. *Brain Bugs: How the Brain's Flaws Shape Our Lives*. New York: W.W. Norton, 2011.

Burnham, Terry, and Jay Phelan. *Mean Genes: From Sex to Money to Food: Taming our Primal Instincts*. New York: Perseus Publishing, 2000.

Burton, Robert A. *On Being Certain: Believing You Are Right Even When You're Not*. New York: St. Martin's Press, 2008.

Butler, Paul. *Chokehold [Policing Black Men]: A Renegade Prosecutor's Radical Thoughts on How to Disrupt the System*. New York: The New Press, 2017.

Cahn, Albert Fox. "How bodycams distort real life." *The New York Times*, August 8, 2019. https://www.nytimes.com/2019/08/08/opinion/bodycams-privacy.html.

Carter, Stephen L. *The Culture of Disbelief: How American Law and Politics Trivialize Religious Devotion*. New York: Basic Books, 1993.

Castells, Manuel. *The Power of Identity*. Malden, MA: Blackwell Publishers, 1997.

Chabris, Christopher, and Daniel Simons. *The Invisible Gorilla: And Other Ways Our Intuitions Deceive Us*. New York: Crown Publishers, 2010.

Chagnon, Napoleon A. *Noble Savages: My Life Among Two Dangerous Tribes—the Yanomamö and the Anthropologists*. New York: Simon & Schuster, 2013.

Chang, Jeff. *We Gon' Be Alright: Notes on Race and Resegregation*. New York: Picador, 2016.

Christakis, Nicholas A. *Blueprint: The Evolutionary Origins of a Good Society.* New York: Little Brown Spark, 2019.

Christian, Brian and Tom Griffiths. *Algorithms to Live By: The Computer Science of Human Decisions.* New York: Henry Holt and Company, LLC, 2016.

Chua, Amy. *Political Tribes: Group Instinct and the Fate of Nations.* New York: Penguin Press, 2018.

Churchland, Patricia S. *Touching a Nerve: Our Brains, Our Selves.* New York: W.W. Norton, 2013.

---. *Conscience: The Origins of Moral Intuition.* New York: W.W. Norton, 2019.

Cialdini, Robert. *Pre-Suasion: A Revolutionary Way to Influence and Persuade.* New York: Simon & Schuster, 2016.

Clarke, David, Jr. *Cop Under Fire: Moving Beyond Hashtags of Race, Crime and Politics for a Better America.* Franklin, TN: Worthy Publishing, 2017.

Coates, Ta-Nehisi. "The Case for Reparations." *The Atlantic,* June 2014. https://www.theatlantic.com/magazine/archive/2014/06/ the-case-for-reparations/361631/.

---. *Between the World and Me.* New York: Random House, 2015.

Combs, Arthur W. *Individual Behavior: A Perceptual Approach to Behavior.* New York: Harper, 1959.

Conn, Stephanie M. *Increasing Resilience in Policing and Emergency Personnel: Strengthening Your Mental Armor.* New York: Routledge, 2018.

Conniff, Richard. *The Ape in the Corner Office: Understanding the Workplace Beast in all of Us.* New York: Crown Business, 2005.

The Constitution of the United States. National Archives. 2019. https://www. archives.gov/founding-docs/constitution.

Coontz, Stephanie. *The Way We Never Were: American Families and the Nostalgia Trap.* New York: Basic Books, 1992.

---. *The Way We Really Are: Coming to Terms with America's Changing Families.* New York: Basic Books, 1997.

---. *A Strange Stirring: The Feminine Mystique and American Women at the Dawn of the 1960s.* New York: Basic Books, 2011.

---, and Peta Henderson, editors. *Women's Work, Men's Property: The Origins of Gender and Class.* London: Verso, 1986.

Couper, David. *Arrested Development: A Veteran Police Chief Sounds Off About Protest, Racism, Corruption and The Seven Steps Necessary to Improve Our Nation's Police.* Blue Mounds, WI: New Journey Press, 2012.

---. *Telling It Like It Is: Couper On Cops.* Blue Mounds, WI: New Journey Press, 2017.

Crick, Francis. "Thinking about the Brain," *Scientific American* offprint, 1984.

Crisp, Dean. *Leadership Lessons from the Thin Blue Line.* New York: Page Publishing, 2017.

Csikszentmihalyi, Mihaly. *Flow: The Psychology of Optimal Experience.* New York: Harper & Row, 1990.

---. *The Evolving Self: A Psychology for the Third Millennium.* New York: HarperCollins, 1993.

–––. *Creativity: Flow and the Psychology of Discovery and Invention.* New York: Harper Collins, 1996.

Daileader, Celia R. *Racism, Misogyny, and the Othello Myth: Inter-racial Couples from Shakespeare to Spike Lee.* UK: Cambridge University Press, 2005.

Damasio, Antonio R. *Descartes' Error: Emotion, Reason, and the Human Brain.* New York: G.P Putnam's Sons, 1994.

–––. *The Strange Order of Things: Life, Feeling, and the Making of Cultures.* New York: Pantheon Books, 2018.

Darwin, Charles. *The Expression of the Emotions in Man and Animals: With an Introduction, Afterward and Commentaries by Paul Erkman.* London: Oxford University Press, 1998.

Davis, Angela J., editor. *Policing the Black Man: Arrest, Prosecution and Imprisonment.* New York: Pantheon, 2017.

De Becker, Gavin. *The Gift of Fear: Survival Signals That Protect Us from Violence.* New York: Dell Publishing, 1997.

De Botton, Alain. *Status Anxiety.* New York: Pantheon Books, 2004.

Deci, Edward L. *Intrinsic Motivation.* New York: Plenum Press, 1975.

–––. *The Psychology of Self-Determination.* Lexington, MA: Lexington Books, 1980.

Degler, Carl. N. *In Search of Human Nature: The Decline and Revival of Darwinism in American Social Thought.* New York: Oxford University Press, 1991.

Delattre, Edwin J. *Character and Cops: Ethics in Policing.* 6th edition. Washington, DC: AEI Press, 2011.

Dennett, Daniel C. *Darwin's Dangerous Idea: Evolution and the Meanings of Life.* New York: Simon & Schuster, 1995.

Depue, Roger L., with Susan Schindehette. *Between Good and Evil: A Master Profiler's Hunt for Society's Most Violent Predators.* New York: Warner Books, 2005.

Derber, Charles. *The Wilding of America: How Greed and Violence Are Eroding Our Nation's Character.* New York: St. Martin's Press, 1996.

DeSteno, David and Piercarlo Valdesolo. *Out of Character: Surprising Truths About the Liar, Cheat, Sinner (and Saint) Lurking in All of Us.* New York: Crown Publishers, 2011.

De Waal, Frans. *Our Inner Ape.* New York: Riverhead Books, 2005.

–––. *Chimpanzee Politics: Power and Sex Among Apes.* Baltimore, MD: The John Hopkins University Press, 2007.

–––. *The Age of Empathy: Nature's Lessons for a Kinder Society.* New York: Harmony Books, 2009.

–––. *The Bonobo and the Atheist: In Search of Humanism Among the Primates.* New York: W.W. Norton, 2013.

–––. *Are We Smart Enough to Know How Smart Animals Are?* New York: W.W. Norton, 2016.

–––. *Mama's Last Hug: Animal Emotions and What They Tell Us about Ourselves.* New York: W.W. Norton, 2019.

Dewan, Shaila. "Prosecutors Block Access to DNA Testing for Inmates." *The New York Times*, May 17, 2009.

Diamond, Jared. *The Third Chimpanzee*. New York: HarperCollins, 1992.

---. *Guns, Germs and Steel: The Fates of Human Societies*. New York: W.W. Norton, 1997.

---. *Collapse: How Societies Choose to Fail or Succeed*. New York: Viking Penguin, 2005.

---. *The World Until Yesterday: What We Can Learn from Traditional Societies*. New York: Viking Penguin, 2012.

DiAngelo, Robin. *White Fragility: Why It's So Hard for White People to Talk About Racism*. Boston, MA: Beacon Press, 2018.

---. "White Fragility." *C-Span* video, 1:28:18. June 30, 2018. https://www.c-span.org/video/?447421-2/robin-diangelo-white-fragility.

Dorsey, Cheryl. *Black and Blue: The Creation of a Social Advocate*. Los Angeles, CA: Dorsey, 2018.

Dunkelman, Marc J. *The Vanishing Neighbor: The Transformation of American Community*. New York: W.W. Norton, 2014.

Dutton, Kevin. *The Wisdom of Psychopaths: What Saints, Spies, and Serial Killers Can Teach Us About Success*. New York: Farrar, Straus and Giroux, 2012.

Dwech, Carol. S. *Mindset: The New Psychology of Success*. New York: Random House, 2006.

Dworkin, Ronald. *Justice for Hedgehogs*. Cambridge, MA: The Belknap Press, 2011.

Dyson, Michael Eric. *What Truth Sounds Like: RFK, James Baldwin, and Our Unfinished Conversation About Race in America*. New York: St. Martin's Press, 2018.

Eagleman, David. *Incognito: The Secret Lives of the Brain*. New York: Random House, 2011.

Easterly, William. *The Tyranny of Experts: Economists, Dictators and the Forgotten Rights of the Poor*. New York: Basic Books, 2013.

Eberhardt, Jennifer L. *Biased: Uncovering the Hidden Prejudice That Shapes What We See, Think, and Do*. New York: Viking, 2019.

The Editorial Board. "The Meaning of the Ferguson Riots." *The New York Times*, November 25, 2014. https://www.nytimes.com/2014/11/26/opinion/the-meaning-of-the-ferguson-riots.html.

Eisenberg, Adam. *A Different Shade of Blue: How Women Changed the Face of Police Work*. Lake Forest, CA: Behler Publications, 2009.

Ellison, Ralph. *Invisible Man*. 2nd edition. New York: Vintage Books, 1995.

Emerson, Ralph Waldo. *Emerson: Essays and Lectures*. New York: The Library of America, 1983.

Epp, Charles R., Steven Maynard-Moody, and Donald Haider-Markel. *Pulled Over: How Police Stops Define Race and Citizenship*. Chicago, IL: The University of Chicago Press, 2014.

Ested, Joseph J. *Police Brutality Matters*. Atlanta, GA: PMB Publications, 2018.

Evatt, Chris. *The Myth of Free Will.* Sausalito, CA: Café Essays, 2010.

Eubanks, Virginia. *Automating Inequality: How High-Tech Tools Profile, Police, and Punish the Poor.* New York: St. Martin's Press, 2017.

Ezekiel, Raphael S. *The Racist Mind: Portraits of American Neo-Nazis and Klansmen.* New York: Viking, 1995.

Falk, Dean. *Braindance: New Discoveries About Human Origins and Brain Evolution.* New York: Henry Holt and Company, 1992.

Falk, Gerhard. *Stigma: How We Treat Outsiders.* Amherst, NY: Prometheus Books, 2001.

Ferguson, Andrew Guthrie. *The Rise of Big Data Policing: Surveillance, Race, and the Future of Law Enforcement.* New York: New York University Press, 2017.

Ferner, Matt. "If You Want to Totally Change America's Criminal Justice System, You Need a Plan." *Huffington Post*, May 29, 2018. https://www.huffingtonpost.com/entry/fair-just-prosecution-criminal-justice-reform_us_5aff5a94e4b0463cdba1e59d.

Festinger, Leon. *A Theory of Cognitive Dissonance.* Stanford, CA: Stanford University Press, 1962.

Fields, R. Douglas. *Why We Snap: Understanding the Rage Circuit in Your Brain.* New York: Dutton, 2015.

Fingarette, Herbert. *Self-Deception.* Berkeley, CA: University of California Press, 2000.

Fiske, Alan Page, and Tage Shakti Rai. *Virtuous Violence.* Cambridge, UK: Cambridge University Press, 2015.

Flam, Faye. *The Score: The Science of the Male Sex Drive.* New York: Avery, 2009.

Forman, James Jr. *Locking Up Our Own: Crime and Punishment in Black America.* New York: Farrar, Straus and Giroux, 2017.

Fortin, Jacey. "Arizona Prisons' Ban on Book About Racism in Criminal Justice Draws Challenge." *The New York Times*, May 22, 2019, https://www.nytimes.com/2019/05/22/us/arizona-bans-chokehold-book.html.

Fox, Robin. *The Tribal Imagination: Civilization and the Savage Mind.* Cambridge, MA: Harvard University Press, 2011.

Fredrickson, George M. *Racism: A Short History.* Princeton, NJ: Princeton University Press, 2002.

Fridell, Lorie A. *Producing Bias-Free Policing: A Science-Based Approach.* Switzerland: Spring International Publishing, 2017.

Friedman, Lawrence J. *The Lives of Erich Fromm: Love's Prophet.* New York: Columbia University Press, 2013.

Friedman, Milton, and Thomas Szasz. *On Liberty and Drugs: Essay of the Free Market and Prohibition.* Washington, D.C. The Drug Policy Foundation, 1992.

Fromm, Erich. *The Sane Society.* New York: Henry Holt, 1955.

---. *The Anatomy of Human Destructiveness.* Greenwich, CT: Fawcett Publications, 1973.

–––. *On Disobedience: And Other Essays.* New York: The Seabury Press, 1981.

Fukuyama, Francis. *Identity: The Demand for Dignity and the Politics of Resentment.* New York: Farrar, Straus and Giroux, 2018.

Fuller, Robert W. *Somebodies and Nobodies: Overcoming the Abuse of Rank.* Gabriola Island, BC, Canada: New Society Publishers, 2004.

Fussell, Paul. *Class: A Guide Through the American Status System.* New York: Ballantine Books, 1983.

Gallagher, Winifred. *Rapt: Attention and the Focused Life.* New York: The Penguin Press, 2009.

Gans, Herbert J. *The War Against the Poor: The Underclass and Antipoverty Policy.* New York: Basic Books, 1995.

Gardner, Howard. *Changing Minds: The Art and Science of Changing Our Own and Other People's Minds.* Boston, MA: Harvard Business School Press, 2004.

Gardner, Howard E., Mihaly Csikszentmihalyi, and William Damon. *Good Work: When Excellence and Ethics Meet.* New York: Basic Books, 2001.

Gates, Henry Louis, Jr. *Stony the Road: Reconstruction, White Supremacy, and the Rise of Jim Crow.* New York: Penguin Press, 2019.

Gaylin, Willard, and Bruce Jennings. *The Perversion of Autonomy: The Proper Uses of Coercion and Constraints in a Liberal Society.* New York: The Free Press, 1996.

Gazzaniga, Michael S. *The Consciousness Instinct: Unraveling the Mystery of How the Brain Makes the Mind.* New York: Farrar, Straus and Giroux, 2018.

Gilligan, Carol. *In a Different Voice: Psychological Theory and Women's Development.* Cambridge MA: Harvard University Press, 1982.

Gilmartin, Kevin M. *Emotional Survival for Law Enforcement: A Guide for Officers and Their Families.* Tucson, AZ: E-S Press, 2002.

Giroux, Henry A. *The Violence of Organized Forgetting: Thinking Beyond America's Disimagination Machine.* San Francisco, CA: City Lights Books, 2014.

Gladwell, Malcolm. *Talking to Strangers: What We Should Know About the People We Don't Know.* New York: Little Brown and Company, 2019.

Goble, Frank G. *The Third Force: The Psychology of Abraham Maslow.* New York: Simon & Schuster, 1971.

Goffman, Erving. *Stigma: Notes on the Management of Spoiled Identity.* New York: Simon & Schuster, Inc., 1963.

Goldwag, Arthur. *The New Hate: A History of Fear and Loathing on the Populist Right.* New York: Pantheon Books, 2012.

Goleman, Daniel. *Vital Lies, Simple Truths.* New York: Simon & Schuster, 1985.

–––. *Emotional Intelligence.* New York: Bantam Books, 1995.

–––. *Social Intelligence.* New York: Bantam Dell, 2006.

Gottschall, Jonathan. *The Professor in the Cage: Why We Fight and Why We Like To Watch.* New York: Penguin Press, 2015.

Gottschall, Jonathan, and David Sloan Wilson, editors. *The Literary Animal: Evolution and the Nature of Narrative*. Evanston, IL: Northwestern University Press, 2005.

Gould, Stephen Jay. *Bully for Brontosaurus: Reflections in Natural History*. New York: W.W Norton, 1981a.

---. *The Mismeasure of Man*. New York: W.W. Norton, 1981b.

---. *Full House: The Spread of Excellence from Plato to Darwin*. New York: Harmony Books, 1996.

Graeber, David. *Debt: The First 5,000 Years*. Brooklyn, NY: Melville House, 2011.

Gramlich, John. "Black and white officers see many key aspects of policing differently." *Pew Research Center*, January 12, 2017. https://www.pewresearch.org/fact-tank/2017/01/12/black-and-white-officers-see-many-key-aspects-of-policing-differently/.

Greenberg, Jeff, Sandel L. Koole, and Tom Pyszczynski, editors. *Handbook of Experimental Existential Psychology*. New York: The Guilford Press, 2004.

Greene, Joshua. *Moral Tribes: Emotion, Reason, and The Gap Between Us and Them*. New York: The Penguin Press, 2013.

Griffin, Joe, and Ivan Tyrrell. *Human Givens: A New Approach to Emotional Health and Clear Thinking*. Great Britain: HG Publishing, 2003.

Grossman, Dave. *On Killing: The Psychological Cost of Learning to Kill in War and Society*. New York: Back Bay Books, 2009.

Grossman, Dave, with Loren W. Christensen. *On Combat: The Psychology and Physiology of Deadly Conflict in War and Peace*. New York: Warrior Science Books, 2008.

Guarino, Mark, and Mark Berman. "Chicago police officer Jason Van Dyke convicted of second-degree murder for killing Laquan MacDonald." *Washington Post*, October 5, 2018. https://www.washingtonpost.com/news/post-nation/wp/2018/10/05/chicago-police-officer-jason-van-dyke-convicted-of-second-degree-murder-for-killing-laquan-mcdonald/?noredirect=on&utm_term=.ec6952bb49fe.

Guinier, Lani. *The Tyranny of the Majority: Fundamental Fairness in Representative Democracy*. New York: The Free Press, 1994.

Hagerman, Margaret. *White Kids: Growing Up with Privilege in a Racially Divided America*. New York: New York University Press, 2018.

Haidt, Jonathan. *The Righteous Mind: Why Good People are Divided by Politics and Religion*. New York: Vintage, 2013.

Hansford, Justin. "5 Years After Ferguson, We're Losing the Fight Against Police Violence." *The New York Times*, August 9, 2019. https://www.nytimes.com/2019/08/09/opinion/ferguson-anniversary-police-race.html.

Harari, Yuval Noah. *Sapiens: A Brief History of Humankind*. New York: HarperCollins, 2015.

———. *Homo Deus: A Brief History of Tomorrow*. New York: HarperCollins, 2017.

———. *21 Lessons for the 21st Century*. New York: Spiegel & Grau, 2018.

Hare, Robert D. *Without Conscience: The Disturbing World of Psychopaths Among Us*. New York: The Guilford Press, 1999.

Hari, Johann. *Chasing the Scream: The First and Last Days of the War on Drugs*. New York: Bloomsbury, 2015.

———. *Lost Connections: Uncovering the Real Causes of Depression—and the Unexpected Solutions*. New York: Bloomsbury, 2018.

Harris, Marvin. *Cows, Pigs, Wars and Witches: The Riddles of Culture*. New York: Vintage Books, 1974.

———. *Cannibals and Kings: The Origins of Cultures*. New York: Vintage Books, 1978.

———. *Our Kind*. New York: HarperCollins, 1989.

Hart, Leslie A. *Human Brain and Human Learning*. New York: Longman, 1983.

Hatter, Melanie S. *Malawi's Sisters*. New York: Four Way Books, 2019.

Hausmann, Issa Kohler. *Misdemeanorland: Criminal Courts and Social Control in an Age of Broken Windows Policing*. Princeton, NJ: Princeton University Press, 2018.

Hayes, Charles D. *Self-University: The Price of Tuition Is the Desire to Learn. Your Degree Is a Better Life* Wasilla, AK: Autodidactic Press, 1989.

———. *Proving You're Qualified: Strategies for Competent People without College Degrees*. Wasilla, AK: Autodidactic Press, 1995.

———. *The Rapture of Maturity: A Legacy of Lifelong Learning*. Wasilla, AK: Autodidactic Press, 2004.

———. "Police Authority and Racism." *LA Progressive*, August 1, 2009, https://www.laprogressive.com/police-racist-abuse/.

———. *Existential Aspirations: Reflections of a Self-taught Philosopher*. Wasilla, AK: Autodidactic Press, 2010a.

———. *September University: Summoning Passion for an Unfinished Life*. Wasilla, AK: Autodidactic Press, 2010b.

Hayes, Chris. *A Colony in a Nation*. New York: W.W. Norton, 2017.

Hedges, Chris. *War is a Force That Gives Us Meaning*. New York: Anchor Books, 2002.

Hinton, Elizabeth. *From the War on Poverty to the War on Crime: The Making of Mass Incarceration in America*. Cambridge, MA: Harvard University Press, 2016.

Hoffer, Eric. *The True Believer: Thoughts on the Nature of Mass Movements*. New York: Harper & Row, 1951. Reset, First Perennial Library, 1989.

Hoffman, Edward. *The Right to be Human: A Biography of Abraham Maslow*. Los Angeles: Tarcher, 1988.

Hofstadter, Richard. *Anti-Intellectualism in American Life*. New York: Vantage Books, 1962.

Holland, Jack. *Misogyny: The World's Oldest Prejudice*. London: Constable & Robinson Ltd., 2006.

Horace, Matthew, and Ron Harris. *The Black and the Blue: A Cop Reveals the*

Crimes, Racism, and Injustice in America's Law Enforcement. New
    York: Hachette Books, 2018.

Horgan, John. *The Undiscovered Mind: How the Human Brain Defies
    Replication, Medication and Explanation.* New York: The Free Press,
    1999.

Horowitz, Juliana Menasce, Anna Brown, and Kiana Cox. "Race in
    America 2019." *Pew Research Center,* April 9, 2019. https://www.
    pewsocialtrends.org/2019/04/09/race-in-america-2019/.

Hughley, D. L., and Doug Moe. *How Not To Get Shot.* New York:
    HarperCollins, 2018.

Hume, David. *A Treatise of Human Nature.* Edited by L.A. Selby-Bigge.
    London: Oxford at the Clarendon Press, 1888.

Hunt, Luke William. *The Retrieval of Liberalism in Policing.* New York: Oxford
    University, 2019.

Hunter, James Davison. *Culture Wars.* New York: Basic Books, 1991.

Hutchinson, Sikivu. *Mortal Combat: Black Atheists, Gender Politics and the
    Values Wars.* Los Angeles, CA Infidel Books, 2011.

Inglehart, Ronald F. *Cultural Evolution: People's Motivations are Changing, and
    Reshaping the World.* Cambridge, UK: Cambridge University Press,
    2018.

Itkowitz, Colby. "Meet the 34-year-old neuroscientist developing a drug to
    prevent depression and PTSD." *Washington Post,* April 25, 2017.
    https://www.washingtonpost.com/news/inspired-life/wp/2017/04/25/
    meet-the-34-year-old-neuroscientist-developing-a-drug-to-prevent-
    depression-and-ptsd/?noredirect=on.

Jackman, Tom. "New Orleans Police Pioneer New Way to Stop Misconduct,
    Remove 'Blue Wall of Silence.'" *Washington Post,* January 24, 2019.
    https://www.washingtonpost.com/crime-law/2019/01/24/new-orleans-
    police-pioneer-new-way-stop-misconduct-remove-blue-wall-silence/.

–––. "Federal task force bans body cameras, so Atlanta police pull out.
    Others may follow." *Washington Post,* June 14, 2019. https://www.
    washingtonpost.com/crime-law/2019/06/14/federal-task-forces-ban-
    body-cameras-so-atlanta-police-pull-out-others-may-follow/.

Jackson, John L., Jr. *Racial Paranoia: The Unintended Consequences of Political
    Correctness.* New York: Basic Civitas, 2008.

Jackson, Maggie. *Distracted: The Erosion of Attention and the Coming Dark
    Age.* Amherst, NY: Prometheus Books, 2008.

Jacobs, Jane. *Dark Age Ahead.* New York: Random House, 2004.

Jamieson, Kathleen Hall. *Cyber War: What We Don't, Can't, and Do Know.*
    New York: Oxford University Press, 2018.

Jarvis, Peter. *Paradoxes of Learning: On Becoming an Individual in Society.* San
    Francisco, CA: Jossey Bass, 1992.

Jerkins, Morgan. *This Will Be My Undoing: Living at the Intersection of
    Black, Female, and Feminist in (White) America.* New York: Harper
    Perennial, 2018.

Juarez, Juan Antonio. *Brotherhood of Corruption: A Cop Breaks the Silence on Police Abuse, Brutality, and Racial Profiling*. Chicago, IL: Chicago Review Press, 2004.

Junger, Sebastian. *War*. New York: Twelve, 2011.

———. *Tribe: On Homecoming and Belonging*. New York: Twelve, 2016.

Kahneman, Daniel. *Thinking Fast and Slow*. New York: Farrar, Straus and Giroux, 2011.

Kahn, Jonathan. *Race on the Brain: What Implicit Bias Gets Wrong about the Struggle for Racial Justice*. New York: Columbia University Press, 2017.

Keen, Sam. *Faces of the Enemy: Reflections of the Hostile Imagination*. New York: Harper & Row, 1986.

Keiser, T.W., and J.L. Keiser. *The Anatomy of Illusion*. Springfield, IL: Charles C. Thomas, 1987.

Kendi, Ibram X. *Stamped from the Beginning: The Definitive History of Racist Ideas in America*. New York: Basic Books, 2016.

———. *How To Be an Antiracist*: New York: One World, 2019.

Kennedy, David M. *Don't Shoot: One Man, A Street Fellowship, and the End of Violence in Inner-City America*. New York: Bloomsbury, 2011.

Kimmel, Michael. *Angry White Men: American Masculinity at the End of an Era*. New York: Perseus Books Group, 2013.

Kinder, Melvyn. *Going Nowhere Fast*. New York: Prentice-Hall Press, 1990.

King, Martin Luther, Jr. "Letter From a Birmingham Jail." The Martin Luther King, Jr. Research and Education Institute. (April 16, 1963) 2019. https://kinginstitute.stanford.edu/king-papers/documents/letter-birmingham-jail.

Kirschman, Ellen, Mark Kamena, and Joel Fay. *Counseling Cops: What Clinicians Need to Know*. New York: The Guilford Press, 2015.

Kohlberg, Lawrence. *The Psychology of Moral Development*. San Francisco: Harper & Row, 1984.

Kohn, Alfie. *Punished by Rewards*. New York: Houghton Mifflin, 1993.

Kristof, Nicholas D., and Sheryl WuDunn. *Half the Sky: Turning Oppression into Opportunity for Women Worldwide*. New York: Vintage Books, 2009.

Krugman, Paul. *The Conscience of a Liberal*. New York: W.W. Norton, 2007.

Lakoff, George, and Mark Johnson. *Metaphors We Live By*. Chicago, IL: Chicago University Press, 1980.

———. *Philosophy in the Flesh: The Embodied Mind and Its Challenge to Western Thought*. New York: Basic Books, 1999.

Langer, Ellen J. *Mindfulness*. New York: Addison-Wesley, 1989.

"Laquan MacDonald shooting video." YouTube video, 1:55. Posted by "Chicago Sun-Times," August 24, 2018. https://www.youtube.com/watch?v=xaXuT9sxCnI.

Larkin, Tim. *When Violence is the Answer: Learning How to Do What It Takes When Your life is at Stake*. New York: Little Brown and Company, 2017.

Leovy, Jill. *Ghettoside: A True Story of Murder in America*. New York: Spiegel & Grau, 2015.

Lieberman, Debra, and Carlton Patrick. *Objection: Disgust, Morality, and the Law*. New York, NY: Oxford University Press, 2018.

Lifton, Robert Jay. *The Broken Connection*. New York: Simon and Schuster, 1979.

Ligotti, Thomas. *The Conspiracy Against the Human Race*. New York: Hippocampus Press, 2010.

Lippmann, Walter. *Public Opinion*. New York: Simon and Schuster, 1922.

Livio, Mario. *Why? What Makes Us Curious*. New York: Simon & Schuster, 2017.

Lobel, Thalma. *Sensation: The New Science of Physical Intelligence*. New York: Atria Books, 2014.

Lopez, Ian Haney. *Dog Whistle Politics: How Coded Racial Appeals Have Reinvented Racism and Wrecked the Middle Class*. New York: Oxford University Press, 2014.

Lorenz, Konrad. *On Aggression*. New York: Bantam Books, 1966.

Lou, Michelle, and Brandon Griggs. "A proposed Tennessee law would make it a felony for police officers to disable their body cams." *CNN*, February 27, 2019. https://www.cnn.com/2019/02/27/us/tennessee-body-cam-felony-trnd/index.html.

Lukianoff, Greg, and Jonathan Haidt. *The Coddling of the American Mind: How Good Intentions and Bad Ideas are Setting Up a Generation for Failure*. New York: Penguin Press, 2018.

Mac Donald, Heather. *The War on Cops: How the New Attack on Law and Order Makes Everyone Less Safe*. New York: Encounter Books, 2016.

Makarechi, Kia. "What the Data Really Says About Police and Racial Bias." *Vanity Fair*, July 14, 2016. https://www.vanityfair.com/news/2016/07/data-police-racial-bias.

Marais, Eugene. *The Soul of the Ape*. New York: Atheneum, 1969.

Markovits, Daniel. *The Meritocracy Trap: How America's Foundational Myth Feeds Inequality, Dismantles the Middle Class, and Devours the Elite*. New York: Penguin Press, 2019.

Marsh, Abigail. *The Fear Factor: How One Emotion Connects Altruists, Psychopaths, and Everyone In-Between*. New York: Basic Books, 2017.

Marsh, Jason, Rodolfo Mendoza-Denton, and Jeremy Adam Smith, editors. *Are We Born Racist? New Insights from Neuroscience and Positive Psychology*. Boston, MA: Beacon Press, 2010.

Martinez, Raoul. *Creating Freedom: The Lottery of Birth, The Illusion of Consent, and the Fight for Our Future*. New York: Vintage Books, 2016.

Maslow, Abraham H. *Motivation and Personality*. New York: Harper and Row, 1954.

–––. *The Farther Reaches of Human Nature*. New York: Penguin Press, 1971.

Massey, Morris. *The People Puzzle: Understanding Yourself and Others*. Reston, VA: Reston Publishing, 1979.

Matthew, Dayna Bowen. *Just Medicine: A Cure for Racial Inequality in American Health Care*. New York: New York University Press, 2015.

Mattis, James N., and Francis J. West. *Call Sign Chaos: Learning to Lead*. New York: Random House 2019.

Maxwell, Angie. *The Indicted South: Public Criticism, Southern Inferiority, and the Politics of Whiteness*. Chapel Hill, NC: The University of North Carolina Press, 2014.

May, Charlie. "FBI investigated white supremacists infiltrating law enforcement agencies: A report." *Salon.com*, January 31, 2017. https://www.salon.com/2017/01/31/fbi-investigating-white-supremacists-infiltrating-law-enforcement-agencies-report/.

McCutcheon, Chuck, and David Mark. *Dog Whistles, Walk-Backs, and Washington Hand Shakes: Decoding the Jargon, Slang and Bluster of America*. Lebanon, NH: University Press of New England, 2014.

Mckesson, Deray. *On the Other Side of Freedom: The Case for Hope*. New York: Viking, 2018.

Meacham, Jon. *The Soul of America: The Battle for Our Better Angels*. New York: Random House, 2018.

Meichenbaum, Donald. *Stress Inoculation Training*. New York: Pergamon Press, 1985.

Meegan, Dan. *America the Fair: Using Brain Science to Create a More Just Nation*. New York: Cornell University Press, 2019.

Metzl, Jonathan M. *Dying of Whiteness: How Politics of Racial Resentment is Killing America's Heartland*. New York: Basic Books, 2019.

Michaels, Walter Benn. *The Trouble with Diversity: How We Learned to Love Identity and Ignore Inequality*. New York: Metropolitan Books, 2006.

Mill, John Stuart. "On Liberty." In *American State Papers and The Federalist*, edited by Robert Maynard. Vol. 43 of *Great Books of the Western World* Chicago, IL: Encyclopedia Britannica, 1952.

Miller, David. *Principles of Social Justice*. Cambridge, MA: Harvard University Press, 1999.

Miller, Rory. *Force Decisions: Understanding How Police Determine Appropriate Use of Force*. Wolfeboro, NH: YMAA Publication Center, Inc., 2012.

Miller, William Ian. *The Anatomy of Disgust*. Cambridge, MA: Harvard University Press, 1997.

Minutaglio, Bill, and Steven L. Davis. *Dallas 1963*. New York: Twelve, 2013.

Mlodinow, Leonard. *Subliminal: How Your Subconscious Rules Your Behavior*. New York: Pantheon Books, 2012.

Morning Joe. "Writer calls for making conservatism unappealing to racists." MSNBC, September 5, 2019. https://www.msnbc.com/morning-joe/watch/writer-calls-for-making-conservatism-unappealing-to-racists-68254277799.

Morrow, Lance. *Evil: An Investigation*. New York: Basic Books, 2003.

Muhammad, Khalil Gibran. *The Condemnation of Blackness: Race, Crime, and the Making of Modern Urban America*. Cambridge, MA: Harvard University Press, 2010.

Mukherjee, Siddhartha. *The Gene: An Intimate History*. New York: Scribner, 2016.

Muller, Jerry Z. *The Tyranny of Metrics*. Princeton, NJ: Princeton University Press, 2018.

Murray, Charles. *Coming Apart: The State of White America 1960-2010*. New York: Crown Forum, 2012.

Murray, Douglas. *The Madness of Crowds: Gender, Race and Identity*. London UK: Bloomsbury Continuum, 2019.

Natapoff, Alexandra. *Punishment Without Crime: How Our Massive Misdemeanor System Traps the Innocent and Makes America More Unequal*. New York: Basic Books, 2018.

Nila, Michael J. *The Nobility of Policing: Guardians of Democracy*. Salt Lake City, UT: FranklinCovey, 2008.

Nisbett, Richard E., and Dov Cohen. *Culture of Honor: The Psychology of Violence in the South*. Boulder, CO: Westview Press, 1996.

Noah, Trevor. *Born a Crime: Stories from a South African Childhood*. New York: Spiegel & Grau, 2016.

Oakley, Barbara. *Evil Genes: Why Rome Fell, Hitler Rose, Enron Failed, and My Sister Stole My Mother's Boyfriend*. Amherst, NY: Prometheus Books, 2008.

Obama, Barack H. *The Audacity of Hope: Thoughts on Reclaiming the American Dream*. New York: Crown Publishing Group, 2006.

O'Donnell, Lawrence. *Deadly Force: A Police Shooting and My Family's Search for the Truth*. New York: William Morrow, 1983.

Oliner, Pearl M., Samuel Oliner, Lawrence Baron, Lawrence A. Blum, Dennis L. Krebs, and M. Zuzanna Smolenska. *Embracing the Other: Philosophical, Psychological and Historical Perspectives on Altruism*. New York: New York University Press, 1992.

Oluo, Ljeoma. *So You Want to Talk about Race*. New York: Seal Press, 2018.

Orlov, Dmitry. *Reinventing Collapse: The Soviet Example and American Prospects*. Gabriola Island, BC, Canada: New Society Publishers, 2008.

Ortiz, Roxanne Dunbar. *An Indigenous People's History of the United States*. Boston, MA: Beacon Press, 2014.

Panksepp, Jaak, and Lucy Biven. *Affective Neuroscience: The Foundation of Human and Animal Emotions*. New York: Oxford University Press, 1998.

---. *The Archaeology of Mind: Neuroevolutionary Origins of Human Emotions*. New York: W.W. Norton, 2012.

Payne, James L. *A History of Force: Exploring the Worldwide Movement Against Habits of Coercion, Bloodshed, and Mayhem*. Sandpoint, Idaho: Lynton Publishing Company, 2004.

Pegues, Jeff. *Black and Blue: Inside the Divide Between the Police and Black America*. New York: Prometheus Books, 2017.

Pfaff, John F. *Locked In: The True Causes of Mass Incarceration and How to Achieve Real Reform*. New York: Basic Books, 2017.

Pinker, Steven. *How the Mind Works*. New York: W.W. Norton, 1997.

———. *The Blank Slate: The Modern Denial of Human Nature.* New York: Viking, 2002.

———. *The Stuff of Thought: Language as a Window into Human Nature.* New York: Viking, 2007.

———. *The Better Angels of Our Nature: Why Violence Has Declined.* New York: Viking, 2011.

———. *Enlightenment Now: The Case for Reason, Science, Humanism, and Progress.* New York: Viking, 2018.

Plantinga, Adam. *400 Things Cops Know.* Fresno, CA: Quill Driver Books, 2014.

———. *Police Craft: What Cops Know About Crime, Community and Violence.* Fresno, CA: Quill Driver Books, 2018.

Plato. "The Dialogues." In *Plato,* translated by Benjamin Jowett. Vol. 7 of *Great Books of the Western World.* Chicago, IL: Encyclopedia Britannica, 1952.

Porges, Stephen W. *The Polyvagal Theory: Neurophysiological Foundations of Emotions, Attachment, Communication, Self-regulation.* New York: W.W. Norton, 2011.

———. *The Pocket Guide to The Polyvagal Theory: The Transformative Power of Feeling Safe.* New York: W.W. Norton, 2017.

President's Commission on Law Enforcement and Administration of Justice. *The Challenge of Crime in a Free Society.* Washington, DC: United States Government Printing Office, 1967. https://www.ncjrs.gov/pdffiles1/nij/42.pdf.

Pugh, George Edgin. *The Biological Origin of Human Values.* New York: Basic Books, 1977.

Pyszczynski, Tom, Sheldon Solomon, and Jeff Greenberg. *In the Wake of 9/11: The Psychology of Terror.* Washington, DC: American Psychological Association, 2003.

Rahr, Sue, and Stephen K. Rice. "From Warriors to Guardians: Recommitting American Police Culture to Democratic Ideals." *New Perspectives in Policing Bulletin.* Washington, DC: U.S. Department of Justice, National Institute of Justice, 2015. NCJ 248654. https://www.ncjrs.gov/pdffiles1/nij/248654.pdf.

Rahtz, Howard. *Understanding the Use of Force.* Boulder, CO: Lynne Rienner Publishers, 2010.

———. *Race, Riots, and the Police.* Boulder, CO: Lynne Rienner Publishers, 2016.

Rana, Aziz. *The Two Faces of American Freedom.* Cambridge, MA: Harvard University Press, 2010.

Rank, Otto. *Beyond Psychology.* New York: Dover, 1941.

Rankine, Claudia. *Citizen: An American Lyric.* Minneapolis, MN: Graywolf Press, 2014.

Rawls, John. *A Theory of Justice.* Cambridge, MA: Belknap Press, 1971.

———. *Political Liberalism.* New York: Columbia University Press, 1993.

Restak, Richard M. *The Brain: The Last Frontier.* New York: Warner Books, 1979.

Roithmayr, Daria. *Reproducing Racism: How Everyday Choices Lock in White Advantage.* New York: New York University Press, 2014.

Rorty, Richard. *Achieving Our Country.* Cambridge, MA: Harvard University Press, 1998.

Ross, Howard J. *Everyday Bias: Identifying and Navigating Unconscious Judgments in Our Daily Lives.* Lanham, Maryland: Rowman & Littlefield, 2014.

Ross, Jeffrey Ian, and Stephen C. Richards. *Beyond Bars: Rejoining Society After Prison.* New York: Penguin, 2009.

Rothenberg, Paula S. *Racism and Sexism: An Integrated Study.* New York: St. Martin's Press, 1988.

Rothstein, Richard. *The Color of Law: A Forgotten History of How Our Government Segregated America.* New York: Liveright Publishing Corporation, 2017.

Rowan, Carl. *The Coming Race War in America: A Wake-up Call.* New York: Little, Brown and Company, 1996

Russell, Harold E., and Allan Beigel. *Understanding Human Behavior for Effective Police Work.* New York: Basic Books, 1990.

Ryan, Christopher. *Civilized to Death: The Price of Progress.* New York: Avid Reader Press, 2019.

Sandoval, Edgar, and Ashley Southall. "Two More N.Y. Police Officers Die by Suicide, Bringing Total to 9 This Year." *The New York Times,* August 13, 2019. https://www.nytimes.com/2019/08/13/nyregion/nypd-officer-suicide.html.

Sapolsky, Robert M. *The Trouble with Testosterone.* New York: Touchstone, 1997.

–––. *Why Zebras Don't Get Ulcers: The Acclaimed Guide to Stress, Stress-Related Diseases, and Coping.* New York: St. Martin's Press, 2004.

–––. *Behave: The Biology of Humans at Our Best and Worst.* New York: Penguin Books, 2017.

Schmidt, Jeff. *Disciplined Minds: A Critical Look at Salaried Professionals and the Soul-Battering System that Shapes their Lives.* Boston, MA: Rowan & Littlefield, 2000.

Schneider, Kirk J. *The Polarized Mind: Why It's Killing Us and What We Can Do About It.* Colorado Springs, CO: University Professors Press, 2013.

Schumaker, John F. *The Age of Insanity: Modernity and Mental Health.* Westport, CT: Praeger Publishers, 2001.

Scott, James C. *Seeing Like a State: How Certain Schemes to Improve the Human Condition Have Failed.* New Haven, CT: Yale University Press, 1998.

Selby, Nick, Ben Singleton, and Ed Flosi. *In Context: Understanding Police Killings of Unarmed Civilians.* St. Augustine, FL: Contextual Press, 2016.

Sen, Amartya. *The Idea of Justice.* Cambridge, MA: Belknap Press, 2009.

Sered, Danielle. *Until We Reckon: Violence, Mass Incarceration, and A Road to Repair.* New York: The New Press, 2019.

Shenkman. Rick. *Political Animals: How Our Stone-Age Brain Gets in the Way of Smart Politics*. New York: Basic Books, 2016.

Shepard, Paul. *Nature and Madness*. Athens, GA: The University of Georgia Press, 1982.

———. *The Only World We've Got*. San Francisco, CA: Sierra Club Books, 1996.

———. *Coming Home to the Pleistocene*. Washington, DC: Island Press, 1998.

Shipp, Robbin, Esq., and Nick Chiles. *Justice While Black: Helping African American Families Navigate and Survive the Criminal Justice System*. Chicago, IL: Bolden, 2014.

The Shootist. Directed by Don Siegel. Hollywood, CA: Paramount Pictures, 1976.

Siegel, Daniel J. *Aware: The Science and Practice of Presence*. New York: TarcherPerigee, 2018.

Siegel, Zachary. "Is the Psychology of Deadly Force Ready for the Courts?" *Scientific American*, December 20, 2018. https://www.scientificamerican.com/article/is-the-psychology-of-deadly-force-ready-for-the-courts/.

Simler, Kevin, and Robin Hanson. *The Elephant in the Brain: Hidden Motives in Everyday Life*. New York: Oxford University Press, 2018.

Simon, David. *Homicide: A Year on the Killing Streets*. New York: Picador, 1991.

Smith, David Livingstone. *Less than Human: Why We Demean, Enslave and Exterminate Others*. New York: St. Martin's Press, 2011.

Snyder, Rachel Louise. *No Visible Bruises: What We Don't Know About Domestic Violence Can Kill Us*. New York: Bloomsbury Publishing, 2019.

Snyder, Timothy. *The Road to Unfreedom: Russia, Europe, America*. New York: Tim Duggen Books, 2018.

Sokol, Jason. *All Eyes Are Upon Us: Race and Politics from Boston to Brooklyn*. New York: Basic Books, 2014.

Solomon, Akiba, and Kenrya Rankin. *How We Fight White Supremacy*. New York: Hachette Books, 2019.

Solomon, Robert C. *A Passion for Justice: Emotions and the Origins of the Social Contract*. New York: Addison-Wesley, 1990.

Sommers, Tamler. *Relative Justice: Cultural Diversity, Free Will, and Moral Responsibility*. Princeton, NJ: Princeton University Press, 2012.

———. *A Very Bad Wizard: Morality Behind the Curtain*. New York: Routledge, 2016.

———. *Why Honor Matters*. New York: Basic Books, 2018.

Southal, Ashley. "Daniel Pantaleo, Officer Who Held Eric Garner in Chokehold, Is Fired." *The New York Times*, August 19, 2019. https://www.nytimes.com/2019/08/19/nyregion/daniel-pantaleo-fired.html.

Stamper, Norm. *Breaking Rank: A Top Cop's Expose of the Dark Side of Policing*. New York: Nation Books, 2005.

———. *To Protect and Serve: How to Fix America's Police*. New York: Nation Books, 2016.

Steele, Shelby. *Shame: How America's Past Sins Have Polarized Our Country*. New York: Basic Books, 2015.

Stevenson, Bryan. *Just Mercy: A Story of Justice and Redemption.* New York: Spiegel & Grau, 2015.

Strother, Logan, Charles Menifield, and Geiguen Shin. "We gathered data on every confirmed, line-of-duty killing of a civilian in 2014 and 205. Here's what we found." *The Washington Post*, August 29, 2018. https://www.washingtonpost.com/news/monkey-cage/wp/2018/08/29/we-gathered-data-on-every-confirmed-line-of-duty-police-killing-of-a-civilian-in-2014-and-2015-heres-what-we-found/?utm_term=.0183ddf25f99.

Stroud, Matt. *Thin Blue Lie: The Failure of High-Tech Policing.* New York: Metropolitan Books, 2019.

Sunstein, Cass, R. *Conformity: The Power of Social Influences.* New York: New York University Press, 2019.

Sunstein, Cass, R. *On Freedom.* Princeton, NJ: Princeton University Press, 2019.

Taibbi, Matt. *The Divide: American Injustice in the Age of the Wealth Gap.* New York: Spiegel & Grau, 2014.

–––. *I Can't Breathe: A Killing on Bay Street.* New York: Spiegel & Grau, 2017.

Tannen, Deborah. *The Argument Culture: Moving from Debate to Dialogue.* New York: Random House, 1998.

Tarvis, Carol. *Anger: The Misunderstood Emotion.* New York: Touchstone, 1982.

Taylor, Kathleen. *Brainwashing: The Science of Thought Control.* New York: Oxford University Press, 2004.

Taylor, Shelley E. *Positive Illusions: Creative Self-Deception and the Healthy Mind.* New York: Basic Books, 1986.

Thomas, Angie. *The Hate U Give.* New York: Balzer & Bray, 2017.

Thomas, David J. *The State of American Policing: Psychology, Behavior, Problems and Solutions.* Santa Barbara, CA: Praeger, 2019.

Thompson, Tracy. *The New Mind of the South.* New York: Simon & Schuster, 2013.

Thoreau, Henry David. *The Portable Thoreau.* Edited by Carl Bode. New York: Penguin Books, 1947.

Thornton, Bruce S. *Plagues of the Mind: The New Epidemic of False Knowledge.* Wilmington, DE: ISI Books, 2000.

Thurston, Baratunde. "How to deconstruct racism, one headline at a time." Filmed April 2019, in Vancouver, BC. TED video, 16:44. https://www.ted.com/talks/baratunde_thurston_how_to_deconstruct_racism_one_headline_at_a_time?language=en.

Tilly, Charles. *Identities, Boundaries, & Social Ties.* Boulder, CO: Paradigm Publishers, 2005.

Todd, Chuck. "Meet the Press – August 11, 2019." *NBC News*, August 11, 2019. https://www.nbcnews.com/meet-the-press/meet-press-august-11-2019-n1041196.

Trivers, Robert. *The Folly of Fools: The Logic of Deceit and Self-Deception in Human Life.* New York: Basic Books, 2011.

Tsiaperas, Tasha. " 'This is a start,' says Jordan Edwards' mother after ex-cop Roy Oliver gets 15 years for murdering 15-year-old." *The Dallas Morning News*, August 30, 2018. https://www.dallasnews.com/news/courts/2018/08/29/defense-hopes-show-jury-real-roy-oliver-seeking-mercy-ex-cop-murdered-jordan-edwards.

United States Department of Justice. "Investigation of the Ferguson Police Department." Civil Rights Division, March 4, 2015. https://www.justice.gov/sites/default/files/opa/press-releases/attachments/2015/03/04/ferguson_police_department_report.pdf.

Vagianos, Alanna. "Why Women Surgeons Around the World Are Recreating This Magazine Cover." *Huffington Post*, April 11, 2017. https://www.huffpost.com/entry/women-around-the-world-re-created-this-magazine-cover-to-show-what-a-surgeon-looks-like_n_58ed0958e4b0c89f9121ef24.

Van Cleave, Kris. "Deaths at red lights have surged since 2012, AAA study finds." *CBS News*, August 29, 2019. https://www.cbsnews.com/news/aaa-study-deaths-at-red-lights-have-surged-2019-08-29/.

Van der Kolk, Bessel A. *The Body Keeps the Score: Brain, Mind, and Body in the Healing of Trauma*. New York: Penguin Books, 2014.

Vitale, Alex S. *The End of Policing*. New York: Verso, 2017.

Wachsmann, Nikolaus. *KL: A History of the Nazi Concentration Camps*. New York: Farrar, Straus, and Giroux, 2015.

Wade, Nicholas. *Before the Dawn: Recovering the Lost History of Our Ancestors*. New York: The Penguin Press, 2006.

–––. *The Faith Instinct: How Religion Evolved and Why It Endures*. New York: The Penguin Press, 2009.

Wade, Peter. "75 Percent of Republicans Say White Americans Are Discriminated Against." *Rolling Stone*, March 9, 2019. https://www.rollingstone.com/politics/politics-news/poll-white-discrimination-806242/.

Walsh, Joan. *What's the Matter with White People? Why We Long for a Golden Age that Never Was*. Hoboken, NJ: John Wiley and Sons, 2012.

Walt, E.R. *The Hall Street Shoot-out: A True Story of the Dallas Police Department's Biggest Gun Battle*. Xlibris Corporation, 2010.

–––. *Holloway's Raiders: A History of the Dallas Police Department's Deadly Shotgun Squads*. West Conshohocken, PA: Infinity Publishing, 2016.

Washington, Booker T. *Up From Slavery: An Autobiography*. New York: Dover, 1995.

Watkins, D. *The Beast Side: Living (and Dying) While Black in America*. New York: Hot Books, 2015.

Weatherford, Jack. *Savages and Civilization: Who Will Survive?* New York: Crown Publishers, 1994.

West, Cornel. *Race Matters*. Boston: Beacon Press, 1993.

Westen, Drew. *The Political Brain: The Role of Emotion in Deciding the Fate of the Nation*. New York: Public Affairs, 2007.

White, Michael D., and Henry F. Fradella. *Stop and Frisk: The Use and Abuse of a Controversial Policing Tactic*. New York: New York University Press, 2016.

Whybrow, Peter C. *The Well-Tuned Brain: Neuroscience and the Life Well Lived*. New York: W. W. Norton, 2015.

Wilde, Oscar. "A Few Maxims for the Instruction of the Over-Educated." Wikisource (November 17, 1894) 2015. https://en.wikisource.org/wiki/A_Few_Maxims_For_The_Instruction_Of_The_Over-Educated.

Wilkerson, Isabel. *The Warmth of Other Suns: The Epic Story of America's Great Migration*. New York: Random House, 2010.

Williams, Kristian. *Our Enemies in Blue: Police and Power in America*. Oakland, CA: AK Press, 2015.

Williams, Robert A., Jr. *Like a Loaded Weapon: The Rehnquist Court, Indian Rights, and the Legal History of Racism in America*. Minneapolis, MN: University of Minnesota Press, 2005.

Wilson, Clint C., II., Felix Gutierrez, and Lena M. Chao. *Racism, Sexism, and the Media: Multicultural Issues Into the New Communications Age*. 4th edition. Thousand Oaks CA: Sage Publications, 2013.

Wilson, Edward O. *Consilience: The Unity of Knowledge*. New York: Alfred A. Knopf, 2002.

– – –. *Nature Revealed: Selected Writings 1949-2006*. Hopkins Fulfillment Service: Baltimore, MD, 2006.

– – –. *The Social Conquest of Earth*. New York: Liveright Publishing, 2012.

– – –. *The Origins of Creativity*. New York: Liveright Publishing, 2017.

– – –. *Genesis: The Deep Origin of Societies*. New York: W.W. Norton, 2019.

Wilson, David Sloan. *This View of Life: Completing the Darwinian Revolution*. New York: Pantheon Books, 2019.

Winn, Denise. *The Manipulated Mind: Brainwashing, Conditioning and Indoctrination*. London: The Octagon Press, 1983.

Winston, Robert. *Human Instinct: How Our Primeval Impulses Shape Our Modern Lives*. New York: Bantam Press, 2002.

Wise, Jeff. *Extreme Fear: The Science of Your Mind in Danger*. New York: Palgrave Macmillan, 2009.

Wise, Tim. *Dear White America: Letter to a New Minority*. San Francisco, CA: City Lights Books, 2012.

Wood, Peter H. *Strange New Land: Africans in Colonial America*. New York: Oxford University Press, 1996.

Wrangham, Richard. *The Goodness Paradox: The Strange Relationship Between Virtue and Violence in Human Evolution*. New York: Pantheon Books, 2019.

Wright, Robert. *The Moral Animal: Evolutionary Psychology and Everyday Life*. New York: Pantheon Books, 1994.

Wuthnow, Robert. *The Left Behind: Decline and Rage in Rural America*. New York: Princeton University Press, 2018.

Yoshino, Kenji. *Covering: The Hidden Assault on Our Civil Rights.* New York: Random House, 2006.

Young, Damon. *What Doesn't Kill You Makes You Blacker: A Memoir in Essays.* New York: Harper Collins, 2019.

Zak, Paul J. *The Moral Molecule: How Trust Works.* New York: Plume, 2013.

Zimbardo, Philip. *The Lucifer Effect: Understanding How Good People Turn Evil.* New York: Random House, 2007.

Zinn, Howard. *A People's History of the United States.* New York: HarperCollins, 1995.

Zuckerberg, Donna. *Not All Dead White Men: Classics and Misogyny in the Digital Age.* Cambridge, MA: Harvard University Press, 2018.

ACKNOWLEDGMENTS

Over a period of more than thirty years LuAnne Dowling edited my books and essays, far exceeding a million words. LuAnne was a terrific editor and a wonderful person. She had an innate and intuitive feel for ethical appropriateness and moral clarity in prose, regardless of the context, and had I not met her, I'm not at all sure that I would have ever learned how to write well. LuAnne passed away in March of 2018 and I will never forget her advice, assistance and friendship.

This book would not likely have been written but for the incident of Professor Henry Louis Gates, Jr. and a police sergeant in Cambridge Massachusetts in 2009. Professor Gates was returning home to his residence when he was reported by a neighbor as a possible burglar and he was arrested when he questioned the police sergeant's authority, after having identified himself. I wrote a blog about the incident that was reposted in the *LA Progressive* followed by a longer blog about police behavior. I had been continuously reflecting on my police experience, but the arrest of Professor Gates set the intensive exploration in motion that led to this book.

Every book in the bibliography is on the shelf in my home library along with a couple thousand more. So, I concur wholeheartedly with General Mattis's advice about the need for extensive reading. Thinking of an education, not as something you get, but as something you take, is at the core of my philosophy of self-education and I can't help but believe that such an attitude is critical for the future of policing. Formal education for the sake of brevity and focus is often much more restricted to relevant disciplines, but the efficacy of self-education knows few bounds when it comes to calling attention to related issues. But for in-service training, especially instruction about diversity and racial bias, so many people in a wide range of occupations attend these sessions begrudgingly, believing they are wasting their time, and that they already understand everything they need to know about these subjects, which is precisely why they are the most in need of training. The lesson, which is hopefully clear by now, boils down to the ability to *believe what we see* instead of *seeing what we believe*. But the perceptual experience in enduring subjects taught for the purposes of career qualifications and simply becoming truly interested in the subject matter is radically different when it comes to objectivity. With a genuine interest in any discipline comes the ability to perceive patterns and connections practically everywhere one looks, offering an enormous advantage in perspective, insightful depth in comprehension and an increased ability for objective analysis, which I hope helps explain the eclectic scope of this book.

I am grateful to the following people who offered comments on early versions of the manuscript: Brian Austin, Jonathon Balcombe, Scott Campbell, David Couper, Mihaly Csikszentmihalyi, Lavonne Currier, Marc-David Freed, Aaron Hayes, Nancy Hayes, John F. Schumaker, Sharon Kyle, Dick Price, John Murphy, Stephen Rhodes, Norm Stamper, Robert M. Sapolsky, Jeff Schmidt, and David Yamada.

And finally, thanks for the thoughtful editing and advice of Sonya Senkowsky and Anna Olson.

ABOUT THE AUTHOR

Charles D. Hayes is a self-taught philosopher and one of America's strongest advocates for lifelong learning. He spent his youth in Texas, serving there as a U.S. Marine and as a police officer before embarking on a career in the oil industry. Alaska has been his home for more than forty years.

Hayes' 1998 book *Beyond the American Dream: Lifelong Learning and the Search for Meaning in a Postmodern World* received recognition by the American Library Association's *CHOICE* magazine as one of the year's most outstanding academic books. His other titles include *Existential Aspirations: Reflections of a Self-Taught Philosopher*; *September University: Summoning Passion for an Unfinished Life*; *The Rapture of Maturity: A Legacy of Lifelong Learning*; *Training Yourself: The 21st Century Credential*; *Proving You're Qualified: Strategies for Competent People without College Degrees*; and *Self-University: The Price of Tuition is Desire, Your Degree is a Better Life*. His fictional work includes the novels *Portals in a Northern Sky* and *A Mile North of Good and Evil*, as well as the novellas *Pansy: Bovine Genius in Wild Alaska*, *Stalking Cindy*, *The Call of Mortality* and *Benzeerilla*.

Promoting the idea that education should be thought of not as something you get but as something you take, Hayes' work has been featured in *The L.A. Progressive*, *USA Today*, and the *UTNE Reader*, on National Public Radio's *Talk of the Nation* and on Alaska

Public Radio's *Talk of Alaska*. His website, www.autodidactic.com, provides resources for self-directed learners—from advice about credentials to philosophy about the value that lifelong learning brings to everyday living.

Amazon Kindle versions are available for all the books mentioned above.

Also by Charles D. Hayes

Fiction

The Call of Mortality

Portals in a Northern Sky

Pansy: Bovine Genius in Wild Alaska

Stalking Cindy

Moose Hunter Homicide

A Mile North of Good and Evil

Benzeerilla

Nonfiction

September University: Summoning Passion for an Unfinished Life

Existential Aspirations: Reflections of a Self-Taught Philosopher

In Defense of Liberal Ideas

The Rapture of Maturity: A Legacy of Lifelong Learning

Training Yourself: The 21st Century Credential

Beyond the American Dream: Lifelong Learning and the Search for Meaning in a Postmodern World

Proving You're Qualified: Strategies for Competent People without College Degrees

Self-University: The Price of Tuition Is the Desire to Learn. Your Degree Is a Better Life

What Others Say About the Work of Charles D. Hayes

"In a world of flabby, fragmentary, and postmodernist thinking, Hayes offers a glowing tribute to old-fashioned curiosity and reason. Clear thinking is as human and healthy as breathing. Charles Hayes encourages us to give it a try."

—BARBARA EHRENREICH, author of *Fear of Falling* and *Blood Rites*

"In the midst of all the frantic hype and fluff that deluge Americans every day and produce so much ovine behavior, it is an inspiration to hear from someone who both cherishes and exemplifies independent thinking."

—PHILIP SLATER, author of *The Pursuit of Loneliness* and *A Dream Deferred*

"Reading *Portals* is like looking through a kaleidoscope in which breakneck adventure and science fiction occasionally reconfigure themselves into patterns of ancient wisdom—don't start unless you have enough time to finish it, because you won't be able to put it down."

—MIHALY CSIKSZENTMIHALYI, author of *Flow* and *The Evolving Self*

"Charles Hayes' voice is one of experienced wisdom, grappling artfully with the 'existential' questions we all grapple with, well or poorly. His answers, his appreciation of the role of Emersonian ecstasy in education, and his reflections on things that matter, are well worth your consideration."

—ROBERT C. SOLOMON author of *Spirituality for the Skeptic: The Thoughtful Love of Life* and coauthor of *A Passion for Wisdom*

"*The Rapture of Maturity* takes the reader on a wonderful intellectual journey through the author's own lived experiences as well as some timeless scholarly works on the mysteries of human existence. The book is a rich tapestry in which threads of insight are interwoven by the author into a fabric of wisdom, providing the reader with a comforting blanket of understanding regarding some of the more distressing aspects of being human."

—JAMES CÔTÉ, author of *Arrested Adulthood: The Changing Nature of Maturity and Identity*

"I agree with Charles Hayes when he says, 'Nothing is as it seems.' He clearly understands that we must make efforts to overcome our conditioning if we are to fulfill our potential. *The Rapture of Maturity* spells out why it is important for all human beings to be stretched (not stressed) throughout our lives, to always inquire about the truth of things, and to serve others."

—IVAN TYRRELL, coauthor of *Human Givens:*
A New Approach to Emotional Health and Clear Thinking

"*The Rapture of Maturity* is one of those rare books that one only realizes, after it gets written, how desperately needed it was. At a time when self-help books for the 'boomers' are both endemic and anemic, this one is a trumpet blast of authenticity, courage, and useable erudition."

—RONALD GROSS, author of *The Lifelong Learner and Socrates' Way*
and chairman at Columbia University Seminar on Innovation

"*The Rapture of Maturity* is an exquisitely thoughtful book. Hayes has a lovely spirit and strong insights into the springs of personal power."

—JOHN TAYLOR GATTO, former New York Teacher of the Year and
author of *The Underground History of American Education*

"*September University* is a nourishing feast of a book, replete with reasons to discover new meaning and purpose in the last chapters of your life, to welcome those years as life's most precious gift—an opportunity to cultivate wisdom and then put it to use in the world."

—WALTER TRUETT ANDERSON, President Emeritus at
World Academy of Art and Science

"*September University* is the first philosophy integrating the university without walls and transformative learning—essential reading for learning in the 21st century."

—DANIEL S. JANIK, MD, PhD, author of *Unlock the Genius Within:*
Neurobiological Trauma, Teaching, and Transformative Learning

"*September University* is a wonderful book. It is wise and passionate and can teach us all about the rare art of growing old."

—Sam Keen, philosopher and author of *Faces of the Enemy*

"It's not too late to make your mark on the world and enjoy a new level of fulfillment in your life. Charles Hayes will inspire you to muster the courage to do it."

—JEFF SCHMIDT, author of *Disciplined Minds*

"*September University*, by leading scholar and visionary Charles Hayes, is a superb intellectual achievement by any standards. With sweeping scope and remarkable depth of knowledge across numerous disciplines, Hayes addresses the totality of the human experience—along with neglected questions surrounding life, death, freedom, authenticity, and truth—as he paves the way for a genuinely mature future in which citizens discover new degrees of potency and thoughtfulness. Rather than shying away from idealism, *September University* sets out a bold and timely blueprint for a post-consumer consciousness that is more culturally aware, media literate, and politically astute. Hayes delves with electrifying intelligence into the nature of meaning, identity, and community as he weaves together a comprehensive philosophy that enables people to transcend evolutionary baggage, social indoctrination, and illusions of limitation. *September University* is one of the finest books in print when it comes to the wisdom and existential bearings required to survive the current age of insanity."

—John F. Schumaker, author of *In Search of Happiness: Understanding an Endangered State of Mind, Wings of Illusion, and The Age of Insanity*

"This is an important work. Wisdom evolves from real-life experience, and Charles Hayes has both. For those who aspire to a better world, this is a must read."

—PETER C. WHYBROW, Director of the Semel Institute for Neuroscience and Human Behavior at UCLA and author of *American Mania: When More Is Not Enough*

"Engaging, convincing, and provocative. Given the collapse of the future most adults thought they had, and the involuntary mandate to shape a new one, *September University* calls those in the second half of life to step away from superficial things and commit to becoming wise guides for the generations that come after them."

—DAVID L. SOLIE, MS, PA, author of *How to Say It to Seniors*

INDEX